Great
Hot Springs
of the West

4th Edition

Great Hot Springs of the West

Arizona California Colorado Montana Idaho
Nevada New Mexico Oregon Utah Washington Wyoming

Bill & Ruth Kaysing

CAPRA PRESS
SANTA BARBARA

Typography and cover design by Frank Goad

Annette Burden, Editor

Amanda Jones, Maps

PHOTOGRAPHIC ACKNOWLEDGEMENTS:
We thank the many hot springs proprietors, tourist offices,
and both professional and amateur photographers who provided
prints for this book.

LIBRARY OF CONGRESS CATALOGING-IN-PUBLICATION DATA

Kaysing, Bill, 1921-
Great hot springs of the West / Bill Kaysing. — 4th ed. rev. and expanded.
p.   cm.
ISBN 0-88496-382-9
1. Hot Springs—West (U.S.)   I. Title
GB1198.3.W47K38   1994
647.9478—dc20   93-42611
                                CIP

CAPRA PRESS
P.O. Box 2068
Santa Barbara, CA 93120

CONTENTS

PREFACE

FOURTH EDITION

*I*T'S BEEN MORE than 20 years since we found ourselves in jolly hot water—rollicking with the success of the first edition of *Great Hot Springs of the West*. Readers' thirst for hot springs continues to grow, so once again we find ourselves revising and expanding the most complete guide to Western hot springs ever published in one volume.

Researching that first edition in 1969, we discovered a spring not listed on any maps. The lovely little outpouring measured about 100°F. Beside it stood the remnants of an old shed or changing room. All around, luxuriant greenery reflected the plentiful supply of both hot and cold water.

In the late 1980s we returned to show the spring to a metaphysically minded friend who wanted to establish a healing center at a remote hot spring. We searched and searched, but the spring had disappeared. I can only guess what happened; most likely the road builders bulldozed our "discovery" in the name of progress.

The fortunes of hot springs depend on a great number of factors. Some, like Old Faithful, perform with enduring regularity. Others dry up, become private or polluted or unusable by hot springs lovers for countless other reasons.

With this edition, we say good-bye to a few old friends. One in California, San Juan Capistrano Hot Springs Resort, had 25 outdoor tubs, a swimming pool and beautiful picnic and camping sites grouped around a 122°F spring. Inquiry revealed it closed for business in mid-1993, then burned down in the November brush fires! Now, here's a suggestion: If you have some spare time and money, why not see what can be done to rebuild on the site (which was leased from the Orange County Parks Department)? Perhaps you could create a health spa or stress-reduction center for all those uptight execs in nearby Irvine.

We're amazed to hear that another old favorite, Matilija Hot Springs in Ojai, California, received a condemnation notice. We remember it fondly as a parklike sanctuary for rare plants and native birds set off by a creek, swimming pool and indoor and outdoor tubs. A happy ending for this one: A private party plans to rebuilt. We look forward to including Matilija in a future edition.

The popularity of several previously listed favorites led to the public's exclusion. California's Warner Springs, for example, now caters exclusively to its membership of 1,650 people. Long ago, a hot spring owner told us he thought creating a private club would solve a lot of his problems at once—including the lack of a reasonably assured regular income. Who can blame them?

Despite these few losses, this fourth edition incorporates a number of new (to us) discoveries as well as hundreds of changes in both developed and undeveloped springs. However, because the maps and tables in this book show nearly 1,700 examples, we'd have to issue daily bulletins to keep you up on the absolute latest word. We encourage you to explore with book in hand and let us know, through the publisher, of any changes you encounter.

What a delight to witness the continuing renaissance of the new hot springs era! Classic new-age resorts like Harbin in California and Breitenbush in Oregon continue to thrive with their combination of hot water and education. Harbin, led and supported by its founder, Ishvara, now welcomes groups in a stunning convention hall. Other historic sites, like California's Vichy Springs and White Sulphur Springs, sport first-class additions and upgraded facilities of their own.

Perhaps the most significant change since the first edition has been the conversion of many hot spring resorts into full-blown health spas. This reminds us of Marilyn Ferguson's prediction in her book *The Aquarian Conspiracy*. She believed that in the '90s people would begin taking responsibility for their own health. You see this not only in the boom in natural health therapies—with their emphasis on prevention and relaxation—but in the astonishing number of new fitness facilities nationwide.

Many hot spring resorts, as part of this trend, now provide a variety of health services. In California, Wilbur Hot Springs will help you kick a drug habit. Glen Ivy offers a full menu of skin-care and exercise supplements. Vichy provides a stress-reduction program along with its expanded facilities. Palm Springs' Spa Hotel & Mineral Springs invites you to choose from a variety of packages—arrays of fitness options plus room and meals at a *prix fixe*. In Colorado, giant Glenwood Springs grew even larger with the addition of a full-scale athletic club (complete with racquetball courts). Even rural New Mexico's historic bathhouse at Jemez Hot Springs now offers massages at a reasonable rate.

So venture forth and take the plunge. We guarantee a hot bath will soothe your body and raise your spirits. At the same time, we think you'll find much more. In the search for the perfect source, you may even find the real you.

Our gratitude goes to Joy A. Ikelman, physical scientist of the National Geophysical and Solar-Terrestrial Data Center in Boulder, Colorado, and all the many other people who helped create *Great Hot Springs of the West*. For this fourth edition, we owe special thanks for the tips and suggestions of readers K. Wright of Charleston, Oregon; Lee W. Williamson of Orem, Utah; Brad Greenwell of Fort Smith, Montana; and Liz Faller of Prescott, Arizona.

—BILL AND RUTH KAYSING
Soquel, California
1994

INTRODUCTION

*I*MAGINE FOR A MOMENT a peaceful valley, miles and miles from twentieth century "civilization." For all you know, the year could be 1994 B.C. instead of A.D. In fact, the valley probably hasn't changed much in 4,000 years.

Stone outcroppings lend the appearance of a great natural monument. A stream of clear hot water gushes from a fissure where granite meets slate. At ten gallons a minute, the flow creates a steaming brook that cascades down several rocky waterfalls. Grasses and shrubs grow thick along the over-100°F stream.

Hot water splashes down to a flume nailed together from weathered planks. It flows smoothly and silently to a shoulder-deep pool lined with well-worn stones. Nearby, an aspen suggests one of its older branches as a convenient hook for your clothes. Kick off those dusty boots, strip off your other clothes and slide into that warm, soothing water. As you lie back wiggling your toes in a mild form of ecstasy, you'll no doubt meditate upon the grand design that produced such a benevolent combination of valley, hot springs, you and your friends.

Beautiful? Hot springs lovers know the sensation as one of the best the world has to offer.

HOT SPRINGS HISTORY

According to legend, the Indians who dwelt in the West before the coming of the white man had an intertribal rule: NO FIGHTING AT A HOT SPRING!

I can just imagine three or four feisty

Flatheads cavorting 200 years ago at Bear Trap Hot Springs near Norris, Montana. Suddenly, a small band of enemy Sioux appears. The Flatheads are naked, their weapons out of reach—easy targets for the spears and arrows of the Sioux warriors. So what happens? The Sioux throw down their weapons, fling off their loin cloths, leap into the deliciously warm water and join their enemies in a rollicking mud fight.

Sitting in the same pool today, if you listen carefully, you can almost hear the whoops of joy echoing down the silence of the valley.

The legend of hot springs as places of peace between tribes may be apocryphal. We know for a fact, however, that Native Americans throughout the West regarded hot springs as sacred, as good medicine. Almost every time someone "discovers" a natural hot spring and decides to develop it, he comes upon dozens of artifacts indicating that people have enjoyed the same spot for centuries. Anthropologists confirm that many of the West's hot springs served as centers for tribal councils, religious rites and healing.

In the late nineteenth century, as more and more settlers poured into the American West, people of European descent brought the custom of "taking the cure." Europe abounds with ancient spas that retain their popularity to this day. The "cure" most often consists of daily soaks in hot pools, the application of hot mud from the area and countless glasses of spring water taken internally.

Naturally, European immigrants delighted in the hot springs they found bubbling up all over the mountains, deserts, valleys and seashores west of the Rockies. Before long, fashionable resorts sprang up at some of them

and flourished. High society from the East, indeed from all over the world, traveled by rail and stage to take the Western waters.

The custom lasted through the early 1900s. Then, for a variety of reasons, the fashion changed. Most of the elegant old spas declined and died. Grand hotels collapsed in ruins. All that remained was the flow of hot water seeping out of the ground, running through rusted pipes and over cracked cement.

Our Indian and European forebears knew something of value when they saw it. That something has not been lost—as witnessed by legions of hot spring lovers in the late twentieth century. While we make no scientific claims for the curative value of Western thermal springs, we rejoice in their renaissance. If nothing else, hot springs provide a palliative for city-wrought ills, a soother for troubled spirits, a purgative for poisoned minds and bodies and an unending source of sensual delight.

We firmly believe thermal springs provide more than just heat and water. Hot springs clearly promote not only luxuriant plant growth but a flowering of human potential. Why do some of the most successful consciousness-raising programs in America take place around hot springs? Perhaps truth seekers benefit from some unknown energy source carried by water that issues from deep within the earth. Or perhaps the body's utter relaxation creates a fertile frame of mind that allows for quantum leaps in understanding.

You may dispute the psychological and metaphysical benefits of thermal springs. But no one will deny the practical applications for an endless supply of free hot water or the timeless enjoyment in a good hot soak.

HOT SPRINGS POTENTIAL

A vast belt of geothermal energy girds the earth, and the energy—both wet and dry—lies relatively close to the surface. If you dig deep enough at any spot on the globe, you'll melt your shovel. But for the present, there's enough heat for everyone's energy needs within a reasonable distance of the earth's surface. The potential is virtually unlimited.

According to a government publication, *Assessment of Geothermal Resources of the U.S.,*

> There are immense quantities of thermal energy in the conduction-dominated and igneous-related environments, but the technology to utilize most of this energy has not yet been demonstrated. At present, the geothermal resource is concentrated in the hydrothermal convection systems and the geopressured and sedimentary basins. Both of these categories represent a significant resource of great importance to the energy economy of the U.S. The immense amount of energy that exists in conduction-dominated environments and in igneous-related systems, particularly at depths greater than three kilometers, provides an exciting goal for future exploration and for the development of advanced drilling and extraction technologies.

How the human race chooses to use this vast resource, once we overcome the technical obstacles, will be a test of our wisdom. Obviously, it would take an entire book to thoroughly explore the economic and social potential of thermal springs. We in the '90s see only the beginning of the hot-water rush, the boom in geothermal energy. In decades to come we can expect more spinning turbines like the ones at the Geysers power plant in northern California. And we'll be grateful, too, for the low-cost clean energy they provide.

Did you know the U.S. Bureau of Land Management can grant free land—including geothermal rights—to people who want to create a facility of benefit to the public? For more information, write to the BLM office in your district or state or the main headquarters in Washington, D.C.

Here's another idea. Iceland—a nation of bountiful hot springs, many of them boiling—uses some of the water to heat greenhouses where tropical fruits of all kinds grow easily and quickly the year around. Imagine walking into your thermally heated greenhouse and picking ripe mangos, papayas or bananas in December! It's possible, and the Icelanders prove it. For more proof, look at the geothermal greenhouses around Susanville, California, and Vale, Oregon, to mention just two.

But let's hope most of our hot springs remain untouched in the wilderness, well away from machinery and progress—like the gentle waters at Rogers Warm Springs in southern Nevada. For, as Thoreau wrote, "In wildness is the preservation of the earth."

WHAT IS A HOT SPRING?

U.S. textbooks on the subject define a hot spring as any spring or well whose water temperature noticeably exceeds the average ambient air temperature. Europe classifies any spring with a temperature above 20°C (68°F) as thermal. In the United States, the springs called thermal or hot are those with temperatures at least 15°F above the mean annual temperature of the air.

This means a hot spring could be as cool as 50°F, like one in Utah; or 70°F, like Ana Hot Springs in Oregon.

So much for textbooks. Most of the springs discussed in this book fall well within the human comfort zone. Some—like 180°F Twin Springs outside Boise, Idaho—must be cooled substantially for bathing.

Where does this hot water originate? There are plenty of theories.

Alchemists and early Greek thinkers believed in certain horned spirits who kept lost souls busy stoking enormous fires down below. The residual heat from these fires provided free hot water—and a reminder—for those still alive and kicking on the surface.

These days, a more popular theory has surface water percolating down along channels to the lower, hotter levels of the earth. We know that a mile beneath the surface, the temperature measures about 85°F higher. At two miles, the rocks could boil water. At 25 miles, the rocks are molten.

Theoretically, the elevated temperatures stem from two major sources. First: stored heat energy transformed from the kinetic energy it took to form the earth. Second: radioactive elements generating energy from the decay of atomic structures (like a nuclear reactor).

The accompanying sketch illustrates the most likely process for the origin of most hot springs. Big Caliente north of Santa Barbara, California, provides a good example of this model.

TYPES OF HOT SPRINGS

Most hot springs appear to follow the pattern previously described. Yet nature presents a great many strange and wonderful variations.

Diana's Punchbowl in central Nevada, for example, forms a symmetrical hill on the flat valley floor. No doubt it began as a surface spring and through the years built its own elevated basin from minerals carried by the hot water. Hot Lake in southeast Oregon poses another example of this self-building process. At present it lies only a few feet above the surrounding desert, but in centuries to come it may create increasingly high sides. Of course, you'll find some of the best and most colorful examples of built-up springs in Yellowstone National Park.

Some hot springs emerge from extraordinary depths. Experts estimate the waters of Fales Hot Spring on the eastern slope of the Sierra Nevada come from 7,000 feet below. It's unlikely that surface water would percolate down that far. Instead, the water gushing from Fales is probably "new" water that has never seen the earth's surface. One theory envisions this virgin water produced from the compression of rocks—rocks do contain entrapped water. Others believe the earth forms the water on a molecular level from a combination of free hydrogen and oxygen.

The same mystery surrounds another famous spring, not hot, but still fascinating. This is the giant spring that heads the Metolius River in central Oregon. Here tens of thousands of gallons of pure, fresh, drinkable water gush from a rocky cave. To date, no one has discovered the source. Small amounts of tracer chemicals introduced into water supplies for miles around have never appeared in the Metolius spring. Perhaps someday some spring in the West, emerging from great and unknown depths, may unlock the secret of the river's source.

A GENERALIZED ILLUSTRATION OF A HOT SPRING TYPE OF GEOTHERMAL SYSTEM WITH A HIGH RATE OF UPFLOW

Hot spring basins come in all sizes. Ward's Springs, at the northwest end of Alkali Flat in northwest Nevada, covers 75 acres. You can take your choice of lukewarm to boiling, depending on your distance from the source.

Some of the smaller pools can be regulated, like one of my favorites in California's Santa Ynez Valley. At Little Caliente, a simple volunteer-built pipe brings cold water from a creek that runs just above the outflow of the spring. Bathers let the stream of hot water build the temperature in the pool, then when it's too hot allow the cold water to flow in.

Temperature control can also result when hot water flows down a small canyon. If you build a series of pools, each will be slightly cooler as the water descends. Cougar Springs in central Oregon exemplifies this principle.

Did you say 75,000 gallons a minute? Yes, that's the flow rate of a fantastic spring in southern Oregon near the village of Summer Lake. Most of the water wells up from beneath a large lake and pours into a pool through a conduit. Other springs gush from a cliff face decorated with heat-loving bushes, grasses and flowers. Though not what most of us call hot, the 66°F water can be wonderfully refreshing in the summertime.

These few represent only a fraction of the amazing varieties of hot springs waiting for you in the Western wilderness.

HOW TO FIND A HOT SPRING

No matter what you want from a hot spring—recreation, adventure, therapy or a chance to change your life through agriculture, a home site, space heating, aquaculture, power generation or the operation of a resort—the first

thing you need to do is find the hot water.

To locate a spring described in the front of this book, begin by looking on the map opening each state's chapter. The descriptions that follow appear in alphabetical order. The book's appendix contains maps covering the 11 Western states. Accompanying lists, arranged by state, give the locations, temperatures and, in most cases, names of the springs. The lists group the springs by generally ascending parallels of latitude. Once you pinpoint the location of the spring or springs of your choice, mark your road map and start driving.

If you find no sign posted when you get there, ask someone in the vicinity. If there's no one ask, look around for wisps of steam, or listen for the shouts of happy hot springers.

We think of this book not only as a recreation guide but as a means to discovery. It presents more than 1,700 hot springs in Western America—and that's just a beginning. Most likely there are hundreds more springs still undiscovered or too small to attract the attention of a cataloger. The West features numerous tracts of wilderness where travel has been minimal or nonexistent. We once found a hot spring in southeast Oregon not mentioned in the U.S. Geological Survey. Yet at one time it was well developed, complete with wooden bathtubs and a bathhouse.

Discovering a new hot spring can be a great thrill. One called Vallecitos, for instance, waits near Agua Caliente Springs in Southern California. We have yet to visit, but we know the temperature (79°F) and the flow rate (about five gallons a minute). Who owns it? Is it on Bureau of Land Management land, perhaps available for development as a resort? Is it a haven for gypsies? Does it have a greenhouse spawning giant mushrooms? Or does it simply flow there with no one around to appreciate it?

Consider this book your invitation to explore. Whether you visit one of the favorites we've described in detail, look into the sites noted briefly in the appendix—or strike out on your own and discover hot water previously unknown to man—we guarantee the experience will enrich your life.

If you carry *Great Hot Springs of the West* in your car, camper, plane, boat or backpack, you can chart a route to include hot springs along your way. We trust that soon you'll be not only a fan but, ultimately, a connoisseur who includes hot springs in nearly every travel itinerary.

HOT SPRINGS EQUIPMENT

You don't need *anything* to enjoy the delicious effects of natural warm water swirling over your body. That's part of the joy. But you may want a few items to ensure greater comfort at an undeveloped spring.

A pair of cheap rubber thongs keeps sharp mineral spikes and other thorny objects out of your tender feet. You can also use them for wading in shallow hot lakes or streams. Another basic: Bring a thick towel for drying off to prevent chilling if breezes blow. The same towel can double as a mat for a snooze after a soak.

Some hot springs have oozy edges—mud, algae and other materials—that make walking difficult. So we often carry along a few lengths of thin, waterproof plywood to lay down as a temporary trail. The planks can also serve as an impromptu wharf at the edge of some difficult-to-use pool.

For the desert, consider bringing a piece of canvas or cloth to set up as a sunshade, especially in the summer. We've found fabric much handier to pack and carry than an umbrella.

A fine wine, mellow cheese, tasty sausage and crusty loaf of sourdough go well anywhere in the world, but they seem to taste best beside a hot spring. In addition, bring plenty of non-alcoholic liquid to drink. Soaking in a hot bath, you may not realize how much body fluid you're losing through perspiration. If you don't take precautions, dehydration may result.

Another reminder: Don't overdo the alcohol. To us there's nothing like a good wine with lunch at a hot spring, or a little brandy late on a cold starry night. But we also know a hot bath can magnify the effects of alcohol on

the body and the brain. If you overdo it, you could suffer an unpleasant or even fatal surprise. Some developed hot springs forbid alcohol entirely for this reason.

Staying overnight or nights? Unless you're fortunate enough to own a trailer or camper, bring sleeping bags, pads and maybe a small tent. Don't worry too much about the cold. One of the most rewarding experiences of your life can be to leap out of a freezing sleeping bag in the middle of the night and jump naked into a really hot spring. Now, *that's* an experience you won't soon forget.

Technically oriented or just plain curious? Bring a quart container and a thermometer along. With the former you can measure the flow rate of springs that don't run too fast. The seconds it takes to fill a quart bottle, divided into 15, will give you the gallons per minute. Leave the bottle full if you have a chemist friend to analyze the water's minerals.

An old kerosene lantern—never one of those hissing, eye-destroying gasoline things, please—a guitar or harmonica and a flagon of

aged brandy would complete most hot springs aficionado's list of good things to take.

Finally, hot springs etiquette *demands* you pack out your own trash. You win extra points for carrying out debris left by others—and the admiration of all.

A WORD TO THE WISE

By now you know we regard hot springs as good for the body as well as the spirit. But before we recommend that you leap into the first hot water you find, a few more warnings.

First, as mentioned above, don't mix too much alcohol on the inside with hot water on the outside. Second, drink plenty of nonalcoholic fluids to avoid dehydration—never from a hot spring unless you know without a doubt that it's safe. Many contain dissolved arsenic and other poisons.

Third, always test the waters. Quite a number of people have been cooked by hot springs—in fact, it almost happened to us at Crane's big pool in eastern Oregon. Always dip a finger or toe into that nice steaming pool before plunging in.

Chat with the locals to learn if remote hot springs have any adverse characteristics. Some may have acid or alkaline extremes, poisons or even radioactivity.

Several of the springs listed in this book rest on private property. As a matter of courtesy, and in some cases of law, you should check with the owner first before crossing any fences.

Another matter of courtesy concerns clothing. Generally speaking, no dress code exists in the wild. However, if the locals wear bathing suits, you should follow custom. If the locals like to skinny-dip, you can wear a bathing suit or not and no one will care. The majority of commercial establishments require suits in public, but leave it up to the individual in private rooms or separate men's and women's bathhouses.

Due to road or trail conditions, you can reach some of the remote springs in this book only in the warmer months. Similarly, some of the commercial establishments shut down during winter. If you have any doubt, call ahead before finalizing any plans.

Lastly, never take the word of this book as final. As you know, businesses open, close and change overnight. Don't forget that Mother Earth, too, can switch temperament, personality and outward appearance without a moment's notice. An earthquake some years ago rocked central Idaho around the Challis area. Mountains grew higher, great cracks opened in the earth and many hot springs increased or decreased their flows and raised or lowered their temperatures. Utah's Pah

Tempe Hot Springs presents another example. The September 1992 earthquake that shook the area south of Zion cut Pah Tempe's legendary 5,000-gallon-per-minute flow to a pleasant stream.

As a favor to other readers, please write us, in care of the publisher, about any changes you find. We'll make every effort to incorporate them in future editions of this book.

HOT SPRINGS GAZETTE

The destinations profiled on the following pages run the gamut, from world-class spas in the city to pristine pools in the wilderness. If you lean toward the remote and obscure end of the scale, you'll like the *Hot Springs Gazette*. Though we're much older, our personal preference in springs seems to run on the same wavelength as the editors and writers of the *Gazette*. We love nothing better than to "discover" a spring like Gandy, which the *Gazette*

A generalized illustration of a hot spring type of geothermal system, with high rate of upflow.

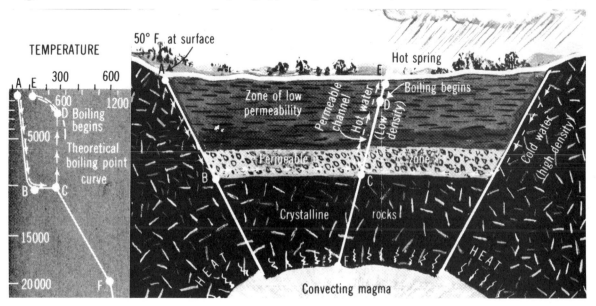

describes as follows:

> Gandy Hot Springs is something else—a marvel of the universe. Go north 30 miles from US 50-6 (in Utah), starting at the junction that shows Garrison (the wrong way). You will see a bunch of planted trees at a ranch to the west. Don't cross Warm Springs Creek where it goes under the Trout Creek dirt road. Go up the big road to the ranch. Near the ranch, the road goes north—you go west on the wagon trail past the big sheep corral. One and a half miles on a road curving like a fishhook toward a volcano-shaped mountain, and there you are! Gandy has underwater caves, two big waterfalls, sand bottom and lots of hot water. You can swim in those caves through maidenhair fern screens. Five Stars.

If Gandy piques your interest, you'll find plenty more like it listed in the *Hot Springs Gazette*. Write for subscription information to 12 S. Benton Ave., Helena, MT 59601. Tell them Ruth and Wild Bill sent you.

THE GOOD LIFE

Marcus Aurelius said, "Little is needed to make a happy life." To the basic list of food, clothing and shelter, might we suggest adding warmth, serenity and fun? You'll find them in great abundance at hot springs all over the West.

HOW TO USE THIS BOOK

The eleven states are presented beginning with California, then traveling north to Oregon and Washington, then through Montana and Wyoming and concluding with the Southwestern states.

Each state opens with a full map. Hot springs are all listed alphabetically within each state. Photographs, too, are arranged alphabetically.

U.S. Geological Survey maps are found at the end of the book showing over 1700 hot spring locations.

CALIFORNIA

*M*ANY YEARS AGO I met a location scout for Warner Brothers who told me that every scenic location in the world could be closely duplicated in California. If you want to film a movie about the Alps, just travel to the High Sierras. For a desert story, drive down to Death Valley. Need lots of water—canals, rivers and the like? The delta between San Francisco and Stockton has thousands of miles of lovely waterways. Many sections resemble the tropics.

The same diversity applies to California's hot springs. Down south, around Palm Springs, you can experience the delightful contrast of chill desert air just before the sun rises and the relaxing warmth of a mineral pool. If it's high desert you want, with pine-clad mountains nearby, fly to the northern end of the state near Alturas. You'll find an abundance of springs, many undeveloped and free for the using.

Between these extremes, California has a variety of hot springs matched by no other state in the West, some developed into luxurious spas, others waiting in the wilderness for you to discover.

WILBUR HOT SPRINGS

Distribution of hot springs in the state of

CALIFORNIA

(Locations are approximate. Consult text and road maps for directions.)

1. Agua Caliente Springs Park
2. Avila Hot Springs Spa
3. Bashford's Hot Mineral Spa
4. Beverly Hot Springs
5. Big Bend Hot Springs
6. Big Caliente
7. Buckeye Hot Spring
8. Campbell Hot Springs
9. Desert Hot Springs Spa
10. Drakesbad Guest Ranch
11. Dr. Wilkinson's Hot Springs
12. Esalen Institute
13. Fountain of Youth Spa
14. Furnace Creek Inn
15. Glen Ivy Hot Spring
16. Grover Hot Spring
17. Harbin Hot Springs
18. Hot Creek
19. International Spa
20. Jacumba Hot Springs Spa
21. Las Cruces Hot Springs
22. Lincoln Avenue Spa
23. Little Caliente
24. Mercey Hot Springs
25. Mono Hot Springs
26. Murrieta Hot Springs
27. Nance's Hot Springs
28. Orr Hot Springs
29. Paraiso Hot Springs
30. Roman Spa Hot Springs
31. Sam's Family Spa
32. Sierra Hot Springs
33. Soda Baths
34. Sonoma Mission Inn
35. Spa Hotel & Mineral Springs
36. Stewart Mineral Springs
37. Sycamore Mineral Springs
38. Tassajara Buddhist Meditation Center
39. Tecopa County Hot Springs
40. Two Bunch Palms
41. Vichy Springs
42. Wheeler Hot Springs
43. White Sulphur Springs
44. Wilbur Hot Springs
45. Woody's Feather River Hot Springs

WILBUR HOT SPRINGS

AGUA CALIENTE SPRINGS PARK

39555 Great Southern State Route of 1849,
Julian, CA 92036
(619) 565-3600

- Outdoor and indoor pools (some with jet pumps), RV hookups, picnic area, campground.
- Bathing suits required.
- Reasonable.
- On County Route S-2 off Highway 8, near the Anza Borrego Desert.

This San Diego County-sponsored facility presents a model of intelligent planning, complete with fly-in capability (airstrip within walking distance) and provisions for the handicapped. Four natural outflows provide water for the scenic desert location: three hot and sulphurous and one pure, cool and drinkable.

Open only between Labor Day and Thanksgiving, Agua Caliente books weekend spaces 90 days in advance. Weekdays are generally open, though, and the county always sets aside a few sites for use on a first-come, first-serve basis. Nevertheless, it's probably a good idea to contact the county office first for current information and reservations.

AVILA HOT SPRINGS SPA & RV RESORT

250 Avila Beach Dr., San Luis Obispo, CA 93405
(805) 595-2359

- Outdoor pools, indoor tubs, RV park, snack bar and grill, massage.
- Bathing suits required in outdoor pools.
- Reasonable.
- On Avila Beach Drive, just off Highway 101.

Conveniently located midway between San Francisco and Los Angeles, Avila operates a family facility suitable for all ages. A large main pool maintains a comfortable 86°F the year around. You'll find the prices reasonable and plenty of room to park your RV or pitch a tent. The resort provides discounts to those planning to stay a while. You'll probably want to.

I found the history of Avila fascinating; ask the manager for a guided tour. And be sure to check out the '30s-style tubs with their multi-colored tiles. These tubs, available for a small fee, have been popular for years with seniors who find the hot mineral water helpful for ailments like arthritis and rheumatism.

Not far away, the Avila Pier overlooks Port San Luis harbor, which is usually alive with fishing and pleasure boats. Personally, I like to shop at the fish stand near the end of the pier for big chunks of well-smoked black cod. The surf that skirts the bay's sandy beaches is gentle enough for even your littlest ones. Close by to the north, the college and retirement town of San Luis Obispo provides an abundance of good restaurants and fine examples of Spanish-era architecture.

BASHFORD'S HOT MINERAL SPA

HCO-1, Box 26, 10590 Hot Mineral Spa Rd., Niland, CA 92257-9707
(619) 354-1315

- Outdoor swimming pool, hydrotherapy pool, soaking tubs, RV park.
- Bathing suits required.
- Reasonable.
- On Mineral Spa Road, 3.5 miles off Highway 111, 15 miles north of Niland.

Bashford's adults-only policy insures peace and quiet and lots of time for walks in the desert beside the Salton Sea and Chocolate Mountains. The mineral springs features a great abundance of 145°F water, cooled and piped to a variety of pools and baths.

Even those in perfect health will feel better after sliding into nature's elixir in the company of warm and friendly people. For older folks with arthritis and related ailments, this could be nirvana.

BEVERLY HOT SPRINGS

308 N. Oxford Ave., Los Angeles, CA 90004
(213) 734-7000
- Indoor hot and cold pools, sauna, massage, health and beauty treatments, restaurant.
- Bathing suits optional.
- Deluxe.
- Right in town, between Beverly Hills and downtown Los Angeles.

Beverly Hot Springs has a lot going for it. For starters, it boasts 100 percent pure alkaline mineral water from the only natural artesian spring in Los Angeles. The water bubbles up from an aquifer 2,200 feet below the earth's surface, at a delightful 105°F.

Separate men's and women's facilities in the modern, well-kept building contain hot and cold mineral pools, wet and dry saunas and immaculate locker and shower rooms. A wide variety of body treatments includes scrubs, shiatsu and oriental herbal medicine. The restaurant specializes in traditional Korean dishes, healthful snacks and teas.

BIG BEND HOT SPRINGS

196 Hot Springs Row, P.O. Box 186, Big Bend, CA 96011
(916) 337-6680
- Indoor and outdoor hot tubs, natural pools, cabins, campground, RV hookups.
- Bathing suits optional.
- Reasonable.
- On Hot Springs Row, just outside Big Bend.

The policy of no smoking, alcohol or drugs at Big Bend Hot Springs recalls its former name—Camp Preventorium. The resort attracts new-age health seekers with massage, diet programs and a community garden of natural organic food. Hot springs enthusiasts find a variety of tubs in and outside the bathhouse, plus natural pools beside the rushing Pit River.

BIG CALIENTE

Santa Ynez Valley, CA 93460
No phone.
- Outdoor concrete tub, changing rooms, toilets.
- Bathing suits required officially; unoffcially, optional.
- Free.
- About 20 miles north of Santa Barbara.

Here's an old favorite of mine—in fact, the scene of my first hot springs adventure. It's just the right distance from Montecito, a suburb of Santa Barbara. The 20 miles or so by dirt road is sufficiently far that when you return you know you've been on a trip, but short enough so it's possible to leave early from work, say 3 p.m., drive over and still be back for dinner.

To reach Big Caliente, you drive up through heavily wooded Romero Canyon. The road is rough, so we suggest a four-wheel drive or motorcycle. After turning left off the only paved section, you climb steeply over a weather-worn road. Within a mile or two you cross a couple of gurgling brooks—at least they gurgle in summertime. Suddenly, as you make a sweeping turn to the left, a spectacular view of the Santa Barbara coastline appears.

Continuing toward Romero Saddle, you pass places where tiny streams gush from hidden springs. A more primitive vista greets your eyes as you continue up and over Romero Saddle. The ranges of Los Padres National Forest, each higher than the last, climb ultimately to Big Pine Mountain at nearly 7,000 feet.

The road descends in a series of loops and straight-aways to the Santa Ynez River Valley. Follow the river's course on an adjacent road for several miles until the valley suddenly widens into meadows dotted with giant oaks and sycamores. The U.S. Forestry Service Station at Pendola lies just beyond. Turn right here and follow Big Caliente Creek for a couple of miles. As the canyon narrows, you cross the creek twice. A fast right turn delivers you to the Big Caliente Hot Spring area, where the powers that be maintain their typically ugly but substantial concrete block house, johns and changing facilities.

Far more attractive are the natural offerings: 118°F water full of skin-soothing soda compounds that flows into a well-used concrete tub. A valve regulates the water's temperature. If it's too hot, shut off the flow and let the water cool. If it's a nippy day in November, you may want to turn the faucet on full.

During the week you may be the only guest, as I had the good fortune to be on my most recent trip. I also enjoyed the pleasant surprise of finding the previously tiny palms and other trees grown into modest giants. On weekends you'll probably have lots of company, the kind you'll enjoy meeting. Officially,

there's no nude bathing; but, in fact, you and whoever's there can decide among yourselves on a dress code that feels comfortable to all.

BUCKEYE HOT SPRING
Mono County, CA
No phone.
- Hot pool.
- No clothing requirements.
- Free.
- Along the trail downstream from Buckeye campground, in Toiyabe National Forest.

Volunteers rebuild the rock dam that creates this lovely pool each year. Grateful bathers soak in a fine spot beneath a hot waterfall, with a pleasant campground nearby.

CAMPBELL HOT SPRINGS
P.O. Box 38, Sierraville, CA 96126
(916) 994-3737
- Outdoor hot swimming pool, indoor and outdoor hot tubs, massage, lodging, meals, picnic area, campground.
- Clothing optional in bathing areas.
- Reasonable.
- Off Lemon Canyon Road, about a mile southeast of Sierraville.

A 680-acre spread of open meadows and wooded hills surrounds Campbell's mineral springs. In addition to hot healing water, visitors find a spiritual community, conscious-breathing training center and Inspiration University. Drawing from a tremendous spectrum of new-age knowledge, program participants study techniques of spiritual enlightenment, including rebirthing and healing methods aimed to integrate spirit, mind and body.

Campbell welcomes visitors anytime; no reservations necessary. Guests find lodging, massage, group and individual consultations, financial opportunities and delicious vegetarian meals made from produce grown at Campbell.

Incidentally, for those who fly, an airport for small planes lies only half a mile away. Or, if you rely on commercial flights, pickup in Reno can be arranged.

DESERT HOT SPRINGS SPA HOTEL
10805 Palm Dr., Desert Hot Springs, CA 92240
(619) 329-6495
(800) 843-6053 (toll-free reservations)
- Outdoor hot swimming pool, seven soak ing pools, sauna, massage, health and beauty treatments, lodging, restaurant, bar.
- Bathing suits required.
- Reasonable.
- Right in town.

Desert Hot Springs' largest full-service spa aptly bills itself "a splash of Shangri-La." Life revolves around seven large soaking pools—a couple of them Jacuzzis—and an Olympic-sized swimming pool. You can lounge around the pools, whether in the palm-studded courtyard or on your own private lanai or balcony, and view spectacular desert sunsets against the snowcapped peaks of the San Jacinto and San Gorgonio mountain ranges.

Crystal-clear and odor-free, the natural hot mineral water rises from 300-foot-deep aquifers at a rate of 120 gallons a minute. Naturally, the resort moderates the 140°F temperature to satisfy a variety of needs and whims.

Pampering extends to massageóSwedish, sports therapy, acupressure, shiatsu and reflexology. Rejuvenating treatments range from body rubs and wraps to facialsóeverything from aloe vera facelifts to glycolic and collagen treatments. To really gild the lily, a beauty shop will cut, color, or perm your hair and do your nails.

Both registered guests and the public have access to the spa treatments, the soaking and the sunbathing around the pools. A complete menu and drinks are served poolside as well as in the restaurant and sports bar. As if that weren't enough, guests also have privileges at nearby tennis courts, Desert Dunes Golf Club and the Mission Lakes Country Club.

DRAKESBAD GUEST RANCH
2150 N. Main St., Red Bluff, CA 96080
(916) 529-1512
- Outdoor swimming pool, indoor tubs, lodging, restaurant.
- Bathing suits required in pool.
- Reasonable.
- At the end of Warner Valley Road in Lassen National Park.

The only resort of its kind within Lassen National Park shows little change since its founding in 1860. Most of Drakesbad's cabins have no electricity. Guests spend their evenings in the warm glow of a kerosene lamp instead of the blue glow of a TV tube.

"Drakesbad is very much secluded," says its brochure, "and nestled into one of the most scenic mountain valleys in all of the country. It is not the place for someone who needs something to do every moment of the day...probably best suited for those who enjoy communing with nature and for those who revel in fresh mountain air and crisp, bright mornings."

AVILA HOT SPRINGS SPA & RV RESORT

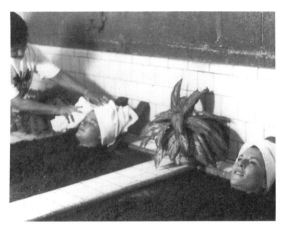

DR. WILKINSON'S HOT SPRINGS

DESERT HOT SPRINGS SPA HOTEL

Registered guests enjoy individual tubs and showers along with the hot springs pool, horseback riding on gentle mounts, fishing in streams practically at their doorstep, hiking to nearby wonders and scarfing up three delicious meals a day. The guest ranch operates on the American plan, and the rates seem like a great bargain, in my opinion.

Drakesbad rests at an altitude of nearly 6,000 feet. It closes in early October and reopens the first week in June. Call ahead for reservations.

DR. WILKINSON'S HOT SPRINGS
1507 Lincoln Ave., Calistoga, CA 94515
(707) 942-4102
• Outdoor pool, bathhouses, lodging, physical therapy, mud baths.
• Bathing suits required in pool.
• Deluxe.
• Right in town.

The mud at Dr. Wilkinson's consists of powdered volcanic ash mixed with naturally heated mineral water. Slide into the thick black warmth, and feel all your cares and toxins drain away. Take a brisk shower and then a mineral tub soak with the whirlpool machine going, and you'll feel like a brand new person.

The difficulty of securing a weekend reservation bears witness to the treatment's success and popularity. Reservations are recommended no matter when you visit.

Calistoga, a thriving resort since the last century's golden age of hot springs, has many things going for it. A visit to an area this scenic and charming can make you feel better even if you never try a hot mineral bath. Miles of surrounding wineries and vineyards backed by wooded hills rival the best of the French and Italian wine country. In addition, Calistoga initiates much of Napa Valley's famous aerial activity, from hot-air ballooning to gliding and ultralight soaring.

Dr. Wilkinson's is but one of many fine health spas in Calistoga. Write the Chamber of Commerce, Calistoga 94515, for a complete list, which with others listed in this book will include the Golden Haven Spa and Royal Polarity Inn (great vegetarian meals).

ESALEN INSTITUTE
Big Sur, CA 93920
(408) 667-3000 (information and seminar reservations)
(408) 667-3047 (hot springs reservations)
• Hot baths, educational center with food and lodging for participants.
• Bathing suits optional.
• Deluxe.
• On Highway 1, 45 miles south of Monterey.

Known as the home of the "human potential movement," the Esalen Institute first opened in October of 1962. Today more than 8,000 people a year flock to the facility, which offers over 500 seminars annually to students from all over the United States and foreign countries. Topics cover the arts, wilderness, ecology, meditation and shamanic practices, psychological process, health and healing massage and more. For a $5 donation, the institute will send its latest catalog of courses, published three times a year and also available by subscription.

The phenomenal beauty of the rugged Big Sur site surely has been one of the secrets of Esalen's success and popularity. Another is the presence of the natural hot-springs water that runs through Esalen's baths. Use of the

ESALEN INSTITUTE

FURNACE CREEK INN & RANCH RESORT

GLEN IVY HOT SPRING

pools—perched on a breathtaking cliff over-looking the Pacific—comes almost exclusively with participation in the institute's programs. The exception: Esalen grants access to the public between 1 and 3 a.m., exclusively by reservation and at a charge of $10 per person.

If you tend to sleep through these hours and so can't make it to the springs, it's still worth a trip down Highway 1—just to experience Big Sur's awesome interface between the western edge of America and the vast Pacific.

FOUNTAIN OF YOUTH SPA

Rte. 1, Box 12, Niland, CA 92257
(619) 348-1340
• Outdoor swimming pools, smaller pools with jets, massage, camp space, RV park.
• Bathing suits required.
• Reasonable.
• At the end of Frink Road off State Highway 111, near the Salton Sea.

Fountain of Youth has most facilities you'd expect from a major RV park—plus lots of hot, mineral-rich water. As the American population ages, we should see more thermal-based spas like this one, developed with the needs of older hot springs lovers in mind.

FURNACE CREEK INN & RANCH RESORT

Death Valley, CA 92329
(619) 786-2345
• Two outdoor swimming pools, sauna, lodging, restaurant, golf, tennis, store, service station.
• Bathing suits required.
• Deluxe.
• On Highway 190, about 30 miles north

west of Highway 127.

The stark desert landscape of Death Valley sets off the luxury of this elegant resort. Magnificent palms shade the oasis's hillside location, fed by a spring of hot natural mineral water.

GLEN IVY HOT SPRING

25000 Glen Ivy Rd., Corona, CA 91719
(909) 277-3529
• Outdoor swimming pool, indoor tubs, restaurant, massage, sauna, showers, aerobics classes.
• Bathing suits required.
• Reasonable.
• On Glen Ivy Road off Temescal Canyon Road, eight miles south of Corona.

Glen Ivy, a favorite with hot springs enthusiasts since 1885, rests in western Riverside County at the base of the Santa Ana Mountains. Long before the commercial resort captured and directed the warm and health-giving mineral waters, the California Indians considered the springs sacred. They called the spot Temescal, in reference to their sweat lodges built for ritual purification.

The mud-and-stick huts of old may be gone, but the tradition of mud and hot water lives on in an updated version. Today's native Californians call Glen Ivy "Club Mud" because of a large red-clay mud bath at the spa. Patrons rub the warm and gooey substance on their bodies from head to toe, then lie in the sun and let the moisture evaporate. As the clay dries, it draws toxins from the pores; once peeled and rubbed off, it leaves the skin remarkably clean, smooth and tight.

Glen Ivy maintains 15 pools and spas,

including an Olympic-sized swimming pool kept at comfortable temperatures the year around. Shoji-screen doors and exotic plants enclose one thermal pool. Or couples can choose from a half-dozen tiled mineral water tubs just right for two. Three larger hot spas round out the picture along with a huge children's wading pool.

Glen Ivy is always improving. Over the last decade it has combined nature's gift of hot mineral water with the latest in health, relaxation and beauty services. A full-service salon offers European facials, hair styling, manicures and other forms of pampering. Spa goers find up-to-date locker rooms and showers, a sauna and cold plunge (for those who like the alternate hot and cold) and free aerobics classes for low-stress, high-fun workouts.

The city of Corona, just a few minutes away, provides plenty of choice in lodgings. Package deals at several hotels include admission to Glen Ivy.

GROVER HOT SPRING STATE PARK

P.O. Box 188, Markleeville, CA 96120
(916) 694-2248
(800) 444-7275 (campground reservations)
• Outdoor soaking and swimming pools, campgrounds, rest rooms, showers.
• Bathing suites required.
• Reasonable.
• On Route E4, Alpine County Road, about four miles west of Markleeville.

Long ago, in the years when we lived an hour's drive away, I frequented Grover quite often. I seldom encountered more than a dozen people in the two pools (one at about 80°F, the other at 104°F). A more recent visit to this Sierra jewel found so many people that I took a hike instead of a soak.

Grover isn't always crowded, though. Even when it is, it's a lovely spot, well worth a stop on a great hot springs tour. You'll find an abundance of hiking trails along with the hot spring pool and swimming pool, tall Sierra peaks (one at more than 10,000 feet) and a lovely large meadow. You can catch a trout if you're lucky and barbecue it in the nearby campgrounds.

The two campsites—Quaking Aspen and Toiyabe—supply stoves, cupboards and tables with piped water, rest rooms and showers. Be sure to call for reservations in the busy season. Both sites close from early October to May, but you can camp in winter—in fact, year-round—in the picnic area adjacent to the park entrance. My own preference for a visit is fall, when the great stands of aspen burst into an explosion of pure gold and vivid scarlet.

HARBIN HOT SPRINGS

P.O. Box 782, Middletown, CA 95461
(707) 987-2477
(800) 622-2477 (toll-free in California)
• Hot and cold outdoor pools, massage, workshops and classes, lodging, camp ground, restaurant, store.
• Clothing optional.
• Reasonable.
• At the end of Big Canyon Road outside Middletown.

It's barely light when you awaken in the comfortable old Victorian Era hotel room. No need to dress; just slip out the door in your birthday suit and tiptoe along the boardwalk in front of the other rooms. Stride boldly up to the soaking pool festooned with elms and laurel, and ease yourself in. Now gaze off through the mist rising from the 100°F-plus water and behold Harbin's acres of gently rolling, tree-clad hills.

This retreat, owned by a nonprofit organization, presents a prime example of what a lot of money and plenty of volunteer work can accomplish. More than 150 residents share the duties of preserving the land as a place of rest and renewal for others—without a single "employee." It's even possible to earn most or even all your keep by contributing labor to the restoration and new construction.

Harbin continues to grow and prosper. Conferences, workshops, events and classes for groups of 14 to over 300 convene in a spacious conference center. Most programs require advance registration, but a few welcome guests on a drop-in basis. While there you might want to sample the Course in Miracles, join a 12-Step meeting or relax with a yoga class. Facility-wide improvements include a gym and weight room open 24 hours, a ban on smoking (except for a section of deck near the entrance), a remodeled pool area, a heart-shaped hot pool and a screened massage deck.

A restaurant prepares fresh and healthful vegetarian meals for breakfast, lunch and dinner. Or cook your own in the guest kitchen—from ingredients purchased at the natural foods store or directly from the organic garden.

Most activity centers around the hot soaking pool, which measures about 20 by 30 feet. A large, unheated pool provides a bracing contrast. Clothing is optional, but during a three-day stay I saw only one bathing suit.

The retreat's 1,160 acres provide abundant hiking trails, a lively stream bounding down a picture-book canyon, a relaxed atmosphere and an aura of tolerance and reason. Need

your muscles relaxed and your consciousness raised, all at a modest fee? Be sure to include Harbin on your hot springs itinerary.

If you'd like to read a fascinating history of Harbin since the mid-1800s, call (707) 987-2477 and ask for a copy of their new book.

HOT CREEK
Inyo National Forest, CA
No phone.
- Hot-springs creek, rest rooms, parking lot.
- Bathing suits required.
- Free.
- Off Long Valley Airport Road, three miles east of Highway 395.

Nature came up with an ingenious design: a near-boiling temperature spring set in the bed of an icy creek. As the scalding water emerges, it meets the 40°F waters that sweep down from the slopes of the eastern Sierras. You may enjoy almost any temperature you wish or dare, from near freezing to heat that would cook a potato.

The evidence of nature's power extends to the surrounding outcroppings of volcanic rock and a row of small geysers near the footbridge. Visitors find a well-built parking lot and bathhouse above the creek.

It's a peculiar sensation to swim about in the rather deep and quick-flowing creek and feel the currents' swiftly changing temperatures—invigorating too. Yet, due to past injuries, both major and minor, the U.S. Forest Service recommends extreme caution and forbids entry to the area between sundown and sunrise. Remember: Even in full daylight, you're on unstable ground with scalding vents—so use your head.

INTERNATIONAL SPA

P.O. Box 856, Calistoga, CA 94515
(707) 942-6122
- Hot mineral baths, massage, mud baths, beauty treatments.
- Reasonable.
- Right in town.

This is one of the best spas in Calistoga for a sampling of hot springs culture and philosophy. Naturally, the facility specializes in hot mineral water soaks and mud baths—time-honored favorites of the region. But International also lives up to its name with possibilities like Japanese enzyme baths and combinations of three major systems of massage (Swedish-Esalen, reflexology and acupressure). Go—and return a new person.

JACUMBA HOT SPRINGS SPA AND MOTEL

44500 Old Hwy. 80, P.O. Box 371, Jacumba, CA 92034
(619) 766-4333
- Outdoor swimming pool, indoor whirlpool, sauna, massage, motel, restaurant, lounge, tennis court.
- Bathing suits required.
- Reasonable.
- On Old Highway 80, three miles off Highway 8.

Jacumba's hot mineral water requires no chemical treatment, as it passes only once through the spacious indoor Jacuzzi and outdoor swimming pool. Other attractions include sauna, massage and nature hikes. Next time you're east of the San Diego area, drop in and enjoy.

LAS CRUCES HOT SPRINGS

Santa Ynez Valley, CA
No phone.
- Soaking pools.
- Bathing suits required officially; unofficially, optional.
- Free.
- Off Highway 101, a few miles north of Gaviota.

Thousands of speeding travelers pass this spring each day. But few take time from their harried schedules to savor the sensual and salubrious waters of Las Cruces.

As you turn off Highway 101 a few miles north of Gaviota—opposite where Highway 1 takes off for Lompoc—you'll see a paved road paralleling the freeway on the east side. Turn south and drive about a block. The road dead-ends at a parking lot complete with trash containers and toilets.

It's easy to locate the trail, which is wide with a gentle grade. As you hike upward through the chaparral and giant sycamores, the sound of the freeway dies away, replaced by bird song, the rustle of leaves and soon the magic of trickling water.

Take the right-hand trail when you come to a Y. A few more steps, and there it is! Inviting tufts of steam arise from both the lower and upper pools if it's a chilly day.

Oh, heaven on earth it is to glide into the mud-and-sand-bottomed lower pool and wallow in the warmth. When you've had enough of the lower pool, climb to the upper, hotter pool where the water is close to body temperature. Lie back and study the infinite shades of green on the sycamores. Listen to the gurgling of the hot water as it bubbles up from the bottom or trickles in from the tiny grotto.

LITTLE CALIENTE

JACUMBA HOT SPRINGS SPA AND MOTEL

LAS CRUCES HOT SPRINGS

HARBIN HOT SPRINGS

Next time you're rushing up or down Highway 101 north of Santa Barbara, take a little time to rest your body and mind. Las Cruces, the Tiffany of natural springs, awaits your pleasure 24 hours a day, seven days a week, all year long.

LINCOLN AVENUE SPA

1339 Lincoln Ave., Calistoga, CA 94515
(707) 942-5296

• Health and beauty treatments.
• Reasonable.
• Right in town.

The extensive menu of specialty treatments at this friendly health spa rivals those of La Costa or the Golden Door. A key difference: Calistoga's legendary waters.

Try the one-hour mud wrap, sea-mud wrap, herbal wrap or mint-and-mud wrap as you recline on a custom-designed Honduran mahogany steam table. Go for a skin-glow rub, therapeutic massage, herbal facial or acupressure facelift. Or sample several treatments at a discount with a Pamper Package. Even if you walk in looking every day of your age, you'll come out younger.

Devotees often book rooms at the many deluxe hotels and motels nearby. Or bring your camper or motor home, as I often do.

LITTLE CALIENTE

Santa Ynez Valley, CA
No phone.

• Natural pool, wooden platform and seats.
• No clothing requirements.
• Free.
• About 20 miles north of Santa Barbara.

Mother Nature blessed Santa Barbara's backcountry with a generous amount of hot water. Less than seven miles from Big Caliente waits a secluded smaller sister, Little Caliente.

From the U.S. Forestry Service Station at Pendola (location described under Big Caliente), make a right and travel alongside the Santa Ynez River. En route you'll pass some friendly campgrounds and places where the road dips almost into the sandy riverbed. The oaks, cottonwoods and sycamores become thicker as you ascend an escarpment separating the Santa Ynez from the Mono River. Soon Mono campground appears to your left. Pass the campground and keep to your right. Within two miles, stop at a locked gate leading to the Ogilvy Ranch. Park and walk about 100 yards to the right. Voila!

Little Caliente changes character from season to season, depending on the state of the river itself. Sometimes it's merely a muddy little pond; at other times it's a delightfully clear pool with temperature control. On a recent visit I found the welcome addition of a redwood platform and seats, which makes dressing and undressing much handier.

In rainy weather, you might call the U.S. Forest Service before setting out, to make sure the road is open. But this is all part of the adventure of hot springing—you never know what you'll find.

MERCEY HOT SPRINGS

P.O. Box 1363, Los Banos, CA 93635
No phone.

• Individual indoor hot tubs, massage, lodging, snack bar, campground, RV park.
• Bathing suits optional.
• Reasonable.

- On Little Panoche Road, 13 miles west of Highway 5.

Here's a good rest stop for motorists traveling up and down Interstate 5. After a hard drive, the funky old resort can make a driver's body feel like new again.

MONO HOT SPRINGS

Mono Hot Springs, CA 93642
No phone.
- Indoor hot tubs, outdoor Jacuzzi, lodging, restaurant, campground, picnic area, grocery store, service station.
- Bathing suits required outside.
- Reasonable.
- Off California State Highway 168 in the Sierra National Forest, about 16 miles east of Huntington Lake.

This scenic resort opens only for the summer season, between late spring and early fall. Visitors enjoy Sierra hiking, fishing and camping along with several geothermal attractions in the area.

MURRIETA HOT SPRINGS

39405 Via Las Flores, Murrieta, CA 92362
(909) 677-7451
- Outdoor swimming, exercise and soaking pools; indoor spas; massage; mud baths; beauty treatments; lodging; restaurants; tennis.
- Bathing suits required.
- Deluxe.
- Right in town.

Many hot springs are great, but some are *especially* great. Like Murrieta. I found the place

closed when I visited in the late '70s; decay and vandalism had taken a sad toll. But thanks to the resurgence of enthusiasm for hot water and alternative health methods, Murrieta rose like a Phoenix from near ruin to the upper echelons of hot springs fame in just a few years.

Today this historic resort practices the latest techniques in health maintenance and restoration. Spa offerings—available both to registered guests and the public—begin with hot, healing mineral baths and proceed to "feel alive" programs, facials, cellulite and lymph cleansing, massage, saunas, body rubs, mud baths and every conceivable form of exercise.

Lynne Vertrees, the spa manager, reports that Murrieta now offers a special treatment involving a substance called Moore Mud. Technicians paint the mud, an Austrian import, onto the body, then tuck the client under a heat blanket. After 20 minutes, the client soaks in a hot mineral bath for another 20 minutes. Now, that should cure just about anything that ails you.

Another new attraction, a personal gym instructor, stands by for one-on-one guidance through training. Today's menu of fine spa cuisine includes vegetarian dishes—accompanied by wine, if you'd like.

NANCE'S HOT SPRINGS

1614 Lincoln Ave., Calistoga, CA 94515
(707) 942-6211
- Indoor whirlpool and individual baths, mud baths, massage, lodging.
- Bathing suits optional.
- Reasonable.
- Right in town.

"The whole neighborhood of Mt. St. Helena is

ORR HOT SPRINGS

PARAISO HOT SPRINGS

PALM SPRINGS SPA HOTEL

ROMAN SPA HOT SPRINGS RESORT

full of sulphur and boiling springs," wrote the health-seeking author Robert Louis Stevenson, "and Calistoga itself seems to repose on a mere film above a boiling subterranean lake."

Even earlier, the Wapoo Indians knew all about it, making pilgrimages to the "Oven Place" to bathe in its mud and waters and finish with a sweat wrap. They called the valley Ta La Ha Lu Si, or "Beautiful Land." Today's visitors continue to benefit from the mud and water, but also from a restorative climate that rivals the most celebrated locales of Italy and the South of France.

Thousands of years ago, erupting volcanoes left a three- to five-foot layer of fine ash all around. This ash, mixed with naturally heated mineral water at Nance's, provides a fomentation of deep penetrating heat. Insulated by a blanket wrap, the poltice purifies the skin and increases circulation to leave the body clean, refreshed and greatly relaxed.

Nance's has everything you need to come away rejuvenated: quiet rooms (with color TV, HBO, kitchenettes and air conditioning), expert massage and an unending supply of mud and hot mineral water.

ORR HOT SPRINGS

13201 Orr Springs Rd., Ukiah, CA 95482
(707) 462-6277
• Outdoor swimming and soaking pools,
  indoor soaking pool and
  hot tubs, massage, lodging,
  community kitchen.
• Bathing suits optional.
• Reasonable.
• On Orr Springs Road, 13 miles west of Ukiah.

The community at Orr Hot Springs believes in the sharing life, one that is easy on old Mother Earth. Redwood trees, a gentle brook, good air and wild flowers provide an idyllic setting for day use or overnight—all enhanced by the easy ambience generated by those who run the place.

Massage techniques available include acupressure, reflexology, polarity and chakra balancing. All this, plus hot and healing waters, make Orr a great place to spend an hour or two—or as long as you like.

PARAISO HOT SPRINGS

Soledad, CA 93960
(408) 678-2882
• Warm outdoor swimming pool,
  indoor and outdoor hot pools,
  lodging, campground.
• Bathing suits required.
• Reasonable.
• At the end of Paraiso Springs Road, eight
  miles southwest of Soledad off
  Arroyo Seco Road.

In my years of driving north and south on Highway 101, I've seldom passed up Soledad, a sleepy town where the pace reminds me of a remote Mexican village in deepest Baja. No one hurries. There's always time to shop at the *panadería*, or bakery, for fresh Mexican pastries or hot tortillas. Then it's into the hills for a visit to Paraiso ("Paradise," in Spanish), just a few miles to the southwest.

After a gradual ascent, you're 1,400 feet above the valley floor. Now you can enjoy views of what we native Californians call Steinbeck Country: the gentle Gavilans to the east and, behind you, the rugged Santa Lucias.

Paraiso reveals glimpses of almost every cultural influence since the days of the

Spaniards. Towering royal palms have survived Paraiso's many periodical fires (the most recent in 1954). Other veterans, Victorian cottages with high ceilings, lie to the north. Mobile homes cluster to the south.

I'm always impressed with the serenity of the springs and surrounding area. No irritating radio sounds or loud talking threatens the almost sacred atmosphere. You can enjoy the delicious warm pools in total relaxation.

Paraiso's indoor soaking pool, available year-round from 9:00 a.m. to 5:45 p.m., steeps at about 108°F. A small outdoor pool, at about 104°F, and an Olympic-sized one, at about 84°F, open year-round at 10:00 a.m. The outdoor pools close at 4:45 p.m. from November through April and at 6:00 p.m. from May through October. For a reasonable fee, visitors can rent a cottage, camp overnight or simply spend the day.

ROMAN SPA HOT SPRINGS RESORT
1300 Washington St., Calistoga, CA 94515
(707) 942-4441
- Outdoor swimming pool and whirlpool, indoor therapy pool, mud baths, sauna, massage, beauty treatments, lodging.
- Bathing suits required.
- Deluxe.
- Right in town.

Guests of Calistoga's Roman Spa relax in the splendor of manicured patios and gardens at the heart of Napa Valley wine country. Along with hot mineral baths, the first-class facility provides sauna and mud baths, herbal facials, massage, reflexology and other health and beauty aids.

SAM'S FAMILY SPA
70-875 Dillon Rd., Desert Hot Springs, CA 92240
(619) 329-6457
- Outdoor swimming and wading pools, sheltered pools, gym, sauna, RV park, motel, picnic area, restaurant.
- Bathing suits required.
- Reasonable.
- On Dillon Road off Palm Drive (exit north from Highway 10), seven miles from the city of Desert Hot Springs.

When you add water to a desert, you create an oasis, a spot of green irresistible to man. When nature supplied the abundant hot mineral water at Desert Hot Springs, she created a spot of human health and scenic beauty unique in all the world.

Sam's is but one of many RV-and-mineral-water camps in the vicinity, an area growing commensurately with America's retirement population. What especially appeals to me about Sam's is the proximity of RV spaces to the outdoor hot mineral water pool—a handy arrangement for the hundreds of seniors who visit the resort each year.

Along with the main pool, the 50-acre park features an outdoor wading or sitting pool and four sheltered therapeutic pools, all heated naturally with various temperatures of water. Sam's wells, at 265 and 300 feet, range from 105°F to 140°F. Guests can also unwind on a children's playground or courts for volleyball, basketball and horseshoes; in the workout room or sauna; and in a recreation hall with Ping Pong and pool tables. A lake attracts numerous ducks and other birds for nature lovers to feed or observe.

While Desert Hot Springs shares the Coachella Valley with Palm Springs, Rancho Mirage and Palm Desert, its higher altitude—1,200 feet—results in a milder climate. Mountains, snow-capped most of the year, frame matchless views of sun-drenched desert in all directions.

The small, friendly town seems quite sensible when it comes to the cost of living. Travelers find more than a hundred hotels and motels, 30 mobile home parks and an excellent selection of restaurants, clubs and recreational activities. Best of all, many of the facilities feature hot tubs and pools filled with the endless supply of hot local waters.

For information on other hot-spring destinations in the area, write the Visitor Information Center, P.O. Box 848, Desert Hot Springs, CA 92240.

SIERRA HOT SPRINGS
P.O. Box 366, Sierraville, CA 96126
(916) 994-3773
- Outdoor hot tubs, massage, lodging, picnic area, campground.
- Bathing suits optional.
- Reasonable.
- Off Lemon Canyon Road on Campbell Hot Springs Road, about a mile southeast of Sierraville.

North of Truckee, the trees of Tahoe National Forest spill down to the edge of a broad alpine valley spotted with horses, fields and a few small towns. A row of rustic hot springs half a mile long hides at the edge of the trees outside Sierraville. If you like hot springs in their natural state, you'll love Sierra Hot Springs.

A spiritual community maintains the hot tubs, massage schedule, lodging, picnic area and campground. Along with the baths, fed by hot mineral springs, nature lovers revel in the 680-acre spread of open meadows and wooded hills.

SODA BATHS
Lake County, CA
No phone.
- Hot pools.
- No clothing requirements.
- Free.
- On a small island just off the shore of Clear Lake, near Kelseyville.

Clear Lake, the largest natural lake within California's borders, once centered an elegant resort area. With its glory days past, the majestic setting remains: mighty Mount Kinockti and some of the most glorious sunsets in the state.

You'll need a boat to reach the Soda Baths, and you can rent one in nearby Kelseyville.

SONOMA MISSION INN AND SPA
P.O. Box 1447, Sonoma, CA 95476
(707) 938-9000
(800) 862-4945 (toll-free in California)
(800) 358-9022 (toll-free outside California)
- Outdoor swimming pool, indoor and outdoor whirlpools, sauna, steam bath, massage, beauty treatments, fitness classes, lodging, restaurants, tennis.
- Bathing suits optional in private spaces.
- Deluxe.
- 18140 Sonoma Highway 12, two miles north of Sonoma.

Built upon a hot springs discovered in 1895, Sonoma Mission Inn's predecessor drew wealthy San Franciscans by stagecoach. In the

1890s, the elite came to Boyes Hot Springs to see and be seen, to take dips in the tepid waters and to wrap themselves in medicinal mud from the springs. A fire in 1923 destroyed the original hotel, but it was rebuilt in 1927. After decades of boom and bust, millions of dollars in improvements and expansion have made Sonoma Mission Inn and Spa one of the premier luxury health resorts in the West.

A massive courtyard with circular drive fronts a magnificent Spanish-revival facade. The lobby—a grand affair—has a vaulted beam ceiling, plush furnishings and a forest of indoor plants. A state-of-the-art, Grecian-style spa caters to an upscale crowd with a full schedule of fitness activities, indoor and out-door whirlpools, sauna, steam room, gym and indoor and outdoor massage. Spa specialties include herbal wraps—of lavender, pepper-mint, sassafras, chamomile, mugwort or other plants—and a mineral-water massage from a pressurized hose.

The gourmet restaurant features Sonoma wine country cuisine—geared for health-minded hedonists, naturally. The first-class refinements go on and on, from complimenta-ry newspapers and croissants at breakfast to laundry, baby-sitting and limousine services.

SPA HOTEL & MINERAL SPRINGS
100 N. Indian Canyon Dr., Palm Springs, CA 92262
(619) 325-1461
- Outdoor swimming pools, indoor pools and tubs, sauna, massage, beauty treatments, lodging, restaurant, tennis.
- Bathing suits required in public areas.
- Moderate.
- Right in town.

Years ago some foresighted Cahuilla Indians built a bathhouse over a natural hot spring in what is now downtown Palm Springs. Settlers, saddle tramps and other travelers flocked to the waters, pleased to find a little comfort and company in a mighty lonely desert region.

Today the old bathhouse and its springs have grown into a full-service spa hotel with a client list of movie stars, presidents, and royalty. Attractions include three outdoor swimming pools (two with natural spring water), 34 "swirlpools," a bathhouse, three lighted tennis courts, a health club, beauty salons, even a euca-lyptus inhalation room. You'll also find massage, exercise classes, herbal wraps and baths, loofah and salt-glow rubs, tanning machines, orthion treatments and aromatherapy along with the use of the various tubs and pools.

Guests of the 230-room hotel receive a complimentary Continental breakfast in the Poolside Tahquitz Room. From 11 a.m. to 4 p.m., the Pool Bar provides light snacks and refreshments like juices, sodas, mineral waters, beer and mixed drinks.

Packages range from the week-long Discover the Springs to Pamper Day and Spa Sampler for those with limited time. All pack-ages include room, breakfast and a healthy dose of the options listed above. Attractive high-season rates turn even more affordable in the summer.

STEWART MINERAL SPRINGS
4617 Stewart Springs Rd., Weed, CA 96094
(916) 938-2222
- Indoor hot tubs, outdoor whirlpool, saunas, sun decks, massage, RV space, picnic sites, lodging, restaurant.

- Bathing suits required in public areas.
- Reasonable.
- Outside Weed on Stewart Springs Road, four miles west of Highway 5's Edgewood exit.

Stewart Mineral Springs closes for the winter. But in the summer it's a great place to soak in the heated mineral-water tubs or frolic in the icy stream. Visit on a Saturday, and you're welcome to join the local Kuruk Indians who come for a weekly purification sweat on their traditional healing grounds in the foothills of Mt. Shasta.

Guests stay in dormitories, cabins, apartments and a five-bedroom A-frame house. All but the dorm rooms have kitchens or kitchenettes.

SYCAMORE MINERAL SPRINGS

1215 Avila Beach Dr., San Luis Obispo, CA 93405
(805) 595-7302
(800) 234-5831 (toll-free)
- Swimming pool, hot tubs, massage, lodging with private mineral spas, restaurant.
- Bathing suits optional in private spaces.
- Reasonable.
- On Avila Beach Drive, a third of a mile west of Highway 101.

Two men drilling for oil in 1897 struck the hot sulphur-based waters of Sycamore Mineral Springs. The resort that resulted attracted turn-of-the-century spa goers, then celebrities like W.C. Fields and guests from nearby Hearst Castle in the 1920s. A more therapeutically minded crowd followed in the '30s.

Rebuilt in the '70s and continually updated, today's resort welcomes overnight guests with 27 comfortable rooms. Each has its own private outdoor patio equipped with an acrylic spa. Fill it with hot mineral water, sit back and relax.

Hotel stays include complimentary Continental breakfast and unlimited mineral water soaks. Those unable to enjoy an overnight stay can rent one of the redwood hot tubs nestled on a tree-covered hillside.

A new restaurant, The Gardens of Avila, specializes in health-conscious California cuisine and includes facilities for meetings and seminars. The oak- and sycamore-laden grounds provide a large gazebo and courtyard area popular for weddings and receptions, banquets and company parties.

Beaches, golf courses, horseback riding, tennis, wine tasting and other activities wait nearby. Yet many never leave the grounds, choosing to play volleyball on the sand courts, lie in the sun around the swimming pool, indulge in a massage or soak to their hearts' content on their own private patio. The soothing waters, idyllic surroundings and friendly, experienced staff make every visit a memorable one.

TASSAJARA BUDDHIST MEDITATION CENTER

Tassajara Springs, Carmel Valley, CA 93924
(415) 431-3771
- Outdoor swimming pool, indoor and outdoor soaking pools, lodging, meals.
- Bathing suits required in swimming pool.
- Deluxe.
- On Tassajara Road, off Carmel Valley Road southeast of Carmel Valley.

Secluded in the mountains behind Big Sur,

this Zen monastery opens to guests from May through August. A visit requires reservations, which you'll need to make far in advance. Tassajara is well worth any wait, though. The experience combines heavenly hot water, delicious vegetarian meals and an ambience of matchless serenity.

TECOPA COUNTY HOT SPRINGS
Tecopa, CA 92389
(619) 852-4264
- Indoor soaking pools, RV park, campground.
- Nude bathing only.
- Free.
- Two miles north of Tecopa off State Highway 127, 57 miles north of Baker.

En route to Death Valley a few years ago, we stopped at Tecopa, a little desert village with lots of RV parks and older people easing their arthritic aches. Two miles outside the village, we found a pair of bathhouses with large hot-spring pools, one for men and one for women. We loved these pools and loved the price—free!

Here the county maintains 40 acres complete with campground and lots of spaces for RVs and tents. You can count on plenty of sunshine (the yearly rainfall averages two inches) and electricity, but no drinking water. If you find yourself in the desert in need of a soothing mineral water bath, however, we highly recommend this spot.

TWO BUNCH PALMS
67425 Two Bunch Palms Trail, Desert Hot Springs, CA 92240
(619) 329-8791
(800) 472-4334 (toll-free in Southern California)

- Outdoor hot pools, beauty treatments, massage, lodging, restaurant.
- Bathing suits customary outside.
- Deluxe.
- On Two Bunch Palms Trail, via Palm Drive off Interstate Highway 10.

On the hot side in summer, this resort is heavenly when coolness returns to the desert. You'll find everything you ever wanted in a laid-back health resort, including swaying palms, blue-water hot pools, sauna, massage, facials and other body treatments.

The accommodations range from modest rooms furnished in Victorian oak to sprawling modern villas complete with mirror-lined bedrooms and private Jacuzzis.

Massage includes everything from Swedish to Jin Shin Do and Trager (in which you're cradled and rocked like a baby). Candlelight and the scent of herbs accompany the rubdowns. Go in haggard, come out reborn!

In the pool, you can relax and chat with other guests as you surreptitiously scout for film stars in the palm-shaded grotto.

VICHY SPRINGS
2605 Vichy Springs Rd., Ukiah, CA 95482
(707) 462-9515
- Outdoor swimming pool, indoor tubs, massage, lodging.
- Bathing suits required.
- Reasonable.
- On Vichy Springs Road, three miles off Highway 101, two hours north of San Francisco.

Vichy Springs, named after the famous spring in France, has a long, long history. The 90°F

SONOMA MISSION INN AND SPA

WOODY'S FEATHER RIVER HOT SPRINGS

VICHY SPRINGS

water issues from a travertine grotto estimated at ten million years old.

Experts say the source lies three to five miles deep, and some believe Vichy's water has never reached the earth's surface before. Today's owners bottle the water. It's naturally carbonated, rich in minerals and tastes great.

For centuries the local natives revered the spring as a holy place and used it for healing. Then in 1854, the waters spawned the resort that has been in operation ever since.

Two cottages—the oldest buildings in Mendocino County—feature charming Victorian decors along with full kitchens, private baths, living rooms and porches. The resort also provides a dozen nonsmoking rooms. Recent improvements include renovations of the cottages and rooms, paved parking lots, a travertine walkway leading to a tiled outdoor hot tub and an Olympic-sized swimming pool.

The 680 wooded acres surrounding Vichy make it ideal for hikers and nature lovers. One visit and you'll agree with author Jack London, who called Vichy his "favorite summer home."

WHEELER HOT SPRINGS
16825 Maricopa Hwy., P.O. Box 250, Ojai, CA 93024
(805) 646-8131
(800) 227-9292 (toll-free)
- Outdoor swimming pool, indoor tubs, massage, skin care center, restaurant.
- Bathing suits required in outdoor pool.
- Reasonable.
- On Highway 33, 6.5 miles east of Ojai.

You can read all about Wheeler's fascinating history while soaking, from the nine-ton brass tub used exclusively by fighter Jack Dempsey to the bomb that finished off a member of the Costello gang during Prohibition.

Wheeler began its roller-coaster existence in 1870, when its namesake, Wheeler Blumberg, discovered the first hot spring while deer hunting. A man of vision and enterprise, he built a huge wood and stone hotel in which each room contained a bath full of hot mineral water. Blumberg added a lodge with tavern, an outdoor ballroom, a bowling alley, even card rooms in the cellar. Though a fire destroyed much of the old facility in 1940, it was rebuilt to a first-class standard.

Wheeler Hot Springs specializes in "health as entertainment": hot-tub soaks; monthly jazz, blues and classical concerts; gourmet dinners; and a variety of massages from licensed technicians. A new skin care center adds a lengthy menu of facials, body wraps, scrubs and peels. Tall sycamores and rushing brooks provide the natural magic of a California canyon environment.

WHITE SULPHUR SPRINGS
3100 White Sulphur Springs Rd., St. Helena, CA 94574
(707) 963-8588 (resort)
(707) 963-4361 (spa appointments)
- Outdoor hot sulphur and mountain-water Jacuzzi pools, massage, mud baths, beauty wraps, lodging.
- Bathing suits required.
- Reasonable.
- At the end of Spring Street on White Sulphur Springs Road, in Napa Valley 2.75 miles off State Highway 29.

The state's oldest mineral springs resort, founded in 1852, pleases history buffs as well as hot springs fans. It typifies the many new-age facilities that set the stage for just about anything one could want, from a quiet weekend with a close friend to an active seminar with dozens of attendees.

A steady stream of hot sulphur water flows through a large outdoor soaking pool (like everything, available to both day users and overnight guests). Another large outdoor pool, filled with clear mountain water, comes with invigorating Jacuzzi action. A new health spa adds locker space, herbal and mud wraps, facials, and massage. A conference center for groups of up to 200 provides a large meeting room, dining room and two rooms for break-out meetings. Banquets call on catering services in nearby St. Helena.

An authentic country feel pervades the two inns (one with shared baths) and nine cottages. While guests in the four largest cottages have full kitchens of their own, others use the resort's common kitchen area or visit the many fine restaurants in town.

Groomed hiking trails lead out through 330 acres of giant redwood, madrone, oak and sycamore. Visitors can also count on mountain bike rental, a year-round creek and waterfall and several delightful picnic spots.

WILBUR HOT SPRINGS
Williams, CA 95987
(916) 473-2306
- Outdoor warm swimming pool, hot soaking tubs, massage, lodging.
- Bathing suits optional.
- Deluxe.
- Five miles by gravel road off the intersection of State Highways 16 and 20.

An elegant old mansion with separate bathhouse and pool nestles in the hills on the west side of the Sacramento River. This is Wilbur Hot Springs, surrounded by 240 acres of rolling terrain, 25 miles from the nearest town and a hundred years out of date.

The water comes out of the ground at 153°F. It's piped to the bathhouse, where it passes through a series of large concrete tanks, cooling as it goes. The coolest bath is body temperature; the hottest, 112°F. There's a strong mineral content to the water that will turn your jewelry black and may straighten your permanent wave, so be careful; otherwise, the water can do you no harm and a lot of good. There's also a swimming pool, kept warm in winter and cool in summer.

Wilbur Hot Springs opened formally in 1865 and flourished during the late nineteenth century. Like a lot of spas, it went into a decline during the '30s and was abandoned in the '60s. Then Richard Louis Miller, a psychologist from Esalen, bought it in the early '70s, intending to establish a therapeutic community based on the Esalen model. In fact, Miller has conducted several healing programs at Wilbur, one of them the highly successful Cokenders, which has helped dozens of cocaine addicts shed their expensive habit.

The people who live at Wilbur full-time serve as innkeepers. Other inhabitants—writers, musicians, painters, clowns, etc.—stay for three months at a time, working half-time for room and board as part of the Wilbur Artists-in-Residence Program.

But the main function of Wilbur Hot Springs is as a restful country inn. Whether you go for a week, a weekend or just an afternoon soak, you'll find the setting relaxing, from the scenery outside to the wood stoves, antiques and kerosene lamps inside, to the salubrious waters of the bathhouse. Overnight guests bring their own food to prepare in the gigantic kitchen. A library full of easy chairs contains good books, a billiard table, a pool table, a piano, guitars and plenty of people to meet if you want to meet people. Skilled professional massage is always available.

The resort confines smoking to one area. Other rules keep glass and alcohol out of the bathhouse, cars parked out of sight in the lot and pets left at home. All visits require reservations. There are also a few customs everyone seems to agree to. Clothing is optional, for example, but people remove their shoes before entering the hotel. Guests who use the kitchen wash their own dishes. Perhaps best of all for those who want to relax in real style,

the people who go to Wilbur respect each other's right to peace and quiet.

WOODY'S FEATHER RIVER HOT SPRINGS

P.O. Box 7, Twain, CA 95984
(916) 283-4115

- Two hot pools, motel, restaurant, bar, campsites, RV park.
- Bathing suits optional.
- Reasonable.
- Just off Highway 70 near Twain.

Here's an opportunity to soak in a hot tub right next to a river. When you get too hot, you can cool off the natural way. Excellent hiking trails explore the upper Feather River Canyon. Recreation extends to good fishing and panning for gold.

OREGON

*T*AKE A LOOK at the Oregon map, and you'll see the majority of hot springs concentrated in the southeast and south-central region. Most of these remain in their natural state, for the simple reason that few people inhabit this part of Oregon. A typical county might have 10,000 residents in 10,000 square miles. Oregon's wide open spaces allow for exploration of the freest kind.

As long as you have a dependable vehicle with good tires, you'll have no problems. Even if you do, the people are friendly and accommodating. We once drove from Frenchglen to Fields, for example, along what has to be one of the West's least traveled roads. When we casually waved at a low-flying plane, it banked, descended steeply and landed on the road right behind us. The pilot had interpreted our off-handed hello as a call for help. The event ended well, despite our embarrassment. The pilot and his friend wanted to chat, curious to know what we were doing with such a large trailer so far away from anywhere.

As you wander Oregon's wild and friendly country, you can expect to find some great hot springs on your own. Or peruse the following section for some previously scouted locations.

KAH-NEE-TA RESORT

Distribution of hot springs in the state of

OREGON

(Locations are approximate. Consult text and road maps for directions.)

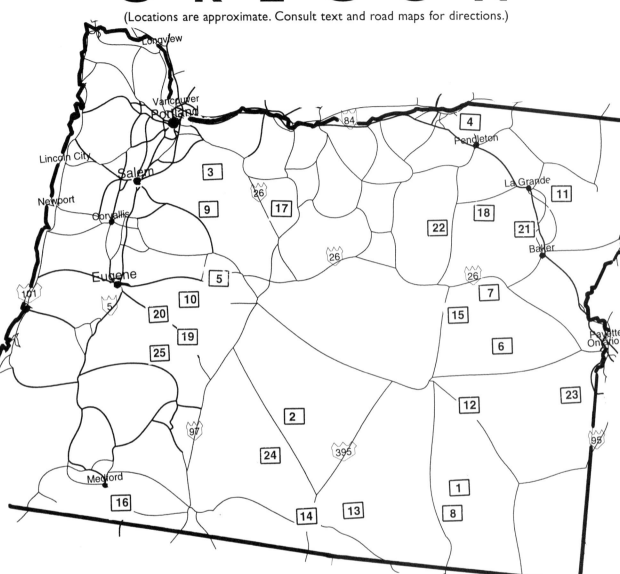

1. **Alvord Hot Springs**
2. **Ana Hot Springs**
3. **Bagby Hot Springs**
4. **Baker's Bar M**
5. **Belknap Lodge & Hot Springs**
6. **Beulah Reservoir Hot Springs**
7. **Blue Mountain Hot Springs**
8. **Borax Lake**
9. **Breitenbush Hot Springs**
10. **Cougar Springs**
11. **Cove Swimming Pool**
12. **Crystal Crane Hot Springs**
13. **Hart Mountain Hot Spring**

14. **Hunter's Lodge**
15. **J Bar L Guest Ranch**
16. **Jackson Hot Springs**
17. **Kah-Nee-Ta Resort**
18. **Lehman Hot Springs**
19. **McCredie Hot Springs**
20. **Meditation Pool at Wall**
21. **Radium Hot Springs**
22. **Ritter Hot Springs**
23. **Snively Hot Springs**
24. **Summer Lake Hot Springs**
25. **Umpqua Warm Spring**

ALVORD HOT SPRINGS
Harney County, OR
No phone.
- Two outdoor concrete tubs.
- No clothing requirements.
- Free.
- Beside the Alvord Desert, about 20 miles north of Fields.

If you're looking for a hot spring in a remote location, this will fill the bill. You can gaze off to the Steens Mountains to the west and the Alvord Desert to the east while soaking in utter detachment from the rest of the world.

Or take a friend. Two concrete pools allow bathers to maintain their personal temperature preference simply by adding more hot water or stopping the flow and allowing the tub to cool.

ANA HOT SPRINGS
Lake County, Oregon
No phone.
- Warm swimming hole, campground.
- No clothing requirements.
- Free.
- A few miles northeast of Summer Lake.

Ana Springs is one of the largest hot springs in the West in terms of flow rate. The water gushes from several places in the desert at the almost unbelievable rate of 50,000 to 75,000 gallons per minute!

Not as hot as many springs, the water, at 70°F, is still considered thermal because it exceeds the average annual air temperature. Most of it flows from an ordinary galvanized pipe about three feet in diameter. The remainder spouts from fissures in the canyon wall.

Heavy growth of trees and shrubs conceals some of these springs, but a little probing will be most rewarding, especially in spring and summer when wild flowers decorate the grotto.

To get to Ana, drive north two miles from the Summer Lake post office and turn right at the Ana Reservoir sign. After about a mile, you'll see a large lake on your right. Turn down any of the dirt roads heading that direction. They all lead to a campground equipped with fire pits. You won't see Ana Springs at first. But as you turn left from the lake, you'll see it set in a miniature version of the Grand Canyon.

What a great swimming hole! And what great sport to try to swim against the current of thousands of gallons of warm water pouring into this fantastic pool. Try it—you'll be amazed.

BAGBY HOT SPRINGS
Clackmas County, OR
(503) 630-4256 (information)
- A dozen indoor hot tubs, rest rooms.
- Bathing suits optional.
- Free.
- In Mt. Hood National Forest, 1.5 miles by road from Pegleg Falls Campground, then 1.5 miles by trail from Bagby's parking lot.

After a fire in the late 1970s burned Bagby to the ground, a volunteer group called the Friends of Bagby rebuilt the facility. The first of Bagby's bathhouses has a large redwood hot tub. The second has another large tub plus four hollow-log tubs ideal for two. A third has six hollow-log tubs in private stalls. Bathers moderate the temperature to their liking with ladles of cold water from buckets.

Sadly, Bagby has suffered greatly from its

popularity in recent years. You'll want to avoid it entirely on Friday and Saturday in the summer, when young people flock to the area for all-night drinking parties and such. Another caveat: Because of vandals, the Forest Service advises against leaving valuables in your car at the trail head. Store items you value elsewhere, or take them with you to the springs. Also, be sure to carry a flashlight; without one the trail can be impossible to negotiate after sundown.

A wisely planned and timed visit, however, can result in a rewarding experience. Bagby's trail winds through a wilderness area of great natural beauty and towering trees. After an hour or two at Bagby, some like to continue on the trail beyond the springs to Bull of the Woods Wilderness—where the lookout tower presents an unforgettable panorama of majestic old-growth forest.

The Friends of Bagby maintain a cabin with hard-working volunteer attendants at the springs. If you want to help, send donations to P.O. Box 15116, Portland, OR 97215.

BAKER'S BAR M
Route 1, Adams, OR 97810
(503) 566-3381
• Outdoor hot swimming pool, lodging, meals, horseback riding.
• Bathing suits required.
• Deluxe.
• On the Umatilla River near Adams, about 25 miles east of Pendleton.

Here's a Wild West guest ranch to bring back memories of cowboy movies you saw as a kid. Minimum one-week stays include your own personal saddle horse and delicious ranch-style meals. After an all-day ride, you'll really

enjoy a long, soothing soak in the 90°F pool. The water flows through continuously, so no chlorine sullies the crystal clarity.

BELKNAP LODGE AND HOT SPRINGS
Belknap Springs, OR 97413
(503) 822-3512
• Two outdoor swimming pools, indoor tubs, lodging, RV park, campground.
• Bathing suits required in pools.
• Reasonable.
• On Highway 126, five miles east of McKenzie Bridge.

Five miles east of the village of McKenzie Bridge, a sign points the way to Belknap Lodge and Hot Springs. Here hot-springs fans benefit from several healthy flows of 75 gallons per minute and temperatures that vary from 147°F to 198°F.

The comfortable, fully developed resort provides both trailer spaces and recently remodeled cottages. In addition to the two swimming pools and hot tubs, visitors come for the great sightseeing, white-water rafting and fishing (with many river guides in the area), excellent hiking, golf at Takatee Golf Course, water sports at a nearby reservoir and snow skiing in winter. Numerous stores and restaurants wait ten miles away while, at Belknap, there's just plain peacefulness.

BEULAH RESERVOIR HOT SPRING
Malheur County, OR
No phone.
• Bathtub.
• No clothing requirements.
• Free.

• At the northeast corner of the Beulah Reservoir, 75 miles northeast of Burns.

Bring a garden hose to siphon water from Beulah's hot springs. The tub stands in the open, next to a ditch that feeds the reservoir.

BLUE MOUNTAIN HOT SPRINGS GUEST RANCH

Star Route, Prairie City, OR 97876
(503) 820-3744
• Outdoor hot swimming pool.
• Bathing suits required.
• Reasonable.
• At the edge of Malheur National Forest along the John Day River, about ten miles southeast of Prairie City.

You'll love the Blue Mountain area any time of year for its enchanting scenery and surrounding wilderness. The weather gets mighty cold in winter—but it only makes the water of this pool feel even greater.

Be sure to call ahead. Now privately owned, the former guest ranch opens its pool to visitors only when the residents are home, and on a reservation-only basis.

BORAX LAKE

Harney County, OR
No phone.
• Warm lake.
• No clothing requirements.
• Free.
• About ten miles north of Fields in south east Oregon.

Imagine swimming in a clear warm lake, whose water rises from great depths at a rate of nearly a thousand gallons a minute. To us it was like a visit to another planet.

To reach this geothermal wonder, drive north from Fields for about ten miles until you see Alvord Lake ahead. It may or may not contain water, depending on recent rainfall. About two and a half miles south of Alvord, watch for a road that turns right. It's bumpy and there's not much clearance for modern cars, but we made it in a '66 Chevy Impala, which proves it's not too bad.

You'll see traces of an abandoned borax works after driving a mile or so. Stop and walk to the cabin constructed from blocks of borax. From here, you can't miss sighting the five-acre lake with its 90°F water and shoreline built up by centuries of mineral deposits. It's somewhat difficult to navigate the soggy ground, crusty bank and muddy shallows. But once you're floating in Borax Lake, you'll find it well worth the trouble.

BREITENBUSH HOT SPRINGS

P.O. Box 578, Detroit, OR 97342
(503) 854-3314
• Swimming pool, soaking pools, hot tubs, sauna, massage, lodging, campsites, restaurant.
• Bathing suits optional.
• Reasonable.
• At Mile Post 10 on Forest Service Road 46, ten miles east of Detroit and about a hundred miles south of Portland.

The Breitenbush Community, a worker-owned cooperative, maintains an educational, consciousness-raising and overall transformational center at Breitenbush Hot Springs. Here in the high Cascades, in midst of 50-plus ther-

BREITENBUSH HOT SPRINGS

COUGAR SPRINGS

CRYSTAL CRANE HOT SPRINGS

COVE SWIMMING POOL

mal springs, you'll find a healing retreat and a conference center dedicated to holistic health, spiritual growth and the celebration of life. Because groups sometimes book the whole retreat for themselves, it's imperative to call ahead for reservations.

The site rests on Mt. Jefferson, surrounded by the Mt. Jefferson Wilderness Area and 1,675,407-acre Willamette National Forest. The community supports its 50 members entirely through its services. Licensed massage therapists offer everything from Swedish to *lomi lomi* to Thai. In addition to special seminars and classes, guests may join in daily yoga and other well-being programs. Visitors, whether staying in the 42 cabins or camping on the grounds, receive three delicious vegetarian meals a day.

Breitenbush's hot-springs menu includes a natural steam sauna, the Medicine Circle (four hot tubs set at cardinal points of the compass) and a meadow with a trio of idyllic hot pools. Outdoor activities range from volleyball to hiking and cross-country skiing in season.

To me, Breitenbush represents the best use possible for a geothermal resource. The community's statement of purpose: "To provide a safe and potent environment for people to evolve in ways they never even imagined." I dream of seeing this type of facility repeated all through the West. Your support and encouragement can make the dream reality. If you or your group plan to hold a retreat, seminar or similar activity, I urge you to consider Breitenbush as one of your first choices.

COUGAR SPRINGS
Lane County, OR
No phone.

- Hot creek, pools.
- No clothing requirements.
- Free.
- On the Cougar Reservoir road, off Highway 126 about 50 miles east of Eugene.

While exploring central Oregon south of the McKenzie River, we stumbled upon a fantastic spring. It originates in the bed of a small creek. The hot water joins the cold creek water to create just the right temperature for bathing. The water descends into three separate pools. Because each pool is cooler than the next, there's something for everyone's taste in temperature.

Our visit found the spot festooned with wild flowers, bits of old Ponderosa bark and students from the University of Oregon at nearby Eugene. We enjoyed chatting with several of them while bathing in the pools surrounded by huge evergreens and great gray granite boulders. They told us that, because the roads are plowed, Cougar Springs can be enjoyed nearly all year long. One young man commented on how delightful it is to trudge through powder snow in winter and then leap into the warm water.

Just across the road, the damming of the south fork of the McKenzie River creates an immense body of water known as Cougar Reservoir. We saw a few fishermen and water skiers that indicated these sports are available for the effort. A small lake with good swimming waits about a quarter of a mile below the springs.

To reach the hot springs, heading east from Eugene, turn right off Highway 126 at the Cougar Reservoir sign. When you reach the dam, turn right again and drive about three miles. You'll see a small lake with a waterfall on its southern shore. Park on the left side of the road and walk back to where the trail begins on the north side of the lake. Don your hiking shoes—some of the trail is steep and slippery—and follow the path for about a quarter of a mile.

COVE SWIMMING POOL
907 Water St., Cove, OR 97824
(503) 568-4890
• Outdoor warm swimming pool, picnic ground.
• Bathing suits required.
• Reasonable.
• On Highway 237, 15 miles east of La Grande.

This country day resort opens from May through Labor Day. Visitors enjoy a picnic ground and pool at a pleasant 86°F.

CRYSTAL CRANE HOT SPRINGS
HC-73-2653 Hwy. 78, Burns, OR 97720
(503) 493-2312
• Outdoor pond, indoor tubs, lodging, RV hookups, campground, snack bar.
• Bathing suits required outdoors.
• Reasonable.
• On Highway 78, 25 miles east of Burns.

The owners are constantly expanding this year-round health-oriented resort. With a motel under construction, they now welcome guests with four cabins, several RV hookups, a beautiful campground and a snack bar. Plans include a vegetarian restaurant that will utilize produce from an existing geothermal greenhouse.

Crystal Crane's 185°F mineral water rises from underground springs at a rate of 150 gallons per minute. With no need for chemicals,

it feeds an 80-foot pond and six private tubs for 2 to 15 people. Temperatures range from 95°F to 105°F, but you can adjust them to your liking—whether 50°F or 114°F.

Travelers find accommodations just about anytime in winter. But be sure to call ahead in the warmer seasons, especially for spring and summer weekends.

HART MOUNTAIN HOT SPRING
Harney County, OR
No phone.
• Hot pool.
• No clothing requirements.
• Free.
• In the Hart Mountain National Antelope Refuge, northeast of Plush.

The 275,000 acres of Hart Mountain National Antelope Refuge bound across desert sage-brush and juniper to alpine streams and meadows. The refuge—a haven for pronghorn antelope, bighorn sheep, mule deer, bobcats, golden eagles, sage grouse and other threatened wildlife—also harbors a super-remote hot spring for humans. A simple cement-lined pool catches the water and maintains it at approximate body temperature.

Next time you feel oppressed by too many people and the pace of modern life, try a retreat at Hart Mountain. You can park your RV for as long as you like, and you'll never run out of hot water.

HUNTER'S LODGE
P.O. Box 1189, Lakeview, OR 97630
(503) 947-2127
• Swimming pool, fresh-water Jacuzzi, lodging, restaurant, lounge.

- Bathing suits required.
- Reasonable.
- On Highway 395, two miles north of Lakeview.

Hunter's Lodge faces an ever-spouting geyser in the middle of a small lake. Naturally heated water not only fills Hunter's 20- by 30-foot swimming pool, it warms the motel rooms and a greenhouse growing tomatoes and other vegetables.

Lakeview, in southern Oregon at an altitude of 4,800 feet, is one of the highest towns in the state. Nearby Fremont National Forest mixes high desert terrain and woodland filled with opportunities for golf, fishing, gliding, hiking, rock hunting and skiing.

J BAR L GUEST RANCH
IZ Route, Canyon City, OR 97820
(503) 575-2517
- Outdoor swimming pool, sauna, lodging, RV hookups, campground.
- Bathing suits required.
- Reasonable.
- On Forest Service Road 15 off U.S. Highway 395, ten miles south of John Day.

My number-one criterion for any place I stay is quiet, and this fully developed guest ranch is particularly blessed. Knowing that urban noise contributes not only to human stress but disease, I'm convinced we should all take long health breaks in the wild—especially where man and nature meet so agreeably at hot mineral springs.

More active vacationers than I enjoy the peace and quiet of J Bar L's pool, meadows and forests, too. The ranch makes a great base for hiking, fishing and hunting adventures nearby.

JACKSON HOT SPRINGS
2253 Hwy. 99 North, Ashland, OR 97520
(503) 482-3776
- Outdoor swimming pool, indoor tubs, massage, lodging, RV park, picnic area.
- Bathing suits required.
- Reasonable.
- Two miles north of Ashland on Highway 99.

The 50- by 100-foot swimming pool at this family vacation spot can easily absorb all your children and then some. Along with massages and hot mineral baths in private rooms, the resort provides well-equipped cabins and space for campers and motor homes.

While staying at Jackson, be sure to take advantage of the famous year-round offerings of Shakespearean and contemporary theater in nearby Ashland. The delightfully upbeat college town also presents great opportunities in dining and shopping for arts and crafts.

KAH-NEE-TA RESORT
P.O. Box K, Warm Springs, OR 97761
(800) 831-0100 (toll-free)
- Outdoor hot swimming pool, indoor baths, lodging, restaurant, tennis, golf, horseback riding.
- Bathing suits required.
- Deluxe.
- On Highway 26, 114 miles east of Portland.

You'll be doing yourself a favor by spending some time at this full-service luxury resort. You'll also be supporting the deserving Indian tribe that put the whole thing together.

Kah-Nee-Ta lies within the boundaries of the Warm Springs Indian Reservation north of Bend. Along with a generous inventory of natural hot mineral baths and pools, visitors find horses, golf, tennis, hiking and a wide choice of accommodations. The strikingly designed lodge contains a number of comfortable rooms. You can also park your RV, stay in one of the private cottages or camp in a tepee—warmed by a fire inside.

Kah-Nee-Ta exemplifies what careful planning, organization and intelligent execution can accomplish with a geothermal resource. Be sure to stop by when you're in central Oregon, if only for a bone-soothing soak.

LEHMAN HOT SPRINGS

P.O. Box 247, Ukiah, OR 97880
(503) 427-3015

- Outdoor hot pools, RV space, campgrounds, restaurant.
- Bathing suits required.
- Reasonable.
- On State Highway 244, 18 miles east of Ukiah.

A traditional favorite with hot springs lovers, Lehman won our hearts with its warm ambience many years ago. Now, new owners promise to continue the steady improvements and updating.

HUNTER'S LODGE

SUMMER LAKE HOT SPRINGS

LEHMAN HOT SPRINGS

UMPQUA WARM SPRING

MᶜCREDIE HOT SPRINGS

McCredie Hot Springs, OR
(503) 465-6388 (information)
- Natural pools.
- Clothing optional.
- Free.
- On Highway 58 in Willamette National Forest, 11 miles southeast of Oakridge.

Located just off the highway in the Rigdon Ranger District of Willamette National Forest, McCredie's 20- by 20-foot natural hot pool and three smaller ones cluster on the banks of Salt Creek. A spacious parking lot accommodates visits to this popular spot.

You can enjoy the camaraderie of fellow hot springs lovers in a setting thick with Douglas firs, then pitch your tent at Blue Pool Campground less than a mile to the west.

MEDITATION POOL AT WALL CREEK

Lane County, OR
No phone.
- Natural pool.
- Bathing suits optional.
- Free.
- Off Forest Service Road 1934, about nine miles northeast of Oakridge in Willamette National Forest.

Oregon's famous foliage surrounds this sylvan bath, where the water steeps at around body temperature. A location well below the snow line makes the experience accessible the year around.

RADIUM HOT SPRINGS

Haines, OR
(503) 856-3609
- Hot swimming pool, RV space, campground.
- Bathing suits required.
- Reasonable.
- On Highway 30, a mile north of Haines.

The good life at Radium Hot Springs centers around a 50- by 120-foot swimming pool filled with naturally heated mineral water. Open from June 1 through Labor Day, the resort offers space for both tents and trailers.

The area often attracts history buffs following the old Oregon Trail. A mile from the resort, the Eastern Oregon Museum in Haines displays a fine collection of pioneer relics.

RITTER HOT SPRINGS

P.O. Box 16, Ritter, OR 97872
(503) 421-3846
- Outdoor swimming pool, indoor soaking pools, lodging, RV spaces, picnic sites.
- Bathing suits required in swimming pool.
- Reasonable.
- Between Pendleton and John Day, ten miles west of Highway 395.

Few people travel from Pendleton to John Day via Highway 395. It's no freeway (thank God). It winds through the rolling ranch land of eastern Oregon, dips down to several creeks and rivers and curves through Umatilla National Forest. It's easy to reach Ritter from either Pendleton or John Day; just look for the middle fork of the John Day River and turn west on the road that borders it. Then take a ten-mile jaunt along the river until you see the signs pointing to Ritter Hot Springs.

We found Ritter clean, inviting and homey—fascinating, too, with its old stagecoach stop hotel, general store, quaint cottages, pioneer log cabin and swinging bridge across the river. Though somewhat spare of plants, the surrounding land is rich in geological interest.

Ritter opens its 85°F, 40- by 60-foot pool from May to Labor Day. If you prefer more privacy, four baths lie across the swinging bridge near the springs themselves. RV hookups at Ritter go for a reasonable rate, or you can rent a cottage for a nominal fee by the day, week, month or more

SNIVELY HOT SPRING
Malheur County, OR
No phone.
- Hot pool, picnic grounds.
- No clothing requirements.
- Free.
- Along the Owyhee River, about 30 miles south of Ontario.

A series of five hot springs contributes to the flow of the Owyhee River, one of the least known rivers in the West. At Snively, a simple rock enclosure traps the hot water, providing a comfortable mix with the flowing river. Water-loving trees shade a picnic area. If you're feeling adventurous, check the map for other springs in the vicinity.

SUMMER LAKE HOT SPRINGS
28513 Hwy. 31, Paisley, OR 97636
(503) 943-3931
- Sheltered hot mineral pool, changing rooms, showers, RV park.
- Bathing suits required.
- Reasonable.
- On Highway 31 six miles north of Paisley, between Summer Lake and Lake Abert.

Local residents like to gather at Summer Lake's hot mineral pool to gossip and soak away the minimal cares of this rural region. Hosts Ed and Carol McDaniel welcome travelers with an RV park, changing rooms and showers.

A roof shelters the pool from inclement weather, including the fierce winds of winter. Though modest in size, the water maintains a bone-relaxing 102°F temperature the year around. Bathers can see the 20-gallon-per-minute flow as it bubbles from a pipe connected to an artesian well.

Despite the scarcity of tourists in this remote area, it's relatively easy to find hookups for your RV. No one ever bothered us no matter where we parked. We found south-central Oregon a great place to play gypsy.

UMPQUA WARM SPRING
Douglas County, OR
No phone.
- Sheltered hot pool.
- No clothing requirements.
- Free.
- Near Toketee Lake in Umpqua National Forest, via Highway 138 east from Roseburg.

If you're tired of developed resorts, it's time to try Umpqua. Here things are pretty much the way the Indians enjoyed them. The water comes from the ground at 108°F and fills a pool under a rustic three-sided shelter.

To reach this wilderness jewel, drive east from Roseburg on Highway 138, then north to Toketee Lake Campground. At that point, you'd better ask directions; they involve a dirt road and a final mile or so on foot.

WASHINGTON

*T*REMENDOUS VARIETY—the only words to summarize this fascinating state. Washington has jagged peaks to rival the Alps, waterfalls of gigantic rivers thundering into vast canyons, windswept beaches meeting crashing surf. In the eastern plains, the horizons almost never end. It's all here, and much more, including a generous number of most welcome hot springs.

At one time I lived in Bellevue, a small town near Seattle. That was before I learned of the wonders of hot springs, so I never knew about places like Soap Lake or Carson Hot Springs. Now I wish I could relive those years, just so I could take an occasional soak in the warm waters.

MYSTERY HOT SPRING

Distribution of hot springs in the state of
WASHINGTON
(Locations are approximate. Consult text and road maps for directions.)

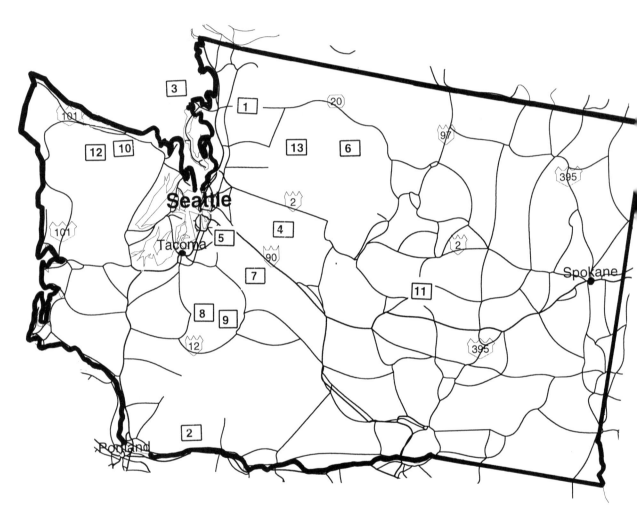

1. **Baker Hot Springs**
2. **Carson Hot Mineral Springs**
3. **Doe Bay Village Resort**
4. **Goldmyer Hot Springs**
5. **Green River Hot Springs**
6. **Kennedy Hot Springs**
7. **Lester Hot Springs**
8. **Longmire Mineral Springs**
9. **Ohanapecosh Hot Springs**
10. **Olympic Hot Springs**
11. **Soap Lake**
12. **Sol Duc Resort**
13. **Sulphur Creek Hot Springs**

CARSON HOT MINERAL SPRINGS RESORT

GOLDMYER HOT SPRINGS

BAKER HOT SPRINGS

Watcom County, WA
(206) 856-5700 (information)
• Hot springs, picnic area.
• No clothing requirements.
• Free.
• Off Forest Service Road 3816, east of Sedro Woolley.

Known at one time as Morovitz Hot Springs, this beautifully isolated spot warrants a visit by those seeking the remote and the obscure.

Baker once had a large tub for a bath, but the Forest Service removed it. Bathing possibilities change with the times. But even if you don't get in a soak, you'll enjoy the picnic tables and views. The surrounding forest epitomizes the character of Pacific Northwest scenery—green, green, green.

To reach the springs, take Highway 20 east from Sedro Woolley to Forest Service Road 385 (Baker Lake Road). Take 385 to Forest Service Road 3816 and drive until you reach the parking area. Park and hike half a mile from that point.

CARSON HOT MINERAL SPRINGS RESORT

P.O. Box 370, Carson, WA 98610
(509) 427-8292
• Indoor hot baths, massage, picnic ground, lodging, campsites, RV park, restaurant.
• Bathing suits required.
• Reasonable.
• In Carson, near the Oregon border east of Vancouver via Highway 14.

Old-timers discovered Carson Hot Springs in 1876. Before long, people seeking the benefits of hot mineral water could visit bathhouses built above the springs on the Wind River.

As word spread, devotees came from all over. They arrived by horseback, covered wagon, and steamboat on the Columbia River. In 1897, a hotel and general store turned Carson into a little town. The 1920s brought cabins and additional bathhouses.

Today's resort calls itself "as comfortable as an old shoe." Prices are comfortable, too, with lodgings from $24 a night. The restaurant features wholesome, home-style meals served in a family atmosphere. After a day of hiking, fishing or bathing, overnight guests retire to the turn-of-the-century hotel or the cabins, campground or trailer park.

For extraordinary lodgings, ask about the $90-a-night Hot Tub Suite with its own kitchen, sitting room, bedroom and private spa. If you simply want to bathe and move on, the charge is only $6 per person.

Carson's mineral water comes from the ground at 126°F, but it's cooled to more manageable levels for the baths. The price of admission includes a bath attendant and all linens—a tradition at Carson for more than 100 years.

DOE BAY VILLAGE RESORT
Star Route, Box 86, Olga, WA 98279
(206) 376-2291
• Hot mineral baths, cold pool, sauna, lodging, general store.
• Bathing suits optional.
• Reasonable.
• Near the town of Olga, on Orcas Island in Puget Sound.

Indulge in the joys of soaking on an island at this picturesque resort. Two of the three mineral baths contain hot sulphur water, the other has cold. While the water comes from a natural spring, it's heated by means other than geothermal. But who cares? It feels great. I guarantee it personally.

Orcas—the largest island in the San Juan Archipelago—spans 57 square miles of picturesque bays and steep, forested ridges. State ferries call on Orcas daily, and several private companies make seasonal runs.

Guests of Doe Bay Village stay in cottages along 2,000 feet of waterfront. The redwood deck in front of the tubs shares the fine view of other islands in the San Juans. Along with the tubs, key resort features include a freshwater stream that tumbles merrily down to a jewel of a saltwater cove, a general store, kayak tours to a wildlife sanctuary and lots of interesting guests throughout the year.

GOLDMYER HOT SPRINGS
North Bend, WA
(206) 789-5631
• Hot outdoor pools, cold pool, campsites, pit toilets.
• Clothing optional.
• Reasonable.
• About 26 miles east of North Bend, a two-hour drive from Seattle.

Goldmyer Hot Springs rests on private property, well hidden by national forest land and the Alpine Lakes Wilderness Area. A nonprofit group, the Northwest Wilderness Programs, monitors the number of visitors by allowing a maximum of 20 people in 24 hours. Call the number above for reservations, directions and current road conditions (which often require

LONGMIRE MINERAL SPRINGS

OLYMPIC HOT SPRINGS

SOL DUC RESORT

UNIDENTIFIED HOT SPRING

SOAP LAKE

four-wheel drive and a wade through a knee-deep river). For a brochure, write 202 N. 85th St., Seattle, WA 98103.

The group dedicates itself to maintaining Goldmyer—a wilderness tract of old-growth forest, unique geological formations and gorgeous waterfalls—as one of the most pristine soaking spots in the West. Water at 110°F spills from a cave into two rock pools, where it progressively cools to about 102°F. A third pool adds a bracing cold-splash alternative. The resident property manager regularly scrubs the rock surface and tests the water's purity.

Taboos include building campfires, bringing glass or pets into the area and eating or drinking alcohol in the pools—mostly common sense, perhaps, but also good reminders of basic hot springs etiquette.

GREEN RIVER HOT SPRINGS
King County, WA
No phone.
- Hot pool.
- Clothing optional.
- Free.
- About three miles from Black Diamond.

Green River Hot Springs makes a lovely retreat from the bustle of urban centers along Puget Sound. The quiet pool rests on a rocky shelf of the Green River Gorge, with a commanding view of forests and the river. Oddly enough, the pool derives its heat from an old underground coal mine that has been burning for many years.

The nearest town, Black Diamond, took its name from the Black Diamond Coal Company, the primary developer of a productive vein discovered in 1890. The town's historical museum displays artifacts from the area's coal-mining days. Nearby, Flaming Geyser State Park centers on an old coal test hole with an eight-inch methane flame.

To reach Green River Hot Springs, drive to Black Diamond on Highway 169. From there, take the Green River Gorge Road about three miles until you reach a footbridge and a parking lot. The trail to the springs begins beyond the bridge on the wooded, higher trail across the road from a resort. The resort owns the property between the road and the springs; so when you ask permission to cross the land, you can also ask for detailed directions to the springs.

KENNEDY HOT SPRINGS
Snohomish County, WA
(206) 436-1155 (information)
- Soaking pool.
- No clothing requirements.
- Free.
- Near White Chuck River, about five miles from Owl Creek Campground in the Darrington Ranger District of Glacier Peak Wilderness.

A small soaking pool collects body-temperature water in the Glacier Peak Wilderness, making a perfect spot to relax and behold the splendors of nature.

Because of the complexity of trails leading to the springs, for directions you'll want to call the Darrington Ranger District at the number listed above. Even better, drop by the office for a Mount Baker–Snoqualmie National Forest visitor's map.

LESTER HOT SPRINGS

King County, WA

No phone.

- Naturally sheltered hot pool.
- No clothing requirements.
- Free.
- Along Green River Road, two miles west of Lester.

A prominent resort—now long gone—once drew its water from this fascinating source. The main flow originates in a cave and fills it, at about 20 gallons per minute, to a depth of about two feet (thanks to a homemade dam of rocks and plastic). Water from the cave and a smaller spring nearby flows directly down slope into the Green River, warming it somewhat.

To find the springs, follow the Green River Road two miles west of Lester. Watch for the water flowing from the hillside above the river on the north side.

LONGMIRE MINERAL SPRINGS

Pierce County, WA

No phone.

- Hot springs exhibit.
- Free.
- Just north of Highway 706, near Longmire Visitor Center in Mount Rainier National Park.

Alas, you can't jump into this spring. But I'm including it anyway because it's a fascinating place for people who love hot springs. Any time you find 50 springs in one small area, it's worth at least a look.

Discovered in 1883, Longmire for a time boasted a hotel, several bathhouses and a reputation for wonder cures. Today the springs

centers an educational exhibit offered by the National Park Service. You'll be glad you took the time to learn more about thermal springs and have a look at the gas bubbling up through the iron-stained waters.

OHANAPECOSH HOT SPRINGS

Lewis County, WA

- Hot pools.
- No clothing requirements.
- Free.
- Beside the Ohanapecosh River in Mount Rainier National Park.

A health resort once operated here, with 30 cabins, a large lodge and bathhouses. Today not a trace remains, except for a self-guided nature trail that circles the 40 acres of seeps, streams and pools.

Between the Ohanapecosh River and a ridge to the east, you'll find a wide variety of pool sizes and flow rates. One hot spring puts out almost 600 gallons a minute at about 120°F. At another place, warm water drains from two seeps into a small creek formed by a nearby cold spring. Don't miss the hot cascade. It falls about 15 feet over a terrace of tufa, then spreads out into a marshy area below.

The nearest campground adjoins Highway 123, 1.5 miles inside the boundary of Mount Rainier National Park and about 12 miles north of Packwood. For information on other accommodations in the park, write Guest Services, Star Route, Ashford, WA 98304; or call (206) 569-2275.

Incidentally, the waters of Ohanapecosh Springs abound in lithium, a plus for people seeking this mineral.

OLYMPIC HOT SPRINGS

Clallam County, WA

(206) 452-2713 (information)

- Rock soaking pools.
- No clothing requirements.
- Free.
- Along the Elwah River in Olympic National Park.

A popular resort in the 1920s, Olympic Hot Springs fell into decline during the Depression. The facilities may be gone, but the springs are still there—running strong in the absence of civilization. Most would agree that it's well worth the eight-mile hike just to feel the warmth of all that hot mineral water in contrast to the moist, chill air of the rain forest.

To reach Olympic Hot Springs from Port Angeles, drive east on Highway 101. Just before Elwah, turn south into the park. Now park and hike along the washed-out road. The cluster of rock soaking pools adjoins the Elwah River. Contact Heart of the Hills Ranger Station at the number listed above for the latest word on conditions.

SOAP LAKE

P.O. Box 433, Soap Lake, WA 98851

(509) 246-1821

- Mineral lake, mud baths, lodging, restaurants, shops.
- Bathing suits required.
- Reasonable.
- Right in town.

Not a hot springs per se, Soap Lake nevertheless has thousands of devotees who come to bathe in its mineral-rich water. The Chamber of Commerce (at the address and number above) keeps a hefty file of letters from people claiming relief from physical ailments—everything from arthritis to skin problems to Buerger's disease. Others say that by drinking the water they've left digestive ills behind.

The area's original inhabitants believed in the lake's therapeutic value, too. They called it *Smokiam*, or "Healing Waters." Because of its soapy feel and "suds" that cover the shoreline on windy days, early settlers changed the name to Soap Lake. Contemporary analysis finds the presence of 28 minerals, including large proportions of sodium, boron and potassium. Black basalt cliffs along the shore bear witness to the lake's volcanic origin.

Lodgings for every taste and pocketbook cluster along the shore in the town of Soap Lake. A few provide water sports equipment like canoes, kayaks and surfboards. Many offer heated mineral water, sauna and mud baths.

I generally shy away from endorsing such health claims. But if I had something seriously wrong with my body, I'd give Soap Lake a try.

SOL DUC RESORT

P.O. Box 2169, Port Angeles, WA 98362

(206) 327-3583

- Outdoor hot swimming pool, massage, lodging, RV park, campsites, picnic area, restaurant, grocery store.
- Bathing suits required.
- Reasonable.
- On Sol Duc River Road in Olympic National Park, 12 miles south of Highway 101.

Olympic National Park spans 923,000 acres of scenic wilderness, from glacier-clad mountains to Pacific shore. At Sol Duc Resort, summer vacationers find lodgings, an RV park, campsites and more—including a large outdoor swimming pool fed by hot springs.

The resort operates at full-service capacity from mid-May through September. It remains closed for the rest of the year, with the exception of April and October weekends when the pool opens from 9 a.m. to 5 p.m.

SULPHUR CREEK HOT SPRINGS
Snohomish County, WA
(206) 436-1155 (information)
- Hot pool.
- No clothing requirements.
- Free.
- About a mile from Sulphur Creek Campground in the Darrington Ranger District of Glacier Peak Wilderness.

Because Sulphur Creek Hot Springs is so remote and hard to find, it's likely you'll have the place to yourself. The hot water stems from a steep slope above the creek, flows along a channel through heavy vegetation and into a pool dug into the creek bank.

To reach the spot, take the dirt trail that leaves Sulphur Creek Campground from the northeast side of the road running along the north side of Sulphur Creek. About three-quarters of a mile up the trail, you'll see a sign marking the Glacier Peak Wilderness Area. A little farther, a log bridge crosses the creek and joins a dirt path, which continues northeast along the creek. The hot spring lies 300 feet up this trail.

A Mount Baker–Snoqualmie National Forest visitor's map will greatly aid your finding this and other hidden springs in the area. Pick one up at the Glacier Peak Wilderness Darrington Ranger District office.

Distribution of hot springs in the state of

I D A H O

(Locations are approximate. Consult text and road maps for directions.)

1. **Baumgartner Hot Springs**
2. **Boiling Springs**
3. **Burgdorf Hot Springs**
4. **Ceilann Hot Spring**
5. **Deer Creek Hot Springs**
6. **Givens Hot Springs**
7. **Gold Fork Hot Springs**
8. **Green Canyon Hot Springs**
9. **Heise Hot Springs**
10. **Idaho Rocky Mt. Ranch**
11. **Jerry Johnson's Hot Springs**
12. **Lava Hot Springs**
13. **Miracle Hot Springs**
14. **Molly's Hot Spring**
15. **Murphy Hot Springs**
16. **Pine Flats Hot Springs**
17. **Red River Hot Springs**
18. **Riggins Hot Springs**
19. **Riverdale Resort**
20. **Riverside Inn & Hot Springs**
21. **Russian John Hot Springs**
22. **Salmon Paradise Inn**
23. **Silver Creek Plunge**
24. **Sligars Thousand Springs**
25. **Trail Creek Hot Springs**
26. **Twin Springs Resort**
27. **Vulcan Hot Springs**
28. **Warm Springs Resort**
29. **White Licks Hot Spring**
30. **Worswick Hot Springs**
31. **Zim 's Hot Springs**

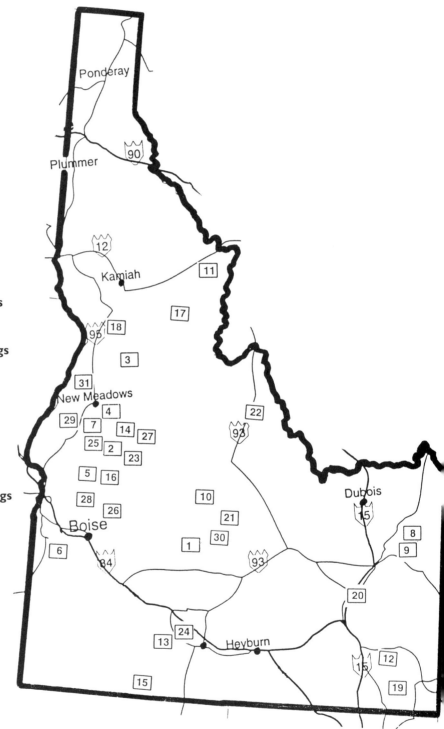

IDAHO

*I*DAHO! This jewellike state has millions of pristine acres to explore. In the process of exploration, you can't help stumbling across hot springs by the dozens. My feeling is that many of Idaho's springs remain undiscovered in the farthest reaches of wilderness. The latest count stands at 257—a bonanza for a state this size.

A number of well-developed springs lie close to Idaho's few major cities. But once you leave the main arteries you have the pleasure of fee-free frolicking. Imagine taking a pack trip into the Selway–Bitteroot Wilderness and finding a natural warm pool with its own waterfall shower. Possible? Of course. In fact, Idaho has several spots that match the description.

Hot springs take many forms in Idaho. Gushers leap from canyon walls above mighty rivers. Pools appear as if by magic in remote flatland regions. In many areas, boiling water surges up to heat nearby creeks and streams. Then there are the gentle flows from lovely hillsides that gather in pools dug centuries ago by the earliest inhabitants.

Although hot springs run 24 hours a day, all year long, in many areas deep snow and frigid weather make their use difficult. Just remember: Playing mountain man can enhance your enjoyment of a wilderness spring, and even the coldest snow can't survive water coming from the ground at 210°F.

Idaho has more hot springs per square mile than any other state. A thorough investigation should take at least a year or two of sheer pleasure.

RIGGINS HOT SPRINGS

BAUMGARTNER HOT SPRINGS

P.O. Box 189, Fairfield, ID 83327
(208) 764-2202 (information)

- Hot and cold pools, campground, rest rooms, picnic area.
- Bathing suits required.
- Free.
- Off Forest Service Road 227,
  12 miles east of Featherville
  in the Fairfield Ranger District of
  Sawtooth National Forest.

Baumgartner Campground bears the name of John E. Baumgartner, the Bavarian-born miner and ranger who lived in the Sawtooth wilderness for more than 40 years. In deeding his tract to the U.S. Forest Service in 1935, he wanted to insure "that it be held in its natural state as far as practicable, consistent with its development for recreation purposes, without profit, and free from dance halls and other objectionable commercial features."

Baumgartner's vision of man in harmony with nature pervades every aspect of the popular facility, from the ban on alcohol to the layout of 30 single, double and multifamily camping units to the self-guided quarter-mile trail (with 24 stops of special interest). Barrier-free handicapped access extends from the rest rooms, camp stoves and water faucets to the trail leading to a fishing pier along the South Fork of the Boise River.

Baumgartner's natural hot pool, fed by a geothermal stream, maintains a constant 103°F temperature—an especially welcome reward for the adventurous souls who cross-country ski and snowmobile in when the road is closed in winter. In summer, children delight in diving into the two deep green-water pools at the upper end of the campground. Ponderosa pines, service berries, trout, salmon and bird life abound.

BOILING SPRINGS

Boise County, ID
No phone.

- Hot pools, campground.
- No clothing requirements.
- Free.
- On Forest Service Road 698 in Boise National Forest.

To reach Boiling Springs, drive north from Crouch on Forest Service Road 698 to the Boiling Springs Campground.

Here you'll find hot water cooling as it flows into a large natural pool. A seasonally built dam forms a second pool, slightly cooler and highly desirable for soaking and frolicking.

BURGDORF HOT SPRINGS

c/o Rick Tidmarsh, McCall, ID 83638
(208) 634-0400 (information)

- Outdoor hot pool, lodging, cooking facilities.
- Bathing suits required during the day.
- Reasonable.
- On the Burgdorf–French Creek Road of the McCall Ranger District in Payette National Forest, reached via a two mile drive on Warren Wagon Road west of Burgdorf Junction.

You'll love this area for its totally primitive, untouched appearance. That's probably why Sylvan "Last of the Mountain Men" Hart chose it for his lifetime retreat. A former New Yorker, Hart fled Manhattan and built a self-sufficient domain on the banks of the South Fork of the

"River of No Return." He made Burgdorf his sole contact point with civilization.

Guests renting Burgdorf's rugged log cabins have exclusive use of the hot pool. It holds a maximum 20 bathers. The managers periodically clean the sand bottom and replace the log sides when necessary.

The cabins come with kerosene lamps, wood-burning stoves and beds, but visitors must bring their own water containers, food and bedding. Winter visitors reach the spot by snowmobile or cross-country skis. Write to the address above for reservations.

CEILANN HOT SPRING
Adams county, ID
No phone.
- Hot pool.
- No clothing requirements.
- Free.
- About three-quarters of a mile from the confluence of Goose Creek and Little Goose Creek, east of Meadows.

National Geographic once ran a color photo of a person enjoying a free shower at this spring. A pipe channels some of the warm water about eight feet above the pool.

To reach Ceilann, drive east from Meadows to where Goose Creek and Little Goose Creek meet. The trail leads about three-quarters of a mile to the spring.

DEER CREEK HOT SPRINGS
Boise County, ID
No phone.
- Hot pools.
- Clothing optional.

- Free.
- On Payette River Road, halfway between Banks and Lowman.

Two very hot springs (185°F) cascade down the cliff above the Payette River, filling pools at the riverside. Popular with campers, this is a great spot for relaxing and cleaning up after a long drive—and the price is right: free.

GIVENS HOT SPRINGS
HC-79 Box 103, Melba, ID 83641
(208) 495-2000
- Indoor hot pool and children's pool, soaking tubs, lodging, RV spaces, campground, picnic area, snack bar.
- Bathing suits required.
- Reasonable.
- On Highway 78, 11 miles southeast of Marsing.

Indians frequented this springs for centuries before the Givens family homesteaded the land along the Oregon Trail. The resort, established in 1881 and now a state historical site, still belongs to descendants of the original settlers. Many local seniors remember coming to the springs as small children and swimming in the old original bathhouse.

The pool house, built in 1952, retains its original charm and popularity after a recent remodeling. The water leaves the ground at 120°F to 140°F, then maintains a comfortable 95°F to 99°F in the pool through regulation of flow.

The facilities extend to an enclosed kiddie pool, soaking tubs, cabins and space for RVs, tents and picnics. Sports areas include a baseball diamond, horseshoe pit, volleyball court and prime fishing spot across the road on the banks of the Snake River.

GOLD FORK HOT SPRING

Adams County, ID

No phone.

- Outdoor hot pools, picnic ground, RV space.
- No clothing requirements.
- Free.
- Southeast of Donnelly, via Highway 55 and Forest Service Road 498.

This free-and-easy, user-built series of pools begins with one at about 110°F at the upper level and ends with one at about 90°F at the lowest.

You can reach the pools by driving south from Donnelly on Highway 55 and turning east on Forest Service Road 498. Warning: Since our last visit, the land has come under private ownership; so be prepared to spend the day simply sightseeing—always a pleasure in these parts of western Idaho.

GREEN CANYON HOT SPRINGS

Box 96, Newdale, ID 83436

(208) 458-4454

- Indoor & outdoor pools, RV hookups, picnic area.
- Bathing suits required.
- Reasonable.
- On Highway 33, 17 miles north of Driggs.

Idaho can get mighty cold. So big pools like this giant indoor version at 93°F are especially welcome in winter. With indoor and outdoor hot pools in a great setting, RV hookups and picnic areas, resorts like Green Canyon act as social centers for Idahoans. They also welcome an occasional Californian or two.

HEISE HOT SPRINGS

5116 Heise Rd., Ririe, ID 83443

(208) 538-7312

- Outdoor warm swimming pool, water slide, hot mineral baths, golf, RV park, campsites, picnic grounds, restaurant.
- Bathing suits required.
- Reasonable.
- On Heise Road just north of Ririe, in eastern Idaho.

Have you ever had snowflakes settle on your nose while basking in 95°F water? This can be one of the many delightful experiences at Heise, a spacious family-type resort with a nine-hole golf course, shaded picnic areas and lots of room to park your RV.

The main pool holds its fresh filtered water at 95°F. Soaking pools deliver 105°F water straight from Mother Nature to you.

IDAHO ROCKY MOUNTAIN RANCH

H/C 64, Box 9934, Stanley, ID 83278

(208) 774-3544

- Outdoor hot swimming pool, lodging, restaurant.
- Bathing suits required.
- Reasonable.
- In the Sawtooth National Recreation Area, nine miles south of Stanley.

Idaho Rocky Mountain Ranch houses guests in an all-log lodge built in 1930. Visitors also stay in a number of cabins with fireplaces. Everyone enjoys a panoramic view of the Sawtooth Mountain Range and casual gourmet dining in the wilderness.

Sportsmen and women work up an appetite with legendary Idaho fishing, boat-

GOLD FORK HOT SPRINGS

LAVA HOT SPRINGS

GIVENS HOT SPRINGS

RED RIVER HOT SPRINGS

ing, riding, hiking and cross-country skiing. I can personally recommend the many hiking trails in the area, where we once marveled at the sight of spawning salmon struggling up a shallow creek.

Especially welcome after a long day on the trail, the 106°F spring offers hot, chemical-free bathing in the swimming pool. Registered guests alone have access to the pool and other facilities, so call ahead for reservations.

JERRY JOHNSON'S HOT SPRING
Idaho County, ID
No phone.
- Hot pools.
- No clothing requirements.
- Free.
- About a mile off the Lewis and Clark Highway (U.S. 12), southwest of Missoula in Clearwater National Forest.

Jerry Johnson's typifies Idaho's many gracious riverside hot springs—springs for those who like to soak far from civilization. If you arrive and find no pool available, build your own from rocks in the stream and regulate the temperature to suit yourself.

To reach Jerry Johnson's, take Highway 12 south of Missoula toward the section of 12 known as the Lewis and Clark Highway. Stop at Warm Springs Creek, where a footbridge crosses the Lochsa River and the trail begins. You'll find the springs about a mile up this trail.

LAVA HOT SPRINGS
Lava Hot Springs, ID 83246
(208) 776-5221
(800) 423-8597 (toll-free outside Idaho)
- Outdoor swimming pools and baths, massage,

lodging, restaurant, RV park, golf, tennis.
- Bathing suits required.
- Deluxe.
- Right in town on Highway 30, ten miles east of Highway 15.

The Lava Hot Springs Foundation runs this state-owned resort so that no tax dollars are needed. It rests in the mile-high Portneuf River Valley in the village of Lava Hot Springs. Climb the Sunken Gardens, a series of terraces built into the walls of an extinct volcano, and take an overview of America's most highly developed natural hot water facilities.

Two pools (open in summer only) comprise nearly a third of an acre of 86°F swimming surface. They include 50-meter racing lanes, a ten-meter diving tower and plenty of play room for children. In another complex, open year-round, bathers stand on soft sand in four steaming hot pools, two with whirlpool jets. Geologists believe the mineral-rich water has been a consistent 110°F for at least 50 million years.

The town's accommodations range from RV parks to quaint old-fashioned hotels, convenient motels and modern condominiums. A premier trout stream, the Portneuf River, flows through the village—in summer, children tumble through on inner tubes. Other pastimes include golf, tennis, hunting, hiking, skiing, snowmobiling and shopping. Yet many do nothing at all but soak up the bountiful minerals, sunshine and scenery.

MIRACLE HOT SPRINGS
P.O. Box 171, Buhl, ID 83316
(208) 543-6002
- Outdoor hot soaking pools, private baths, massage, RV park, campground.
- Bathing suits required in public pools.

- Reasonable.
- On Highway 30, ten miles northwest of Buhl.

Miracle Hot Springs makes a great place for family vacations, reunions and other parties. Overnight visitors park their RVs and pitch tents at a comfortable campground. Though closed on Sundays, the facility operates six days a week the year around.

At a depth of 4.5 feet, both the outdoor pools and 19 private baths prove ideal for therapeutic soaking. A flow-through design requires no chlorine or other chemical additives. Dressing rooms adjoin the private baths, which measure eight by ten feet each.

Scenic Salmon Falls Creek—in fact, most of the Hagerman Valley—provides excellent fishing, hiking, boating and other water sports.

MOLLY'S HOT SPRING

Valley County, ID
No phone.
- Hot pool.
- Bathing suits optional.
- Free.
- On the South Fork of the Salmon River, in Boise National Forest.

From Cascade, drive along Forest Service Road 22 to the South Fork of the Salmon River. Turn south at Forest Service Road 474 and drive along the river about two miles. Park and climb the slope to Molly's rock pool.

Several springs provide the hot water for this primitive, scenic, totally remote yet accessible pool. You're only two miles from a fine campground.

MURPHY HOT SPRINGS

Rogerson, ID 83302
(208) 857-2233
- Outdoor hot swimming pool, indoor baths, lodging, RV park, campsite, picnic ground, restaurant.
- Bathing suits required.
- Reasonable.
- South of Twin Falls and 49 miles west of Rogerson, near the Nevada border.

Murphy Hot Springs hides off in a remote canyon, the very model of an old-fashioned Western homestead. After such a long drive, you should plan to stay several days.

A pipe carries hot water to one lovely 90°F pool by a stream. The facilities include two other outdoor pools, a number of indoor hot tubs, meals, lodging, RV park and campground.

PINE FLATS HOT SPRINGS

Lowman, ID
No phone.
- Hot pools.
- Clothing optional.
- Free.
- A third of a mile from Pine Flats Campground, near Lowman in Boise National Forest.

At Pine Flats Hot Springs, a natural geothermal cascade fills rock pools above the Payette River. Several of these hot, free-flowing showers bless the state of Idaho, and Pine Flats is one of the best. A campground nearby insures comfortable living. I guarantee you won't want to leave this spectacular wilderness setting.

RUSSIAN JOHN HOT SPRINGS

SILVER CREEK PLUNGE

TERRACE LAKES RESORT

UNIDENTIFIED IDAHO LAKE SITE

RED RIVER HOT SPRINGS

Elk City, ID 83525

(208) 842-2587

- Outdoor hot swimming pool, indoor soaking pools, lodging, RV park, restaurant.
- Bathing suits required.
- Reasonable.
- At the end of Red River Road, east of Elk City near the Selway–Bitterroot Wilderness.

Who doesn't like the concept of a year-round hot springs resort at the edge of a great wilderness? You have easy access (except in winter when you may need snowshoes) and the greatest comfort known to man (hot water), but you still have the sense of adventuring on the frontier.

Facilities include cabins, RV hookups and a restaurant with home-styling cooking and delicious baked goods. An outdoor pool and indoor tubs soothe muscle and bone after a long, satisfying hike in the wilderness. Visitors from a nearby campground enjoy the pool and tubs as well.

RIGGINS HOT SPRINGS

P.O. Box 1247, Riggins, ID 83549

(208) 628-3785

- Warm pool, bathhouse, spa, lodging, meals.
- Bathing suits required.
- Deluxe.
- On the Salmon River east of Riggins, in Payette National Forest.

A visit to this elegantly planned and managed resort guarantees a cure for the overworked or overstressed. John Muir himself prescribed a return to the mountains and nature as the best mode of healing. Add deluxe facilities with moderate prices, and you have a retreat that makes you wonder what you're waiting for.

Riggins belongs on every tour of ultimate hot springs resorts. It has just about everything a dedicated hot springs lover would enjoy. A partial list of attractions includes exclusivity for registered guests, a huge pool maintained at about 95°F, a spa at 105°F, a bathhouse, game room and accommodations with private baths in the main lodge. A stay requires reservations. The room rate includes meals.

Anglers find a stocked trout pond right on the property. Easy access to the Salmon, the "River of No Return," suggests a day of wilderness fishing or white-water rafting. The forested countryside beckons with further adventures like hiking, horseback riding, mountain biking, skiing, snowmobiling and on and on.

RIVERDALE RESORT

3696 N. 1600 E, Preston, ID 83263

(208) 852-0266

- Hot pools, water slides, RV park, campground, picnic area.
- Bathing suits required.
- Reasonable.
- On Highway 34, six miles north of Preston.

Riverdale's the place to take the entire family, from toddlers to great-grandpa. You'll find everything you need for a day, weekend or longer. The facilities include pavilions for family reunions and parties, picnic areas, full hookup for your RV, two water slides and three hot pools—over 11,000 square feet of water surface.

RIVERSIDE INN AND HOT SPRINGS

255 Portneuf Ave., P.O. Box 127, Lava Hot Springs, ID 83246
(208) 776-5504
(800) 733-5504 (toll-free)
- Indoor and outdoor hot tubs, lodging.
- Bathing suits optional in private baths.
- Deluxe.
- Right in town, near the state-owned Lava Hot Springs resort.

Known as the Honeymoon Hotel since 1914 and now on the National Historical Register, Riverside Inn reopened with a complete renovation of its building. Guests enjoy two private and one public hot tub indoors and a fourth one outside in summer. All tubs draw on Lava Hot Springs' naturally thermal, odor-free mineral water.

A wide porch overlooks the Portneuf River, near a spacious lobby with color TV, library and Continental breakfast served free to guests. The 16 rooms (12 with private baths) come with colorful quilts, antique dressers, ceiling fans and individual heat control.

The absence of TVs and phones in the rooms allows a complete break from what I call the devil box and the devil's trumpet. Smoking is banned throughout. Another plus: Guests need no car to reach the many fine restaurants in the area or the big pools at nearby Lava Hot Springs resort.

Mandatory reservations require a deposit—Visa and MasterCard accepted. The prices, good value for this level of luxury, range from $33.75 for a double room with shared bath to $85 for the Honeymoon Suite.

RUSSIAN JOHN HOT SPRINGS

Blaine County, ID
No phone.
- Hot pool.
- Clothing optional.
- Free.
- On Highway 93, just inside the boundary of Sawtooth National Recreation Area north of Ketchum.

The pattern of hot springs looks like buckshot over a map of central Idaho. Many of them center around the fabulous resort town of Sun Valley.

Eighteen miles northwest, for example, you'll find Russian John, a 50-gallon-per-minute, 102°F spring. It gushes from a meadow on the grounds of Russian John Guard Station in Sawtooth National Recreation Area and warms a natural clay-bottomed pool to about body temperature.

SALMON HOT SPRINGS PARADISE INN

Rt. 1, P.O. Box 223-B, Salmon, ID 83467-9709
(208) 756-4449
- Sheltered hot swimming pool, lodging, RV space, campground.
- Bathing suits optional
- Reasonable.
- On Warm Springs Creek Road, about nine miles south of Salmon in Salmon National Forest.

The historic facilities at Salmon Hot Springs lay dormant for 20 years, until the present owner bought them in the late 1980s. Since the spring's discovery in 1876, the 340 acres have held several hot pools, a pair of dance halls, an inn—even the local poor farm.

Today's visitors find a newly renovated hot plunge maintained at 98°F to 100°F. The water requires no chemical treatment, as the managers drain and refill the semi-enclosed pool from the 117°F springs every night.

Restoration continues on the enclosed hot pool (dating from 1896), the nine-room inn, a blacksmith shop, and several cabins. Plans include a bar, restaurant and access to saddle trips on the present hiking trails. Overnight guests stay in two renovated cabins or at a campground with space for RVs and tents.

To reach the springs, drive four miles south of Salmon on Highway 93. Turn left on Airport Road and drive nearly a mile to a three-way intersection. Turn left on Warm Springs Creek Road and follow it three and a half miles to the springs.

SILVER CREEK PLUNGE
Garden Valley, ID 83622
(208) 344-8688
• Outdoor swimming pool, lodging, picnic ground, campsites.
• Bathing suits required.
• Reasonable.
• Near Lodgepole Springs Campground in Boise National Forest.

This family-style resort lies in an area renowned for its cross-country skiing, fishing and white-water rafting. The swimming pool, fed by 102°F spring water, gears its comfort level to the air temperature the year around.

Silver Creek nestles in Boise National Forest, so you're surrounded by stately evergreens. Remote sections of the woods harbor black bears, wolves, mountain goats and

bighorn sheep. Rivers and streams abound with kokanee salmon and trout.

SLIGARS THOUSAND SPRINGS RESORT
Route 1, Box 90, Hagerman, ID 83332
(208) 837-4987
• Indoor swimming pool and whirlpool tubs, RV park, campground.
• Bathing suits required.
• Reasonable.
• On Highway 30, five miles south of Hagerman.

Idaho has many geological wonders, and you'll see one of them at this resort—gushing waterfalls leaping from cliffs above the mighty Snake River. Resort facilities encompass an indoor swimming pool, whirlpool tubs, RV park and campgrounds.

If you're the adventurous type, the Thousand Springs area is ideal for exploration. Highlights include the nearby 5,000-acre Hagerman Fossil Beds National Monument, one of the best sites for fossilized fish and small mammals in North America. The beds have also yielded the remains of predecessors to the modern horse, camel, peccary, beaver and turtle.

TRAIL CREEK HOT SPRINGS
Valley County, ID
No phone.
• Hot pool.
• No clothing requirements.
• Free.
• Along Forest Service Road 22, east of Cascade in Boise National Forest.

Here you enter the haunts of one of the most famous mountain men of all time. Sylvan Hart, the recluse profiled in *Last of the Mountain Men*, lived in a quaint house on the South Fork of the Salmon. It's likely he took his baths in Trail Creek.

Trail Creek Hot Springs bubbles from a rocky crevice to fill a rock pool beside the creek. Visitors adjust the 122°F temperature to their liking with creek water. Wear good shoes; they'll make the trail down from the parking area a lot easier to manage.

TWIN SPRINGS RESORT

c/o Atlanta Stage, Boise, ID 83706
(208) 888-0857
• Hot pool, hot tubs, lodging, tavern.
• Bathing suits optional.
• Reasonable.
• On the Middle Fork of the Boise River, east of Atlanta in Boise National Forest.

Twin Springs, like many other hot springs resorts, uses geothermal heat in a variety of ways. Here they raise tropical food fish in ponds filled with the steady supply of hot spring water.

The super-hot springs (180°F) also feed a soaking pool and hot tubs for humans. The facilities include cabins and a rustic tavern. For reservations, contact the address or phone number above.

VULCAN HOT SPRINGS

Valley County, ID
No phone.
• Hot pool.
• Clothing optional.
• Free.

• Near the South Fork of the Salmon River, northeast of Cascade in Boise National Forest.

Boiling water leaves the earth to join a tributary of the Salmon River. The meeting cools the temperature to a comfortable 100°F to 105°F, depending on the air temperature. A dam built by volunteers captures the result in a pool good for soaking.

To reach Vulcan Hot Springs (and a nearby campground) from Cascade, go east on Forest Service Road 22 to Forest Service Road 474. Turn south and drive about seven miles to the parking area. Now walk half a mile west across the South Fork of the Salmon.

WARM SPRINGS RESORT

P.O. Box 28, Idaho City, ID 83631
(208) 392-4437
• Hot outdoor swimming pool, lodging, RV space, campground, picnic areas, snack bar.
• Bathing suits required.
• Reasonable.
• At Mile Post 37 on Highway 21, 1.5 miles southwest of Idaho City in Boise National Forest.

Carbon dated to over 10,000 years of age, the water at this mountain resort rises from an aquifer about two kilometers deep. It emerges from the earth at 109°F and flows through a spacious outdoor swimming pool, maintained at 94°F in summer and 97°F in winter.

Warm Springs Resort began by providing laundry and baths for the gold rush miners of Boise Basin. In its near-130 year history, it's been a saloon, dance hall, hospital, stage stop and inn.

The current owner bought the place in 1961 and remodeled and enlarged the old bathhouse, which now includes a snack bar, gift shop and manager's apartments. He also converted the rock piles left by early dredge mining into a charming and well-kept RV, picnic and tent-camping park. Plans include restoration of the old stage stop inn and additional sleeping cabins to expand on the current offering of two.

With so many prices out of sight these days, it's great to find a truly affordable resort. The Warm Springs cabins rent for $45 and $30 a night, the RV hookups for $15 a day or $150 a month. If you don't wish to stay overnight, you can still spend all day cavorting in the pool for only $3 or use the hiking trails to explore surrounding Boise National Forest.

WHITE LICKS HOT SPRING
Adams County, Idaho
No phone.
- Two bathhouses, picnic ground, campsites.
- Clothing optional in bathhouses.
- Free.
- About halfway between Council and Donnelly on Forest Service Road 186.

This well-designed hot soak facility allows you to select any temperature you wish. Two pipes bring warm and hot water to the covered tubs. You simply plug the pipes or let them flow to suit yourself.

Bring a picnic lunch or the makings of a barbecue. You'll find plenty of parking space, a good campground and lovely evergreen scenery.

WORSWICK HOT SPRINGS
Camas County, ID
No phone.
- Hot-spring flows.
- Clothing optional.
- Free.
- Past the abandoned site of Carrietown west of Sun Valley.

During a week-long stay in Sun Valley, we examined our hot spring map for springs nearby. A large one, Worswick, attracted our attention because of its 250-gallon-per-minute flow. Any time a spring produces five 50-gallon drums of 150°F water in one minute, it must be worth seeing. And it was.

The drive west from Sun Valley wound along a small river, then ascended a steep mountain pass by a series of switchbacks. An old map said we would encounter an abandoned mining and lumbering community called Carrietown, but a diligent search of the map's locale revealed not a trace. A few miles farther along the road, however, we saw to our right the unmistakable indications of a hot spring—wisps of steam rising from a near-boiling flow.

The figure of 250 gallons a minute represents a cumulative flow from about 50 outlets. We ran here and there sticking fingers and toes into springs of all sizes. At one or two spots we found evidence of quickly dug bathing pools. Since Worswick lies in a shallow canyon, winter rains soon dispose of such puny efforts.

As we explored, we visualized what an intelligent, long-range program of development could do for this primitive and now unusable site. Simple cabins and other space for visitors, perhaps a series of natural stone pools, would be all that's needed to make Worswick a comfortable recreational spa. To our understanding, Worswick is available for long-term lease through the U.S. Bureau of Land Management.

As with almost any unimproved hot springs, visitors are welcome to dig a pool or two for impromptu use—a procedure we heartily recommend at Worswick.

ZIM'S HOT SPRINGS

P.O. Box 314, New Meadows, ID 83654
(208) 347-9447
• Outdoor hot swimming pool, soaking pool, lodging, RV park, campsites, picnic ground, restaurant.
• Bathing suits required.
• Reasonable.
• Off Highway 95, four miles north of New Meadows.

Zim's rests in Idaho's heartland, nestled among mountains and pines with a spectacular view of Granite Mountain. Overnight guests of the family-owned and operated facility stay at the Log Lodge (with recreation hall, video games, pool tables and snack bar), the RV park or the campground.

Zim's maintains its swimming pool at 90°F to 95°F; the soaking pool a little hotter, at 105°F. Winter visitors often come for the excellent skiing nearby.

MONTANA

CALIFORNIANS, particularly those who live in the Los Angeles area, often dream of pine-clad slopes and huge blue lakes under skies of towering clouds. For most, this fantasy of clean air and sparkling scenery remains a dream. A few do make the break, however, and some escape to western Montana.

Distribution of hot springs

(Locations are approximate. Consult text and road maps for directions.)

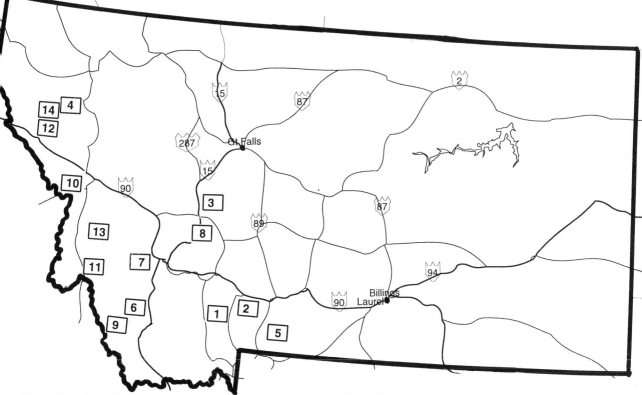

1. Bear Trap Hot Springs
2. Bozeman Hot Springs
3. Broadwater Athletic Club
4. Camp Aqua
5. Chico Hot Springs
6. Elkhorn Hot Springs
7. Fairmont Hot Springs
8. Hillbrook Nursing Home
9. Jackson Hot Springs
10. Lolo Hot Springs
11. Los Trail Hot Springs
12. Quinn's Hot Springs
13. Sleeping Child
14. Symes Hot & Medicinal Springs

BEAR TRAP HOT SPRING

P.O. Box 24, Norris, MT 59745
(406) 685-3303

- Outdoor hot swimming pool, RV park, campground, picnic ground, grocery store.
- Bathing suits required.
- Reasonable.
- On Highway 84, just east of Norris on Highway 287.

The Bostonian who fell in love with Bear Trap's spiritual ambience made a vow to care for it in the same respectful way the Indians did for many centuries. Travelers passing through have been soaking their bones in these waters since the early 1800s.

A half-million gallons of clear, odorless, 130°F water flow each day from the source. The water cools as it sprays into a 4-foot deep, 30- by 40-foot pool. Facilities include a grocery store, picnic area, RV park and campground.

BOZEMAN HOT SPRINGS

81123 Gallatin Rd., Bozeman, MT 59715
(406) 586-6492

- Indoor hot swimming pool, four soaking pools, cold pool, campground, RV park, picnic ground, grocery store.
- Bathing suits required.
- Reasonable.
- On Highway 191, eight miles west of Bozeman.

As a KOA campground, Bozeman Hot Springs has everything for the traveler, from chewing gum to tire patches to plenty of hot water. Management keeps the indoor swimming pool at 90°F. A smaller pool, at 60°F, provides a bracing contrast to four soaking pools gradu-

ated between 95°F and 112°F.

The facility closes early Friday night and reopens Saturday evening, but otherwise operates the year around.

BROADWATER ATHLETIC CLUB & HOT SPRING

4920 Highway 12 W., Helena, MT 59601
(406) 443-5777

- Two outdoor hot swimming pools, water slide, partially enclosed lap pool, hot tub Jacuzzis, steam baths, saunas, massage, indoor and outdoor running tracks, squash and racquetball courts, gym, snack bar.
- Bathing suits required.
- Reasonable.
- On Highway 12, two miles west of Helena.

Manager Chris Kozora says this private health club gladly opens its doors to hot springs enthusiasts. "We like to show off the water," he says.

There's a lot to show off. The springs produce copious amounts of 150°F to 155°F mineral water. The club cools it seasonally to 92°F or 96°F for the 88,000-gallon recreation pool and about 86°F for the lap pool year-round. A five-story free-fall drop from a hot water slide highlights a third pool, open only in summer. The springs also fill several private indoor Jacuzzis and fuel the steam baths.

Dry facilities include separate men's and women's saunas; tanning beds; a full gym with Nautilus, Universal and other equipment; an outdoor dirt running track and an indoor padded track; squash, racquetball and volleyball courts; and two exercise studios with classes from 6:00 a.m. to 6:30 p.m.

While you're there, take a moment to look for up to 50 elk grazing on a hillside near the main pool.

CAMP AQUA

Drawer K, Hot Springs, MT 59845
(406) 741-3480

- Indoor hot pools, steam baths, saunas, lodging, RV park, picnic ground.
- Clothing optional in private tubs.
- Reasonable.
- East of Highway 28, about 2.6 miles north of Hot Springs Junction.

Camp Aqua bills its six indoor pools as private family plunges. All have attached saunas. If the hot water makes you sleepy, rent a room and stay a while or snooze in your RV. The resort has full hookups.

The surroundings typify Montana scenery: big sky and rolling hills that stretch to the horizon and well beyond.

CHICO HOT SPRINGS

Pray, Montana 59065
(406) 333-4933

- Indoor and outdoor hot swimming and soaking pools, massage, lodging, restaurant, bar.
- Bathing suits required.
- Deluxe.
- Off Highway 89, 26 miles south of Livingston.

A former Clevelander gave up the rat race to manage this historic Montana resort. Happily, he brought along his taste for good food. People actually fly in from Denver and Salt Lake City just to have dinner at Chico. They land on the highway. Others drive 150 miles

BEAR TRAP HOT SPRING

CHICO HOT SPRINGS

ELKHORN HOT SPRINGS

FAIRMONT HOT SPRINGS RESORT

from Billings and home again.

An evening might begin with salad, smoked salmon or French onion soup. Entrees include the likes of beef Wellington, fresh seafood or chicken stuffed with boursin cheese and spinach and served with a tarragon sauce. Homemade breads, pastries and caramel cashew cheesecake complete the exceptional menu.

Hot baths? Of course. A large flow-through pool hovers at about 90°F, a soaking pool at 108°F. Chico's spring is one of the largest in a region noted for big ones.

Overnight guests choose from a variety of lodgings: rooms in the restored 1880-style hotel, new chalets that sleep up to ten or an authentic log cabin. Guests—when not sleeping, eating or soaking—disperse over the countryside for fishing, rafting, hunting, skiing and horseback riding.

ELKHORN HOT SPRINGS

P.O. Box 514, Polaris, MT 59746
(406) 834-3434

- Two outdoor hot swimming pools, sauna, lodging, restaurant, bar.
- Bathing suits required.
- Deluxe.
- About ten miles north of Polaris.

Surrounded by Beaverhead National Forest, Elkhorn rests at about 7,500 feet. That means miles and miles of thick evergreens, shiny-leaf shrubs and mountain wildlife. After a brisk walk, try the outdoor soaking pool held at about 100°F or one of the wet saunas inside.

Elkhorn provides rooms for the weary, a restaurant for the hungry, space for your RV and even pine needles to cushion your tent.

Favorite activities include winter sports like cross-country skiing and warm-weather pursuits like hunting, fishing and exploring with backpack and compass.

FAIRMONT HOT SPRINGS RESORT

1500 Fairmont Rd., Gregson, MT 59711
(406) 797-3241
(800) 332-3272 (toll-free in Montana)
(800) 443-2381 (toll-free outside Montana)

- Indoor and outdoor swimming pools, indoor and outdoor soaking pools, water slide, sauna, lodging, RV park, camp ground, picnic area, restaurants, bar.
- Bathing suits required.
- Deluxe.
- On Fairmont Road off Highway 90, 12 miles east of Butte.

Everything at Fairmont reflects the Montana way of thinking—big. The pools are huge, two Olympic-sized for swimming and two for soaking. Thrill seekers enter the outdoor swimming pool by an enclosed 350-foot water slide. The slide and pools draw on a virtually unlimited supply of 155°F natural spring water, cooled to various temperatures for maximum enjoyment.

Resort buildings cover 20 of the 500 acres with 158 guest rooms, restaurant, coffee shop, cocktail lounge and convention facilities (for groups of up to 500). An 18-hole golf course carpets another 150 acres—and still there's room for tennis, croquet, horseshoes, volleyball, badminton, a tepee camp, hookups for 100 RVs, picnic area, children's playground— even a wildlife zoo.

Montana's immensity stretches in every direction. The adjacent Pintler Wilderness area encompasses 150,000 acres. If you tire of soaking, or recreating on the grounds, you may want to try something a little more active, like mountain biking, guided trail rides, hay rides, pack trips, float trips, hunting, fishing or skiing. Here visitors can either relax their minds and bodies or stretch them to the limit.

HILLBROOK NURSING HOME
Clancy, MT 59634
(406) 933-8311
• Indoor hydrotherapy pool, physical therapy.
• Reasonable medical fees.
• Off Highway 15, south of Helena.

If you need skilled professional health care in addition to a hot soak, Hillbrook could be the answer to your aches and pains. The facility accepts patients only under doctor's orders and through Medicare, VA and similar programs. Hillbrook may put the emphasis on serious therapy, but for me the indoor treatment tub's air jets produced instant fun!

JACKSON HOT SPRINGS
P.O. Box 808, Jackson, MT 59736
(406) 834-3151
• Indoor-outdoor swimming pool, lodging, RV hookups, campground, restaurant.
• Bathing suits required.
• Reasonable.
• On Highway 278, right in town.

Free of chemicals or sulphur odor, the renovated pool at Jackson contains water cooled to about 100°F from its 140°F source. Guests stay at an RV park, campground or in reasonably priced cabins.

The restaurant features a prime rib dinner and salad bar supplied fresh from a hot spring-heated greenhouse. Once or twice a month, live bands entertain a packed dance floor.

The location right in town suggests a walking tour of Jackson. A ten-mile drive leads to the evergreen mountains of Beaverhead National Forest, which flanks the resort on three sides.

If you have a million-plus dollars to invest in a hot spring resort of your own, call the number above for details.

LOLO HOT SPRINGS RESORT
38500 W. Hwy. 12, Lolo, MT 59847
(406) 273-2290
• Outdoor swimming pool, indoor soaking pool, lodging, RV park, picnic grounds, campsites, restaurant, bar.
• Bathing suits required.
• Deluxe.
• On Highway 12, 37 miles southwest of Missoula.

Lolo Hot Springs edges one of the largest wilderness areas in the country, the Selway-Bitterroot. So in addition to some spectacular scenery, you're likely to see an abundance of wildlife, from deer and elk to bear and cougar. Moose graze on Lolo's lawns.

Huge boulders surround the outdoor pool, remodeled in recent years by owners Don and Angie Stoen (like nearly everything else at Lolo). A smaller, indoor pool varies between 100°F and 105°F. Along with new lodgings, a full restaurant and saloon, guests find an RV park and lovely grounds for camping and picnicking.

As a year-round resort, Lolo provides everything from hiking, fishing and hunting to superb cross-country skiing. Guests can count on snowmobile, mountain bike and trail horse rental. Specialties of the house include summer pack trips, steak rides and white-water rafting.

Perhaps best of all, Lolo features Montana-blue skies and air like nothing you've ever breathed in the city. A peaceful, natural ambience invites the traveler to pause and take a lesson from nature.

LOST TRAIL HOT SPRINGS RESORT
Sula, MT 59871
(406) 821-3574
- Outdoor hot swimming pool, indoor soaking pool, sauna, lodging, RV park, picnic ground, restaurant.
- Bathing suits required.
- Reasonable.
- On Highway 93, six miles north of Lost Trail Pass.

The water's always fine in Lost Trail's outdoor pool—about 95°F. If you like it hotter, try the indoor pools with jets.

Amenities include sauna, cabins, lodge, campground with RV hookups and a restaurant with hearty family-style meals. A price tag of $1.25 million follows extensive updating and remodeling. Call (406) 363-4630 if you're interested.

QUINN'S HOT SPRINGS
P.O. Box 187, Paradise, MT 59856
(406) 826-3150
- Outdoor swimming pool and soaking pool, private Jacuzzis, lodging, RV park, picnic ground, restaurant, bar, supper club, store.
- Bathing suits required.
- Reasonable.

- On Highway 135 in Lolo National Forest, about six miles south of Paradise.

If you like scenery with your hot soak, you'll find Quinn's ideal. It rests on the Clark Fork River with heavy forests nearby. The hot soaking pool outside has jets so you can soak, get massaged and take in the view at the same time.

The springs feed private Jacuzzis and an outdoor swimming pool as well. Resort amenities extend to an RV park, picnic area, restaurant, bar and supper club. Visitors fish, hike, smell the conifers and luxuriate in the soft, warm natural mineral water. What more can you ask?

SLEEPING CHILD
P.O. Box 1468, Hamilton, MT 59840
(406) 363-6250
- Outdoor heated swimming pool and soaking pools, sauna, lodging, restaurant, bar.
- Bathing suits required.
- Deluxe.
- On Highway 501, 13 miles southeast of Hamilton.

In the 1870s, Chief Joseph of the Nez Percé Indian tribe had to protect his people from the U.S. Army. Faced with a battle, he split the tribe into two groups; one group left their infants by a hot spring. When they returned, the infants were safe, sleeping peacefully. The spring bears the name Sleeping Child to this day.

The safe, warm, peaceful place now cradles a small resort. Located in the Bitterroot Mountains near Hamilton, Sleeping Child encourages a variety of activities. Guests not only soak but hike, fish, hunt and cross-country ski on grounds that encompass 40 acres adjacent to 1.7 million acres of national forest.

The water flows from the springs at 125°F. It cools to 110°F for the soaking pool and about 100°F for the large outdoor swimming pool.

SYMES HOTEL & MEDICINAL SPRINGS

P.O. Box 36, Hot Springs, MT 59845
(406) 741-2361
• Indoor baths, lodging, sun room.
• Bathing suits optional.
• Reasonable.
• Right in town.

This comfortable, single-story, old-style spa hotel has separate men's and women's baths off the lobby. Guests come to get away from TVs and phones, enjoy the baths and quiet sun room and explore the area, on the Flathead Indian Reservation near Lolo National Forest.

Those wishing to stay a while can rent an apartment. Overnight guests book rooms or nearby cabins and take their meals at three cafes in town.

LOST TRAIL HOT SPRINGS RESORT

QUINN'S HOT SPRINGS

SLEEPING CHILD

Distribution of hot springs in the state of
WYOMING
(Locations are approximate. Consult text and road maps for directions.)

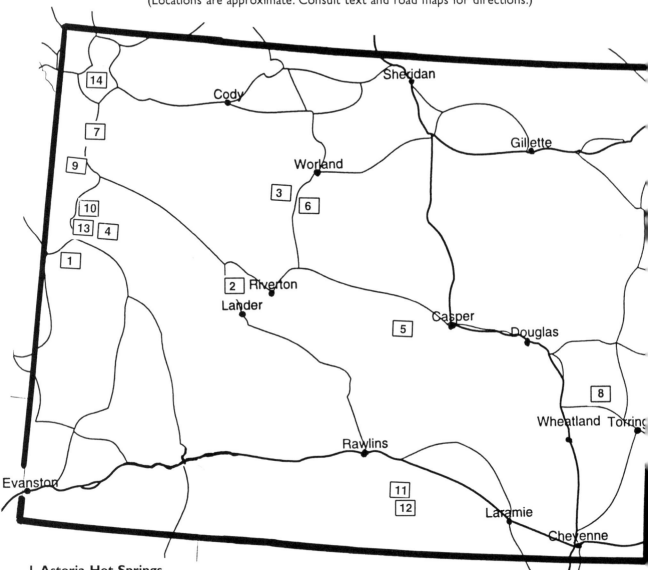

1. Astoria Hot Springs
2. Chief Washakie Plunge
3. Fountain of Youth
4. Granite Creek Hot Springs
5. Horse Creek Springs
6. Hot Springs State Park
7. Huckleberry Hot Springs
8. Immigrant's Washtub
9. Jackson Lake Hot Springs
10. Kelly Warm Spring
11. Saratoga Hot Springs
12. Saratoga Inn
13. Teton Valley Warm Springs
14. Yellowstone National Park

WYOMING

A BRIEF LOOK AT A MAP of Wyoming will tell you what a great state this is for hot springs. To begin, there's fabled Yellowstone National Park, home of the world's most famous geothermal phenomenon, Old Faithful. Yellowstone has an estimated 10,000 hot water features within its boundaries. You could spend a lifetime and never see it all. By the time you finished giving Yellowstone the once-over, many mud pots, geysers and springs would have changed character and grown larger, smaller, hotter, cooler.

Wyoming has lots more hot water beyond the park. The map reveals another section of the state called Hot Springs County, wherein lies Hot Springs State Park and a city called Thermopolis—which means Hot City. Here a U.S. treaty with the Shoshone and Arapaho nations ensured the present park's hot water would remain available to all in perpetuity.

Some of the most beautiful pools you'll ever see appear in other parts of the state. Some shimmer with an intense emerald green, others in shades of blue that defy comparison. Add to these geothermal wonders the splendid scenery of Jackson Hole, the Tetons and Wyoming's plains, deserts, forests and rivers—and you have a state well worth a good long stay.

100° HOT RIVER IN WYOMING'S PITCHSTONE PLATEAU AREA

ASTORIA HOT SPRINGS

Star Route, Box 18, Jackson, WY 83001
(307) 733-2659

- Outdoor hot swimming pool and children's pool, RV park, campground, picnic sites, grocery store.
- Bathing suits required.
- Reasonable.
- On Highway 26, 17 miles south of Jackson.

Astoria's location allows for easy access to the town of Jackson, just 30 minutes away. As the southern gateway to Grand Teton National Park, Jackson serves as the hub of vacation activity in Jackson Hole country.

Scenery of incredible grandeur surrounds Astoria's 40-by-80-foot 95°F pool. A smaller pool, about 18 inches deep, entertains the small fry.

Guests stay at a campground or RV park with 100 hookups. When not soaking, they fish, float down the adjacent river, hike in the nearby mountains and pursue a wide variety of other outdoor sports.

CHIEF WASHAKIE PLUNGE

P.O. Box 217, Fort Washakie, WY 82514
(307) 332-2735

- Outdoor hot swimming and soaking pools, indoor tubs, picnic ground.
- Bathing suits required.
- Reasonable.
- Off Highway 287 on the Wind River Indian Reservation, three miles east of Fort Washakie.

A bathhouse and concrete pool adjoin a natural soaking pool used by Native Americans for centuries. The ancient pool measures about 100 feet across and 3 feet deep. Abundant algae on its gravelly bottom lends a striking green color; several vents bubble gently near the center.

FOUNTAIN OF YOUTH

P.O. Box 711, Thermopolis, WY 82443
(307) 864-3265

- Outdoor hot swimming pool, RV park, tent space.
- Bathing suits required.
- Reasonable.
- On Highway 20, two miles north of Thermopolis.

Sacajawea Well looks like a miniature volcano. The Fountain of Youth flows from this mineral cone to fill the largest swimming pool in the state. The pool—at 235 by 72 feet—holds more than 84,000 cubic feet of eminently swimmable water, replaced every 11 hours by the 1.4 million-gallon flow.

Pitch a tent. Or park your RV in one of 40 spaces with full hookups or 26 with water and electricity only. Day campers pay a small fee for use of the pool.

This spot makes a natural choice for campers planning a visit to nearby Hot Springs State Park.

GRANITE CREEK HOT SPRING

Teton County, WY
No phone.

- Outdoor hot swimming pool.
- Bathing suits required.
- Reasonable.
- Along Granite Creek about 12 miles northeast of Highway 189, in Bridger–Teton National Forest.

ASTORIA HOT SPRINGS

HUCKLEBERRY HOT SPRINGS

GRANITE CREEK HOT SPRING

FOUNTAIN OF YOUTH

The Civilian Conservation Corps built this swimming pool during the Great Depression, and it's provided low-cost recreation for innumerable people ever since.

Today a private firm leases the land from the Forest Service and manages the facility. It charges a small fee for admittance and maintains the water at about 100°F. Visitors enjoy a picnic area nearby and scenery worth at least one roll of film.

To reach the pool, drive south from Jackson on Highway 189. Turn left where the highway first crosses Hoback River and go to the end of the road, about 12 miles up Granite Creek.

HORSE CREEK SPRINGS
Natrona County, WY
No phone.
- Hot soaking pool.
- No clothing requirements.
- Free.
- In the Rattlesnake Hills, between Ervay and Alcova west of Casper.

If you're looking for privacy, you'll love this totally isolated spot. Two spring areas about 30 feet apart feed a large shallow pool with a white sandy bottom. The clear, warm spring water runs over soft mats of watercress and moss—a pleasing contrast to the dry sagebrush-covered hills all around.

To reach the springs, drive southwest from Casper to Alcova and inquire locally. The springs are privately owned, so ask for permission. Then be prepared for a good long hike or horseback ride into the Rattlesnake Hills. If you're coming from Riverton on Highway 136, you can make the same inquiries at Ervay.

HOT SPRINGS STATE PARK
Thermopolis, WY 82443
(307) 864-2176 (information)
- Hot swimming pools, soaking pools, Jacuzzis, water park, geothermal phenomena, lodging, restaurants.
- Bathing suiys required.
- Free to reasonable to deluxe.
- Off Highway 20 at the northeast edge of Thermopolis.

One of the largest hot springs in the world feeds the facilities at Hot Springs State Park. Bighorn Hot Spring releases nearly three million gallons a day.

First, Bighorn's 130°F water flows to a state-run facility of fee-free indoor and outdoor soaking pools and tubs. Two somewhat more elaborate concessions charge admission: the Star Plunge swimming pool and Hot Springs Water Park, an aquatic playground of water slides, basketball courts, soaking space and more.

Two hotels draw on Bighorn's waters as well. A Holiday Inn provides its guests with a large Jacuzzi, while the Plaza Inn features individual soaking tubs.

Adjacent to the main spring, with its spectacular Rainbow Terrace, Black Sulphur Springs bubbles slowly from the earth to form an enchanting crystal-blue pool. Another worthy sight, White Sulphur Springs, waits on the northern side of the park.

Yet another favorite, Bathtub Spring, issues from the base of a relict travertine terrace, 15 feet above the level of the Bighorn River. The water fills a bathtub-size declivity chipped into the travertine, where visitors like to test their endurance in the superhot water.

HOT SPRINGS STATE PARK

IMMIGRANT'S WASHTUB

JACKSON LAKE HOT SPRINGS

SARATOGA INN

The park's 1,025 acres contain numerous hiking trails, excellent fishing waters and the state's herd of bison. Nearby Thermopolis adds a nine-hole golf course and a museum whose displays include a cherry wood bar used by the Hole in the Wall Gang.

HUCKLEBERRY HOT SPRINGS
Teton County, WY
(307) 739-3300 (information)
• Hot pool.
• Bathing suits required.
• Free.
• On Highway 89, two miles south of Yellowstone National Park.

Originally called Polecat Springs for the creek it feeds, this spot took on the name Flagg Ranch Hot Springs after a dude ranch opened nearby. It gained its present name when a resort sprang up around the springs in the 1960s.

Some years ago, the lease on the U.S. Forest Service land ran out and the National Park Service restored the springs and surroundings to their natural state. That's the good news.

The bad news: While the park service stops short of forbidding public use of the springs, it warns that tests revealed not only radioactivity but "bacteria related to spinal meningitis." Locals continue to bathe in the springs. You, however, may want to visit simply to see it and for the marvelous views of pine-clad slopes stretching between Yellowstone and Grand Teton National Park.

TETON VALLEY WARM SPRINGS

YELLOWSTONE NATIONAL PARK

YELLOWSTONE NATIONAL PARK

IMMIGRANT'S WASHTUB

Platte County, WY

No phone.

- Warm pools.
- No clothing requirements.
- Free.
- Off Highway 26, east of Dwyer Junction near Guernsey.

Immigrants on the Oregon Trail looked forward to this spring as a great place to soak weary bodies and wash all those trail-soiled clothes. In the 1840s, the explorer Fremont described it as "gushing forth furnishing a beautiful stream shaded by precipitous rocks."

The flow has diminished since Fremont's day; the ponds serve mainly as watering holes for cattle. But their welcome appearance and history make them worth a visit. To reach the spring, drive east on Highway 26 from Dwyer Junction. The pools flank the road on the right, just before you reach the Platte River.

JACKSON LAKE HOT SPRINGS

Teton County, WY

(307) 739-3300 (information)

- Warm lake.
- No clothing requirements.
- Free.
- Across Jackson Lake from Highway 89, in Grand Teton National Park.

This one presents a challenge. It's on the opposite side of Jackson Lake from Highway 89, so you'll need a canoe or hiking boots. You'll also need a little luck, because the level of the lake must be low enough not only to reveal the springs, but for the temperature to be right.

A diminished water level in the early 1960s led to the springs' discovery. There they were, gushing out along the shoreline for almost 900 feet, with temperatures ranging between 75°F and 120°F.

If you're both adventurous and lucky, you're in for a treat. In any case, there's no place like the Tetons breathtaking scenery.

KELLY WARM SPRING

Teton County, Wyoming

(307) 739-3300 (information)

- Warm pool.
- No clothing requirements.
- Free.
- On Gros Ventre Road in Grand Teton National Park, near Kelly about ten miles from Jackson via Highway 89.

Almost an acre in size and eight feet deep, this lukewarm pool provides a unique recreation spot for visitors to Grand Teton National Park. People sometimes practice with kayaks, since there's plenty of space for everyone.

A clean gravel bottom underlies the water, which is constantly replenished through numerous gently bubbling sources. A sign says, "Unfit for drinking," but that doesn't discourage its popularity as a swimming hole.

In other parts of the park requiring an admission fee, five campgrounds operate on a first-come, first-serve basis. Opening dates range from mid-May to mid-June; closing dates from early September to mid-October.

SARATOGA HOT SPRINGS

Saratoga, WY

(307) 326-8855 (information)

- Hot swimming pool, soaking pool, bathhouse.

- Bathing suits required.
- Free to reasonable.
- Right in town.

The town of Saratoga keeps its hot soaking pool open 24 hours a day. Free for visitors and residents alike, the pool retains a comfortable bathing temperature the year around.

In summer, a nominal fee gains you admission to the community's spring-fed swimming pool. Commercial lodgings wait two blocks west and a picnic ground across the North Platte River, within sight of the pools.

The local Chamber of Commerce prefers the name Saratoga Hot Springs to the historic, if somewhat less dignified, Hobo Pool. For more information, call the number above.

SARATOGA INN

P.O. Box 869, Saratoga, WY 82331
(307) 326-5261
- Outdoor hot swimming pool, lodging, RV park, restaurant, bar, golf, tennis.
- Bathing suits required.
- Deluxe.
- Right in town.

This friendly resort offers golf, tennis and a large 95°F mineral-water pool for recreation. The year-round facilities include rooms, an RV park, a restaurant and bar.

The town presents additional bathing facilities free of charge, and the surroundings promise unforgettable hunting, trout fishing and just plain relaxing.

TETON VALLEY WARM SPRINGS

Teton County, WY
(307) 733-4572 (information)
- Warm pond, dock.
- No clothing requirements.
- Free.
- Near Kelly, about 15 miles from Jackson via Highway 89.

These springs arise on Teton Valley Ranch, near a children's summer camp owned by Phillip Wilson. Before irrigating the ranch's crops, the water collects in a large pond outfitted with a dock.

Call the number above for more information and permission to visit the privately owned spring.

YELLOWSTONE NATIONAL PARK

c/o TW Recreational Services, Inc.,
Yellowstone National Park, WY 82190
(307) 344-7311
- Warm rivers and swimming holes, geothermal phenomena, lodging, campgrounds, restaurants.
- Bathing suits required.
- Reasonable to deluxe.
- In the northwest corner of Wyoming.

Yellowstone National Park—the mecca of hot springs enthusiasts—contains an estimated 10,000 thermal features, from bubbling mud, geysers and fumaroles to hot pools, waterfalls and boiling rivers.

Before describing a few favorite swimming holes, we must pass on a caution from the National Park Service: "The swimming or bathing in a natural, historical, or archaeological thermal pool or stream that has waters originating entirely from a thermal spring or pool is prohibited."

In other words, you may not jump into a hot spring in Yellowstone.

YELLOWSTONE NATIONAL PARK

This law protects not only you—who could be boiled alive or badly harmed by acids or alkalies—but also rare and in some cases endangered species of plants and animals. So, as a general rule, look, sniff, but stay dry.

On the other hand, don't despair; there are places in Yellowstone where you can have a great time bathing in hot water. The trick is finding where the springs mix with cold rivers to create the perfect temperature for a swim. Any of the park's visitor centers or ranger stations can advise you about current accessibility.

Boiling River, just north of Mammoth Hot Springs, provides a popular spot for dipping (daylight hours only). Here, where the hot water from Mammoth enters the Gardner River, a wonderful swimming hole offers the ideal temperature. Also, look for Firehole River and Madison River near Madison campground. Wear your bathing suit, and always test the water first with your big toe.

For information on Yellowstone's wide variety of hotels, motels and campgrounds, contact the address or phone number above. Tourists pack the park in summer, especially July and August; so if you want to visit at that time, you'll need reservations well in advance.

Camp in the backcountry, however, and you'll have over 1,200 miles of trails practically to yourself. Stop by any ranger station within 48 hours of departure to obtain a free backcountry permit. While there, ask for directions to Bechler and Warm rivers, both likely areas for remote, swimmable pools.

Yellowstone has lots to offer even those who don't want to spend all day, every day exploring the geothermal wonders. Thousands visit Yellowstone every year. Nobody leaves disappointed.

Distribution of hot springs in the state of

COLORADO

(Locations are approximate. Consult text and road maps for directions.)

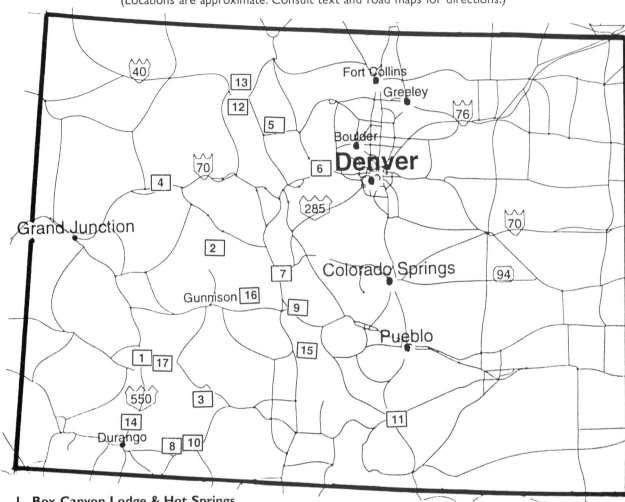

1. Box Canyon Lodge & Hot Springs
2. Conundrum Hot Springs
3. 4UR Guest Ranch
4. Glenwood Hot Springs Lodge
5. Hot Sulphur Springs
6. Indian Springs Resort
7. Mt. Princeton Hot Springs
8. Pagosa Hot Springs
9. Salida Hot Springs
10. The Spa Motel
11. Splashland
12. Steamboat Springs
13. Strawberry Park Hot Springs
14. Trimble Hot Springs
15. Valley View Hot Springs
16. Waunita Hot Springs Ranch
17. Wiesbaden Hot Springs

COLORADO

*T*HE UNITED STATES GEOLOGICAL SURVEY counts 47 hot springs in the state of Colorado. Compare that with 312 in Nevada, and it doesn't sound like much. On the other hand, Colorado has 47 more than the state of Oklahoma right next door.

Besides, some of the finest mountain scenery in the world surrounds Colorado's hot springs. The mountains promise superb camping in the summer and world-class skiing in the winter. Once you find it, the water's hot all year long.

The state's hot-spring developments run the gamut, from none at all in the remote wilds of Conundrum Hot Springs to the commercially developed athletic club at Glenwood Springs, from the new-age ambience of Valley View to the luxurious dude ranch atmosphere of 4UR Guest Ranch. No matter what your taste, you'll find a hot spring to your liking in Colorado.

BOX CANYON
LODGE & HOT SPRINGS

45 Third Ave., P.O. Box 439, Ouray, CO 81427

(303) 325-4981

(800) 327-5080 (toll-free)

- Four jetted hot tubs, lodging, picnic area.
- Bathing suits required.
- Deluxe.
- At the southwest corner of town.

The city owns nearly all rights to the hot mineral water of Ouray, and uses much of it in its public pool. Only three motels and one or two individuals have rights to the springs on their property. One of these, Box Canyon Lodge, puts its resident 140°F spring to good use heating the rooms geothermally and, with the aid of Swedish-made heat exchangers, its city water supply.

The spring water itself—brimming with beneficial minerals—spills into four flow-through redwood tubs. Registered guests soak outdoors on hillside decks, drinking in 360° views of the city and its alpine backdrop. Air jets and temperatures of 103°F to 107°F insure complete relaxation.

The accommodations earn a three-diamond endorsement from the American Automobile Association. Options include kitchenettes, stone fireplaces and complimentary morning tea and coffee in the lobby. In warm weather, several hiking trails tempt guests away from the peaceful, congenial atmosphere. In winter, skiers can buy lift tickets at half the Telluride ticket window price.

CONUNDRUM HOT SPRINGS

Pitkin County, CO

No phone.

- Hot pools.
- No clothing requirements.
- Free.
- At the source of Conundrum Creek, in the Maroon Bells–Snowmass Wilderness of White River National Forest.

If you're in Aspen during the summer, you may want to get away from the crowd and enjoy this wilderness hot spring. It surfaces near the Continental Divide at the source of Conundrum Creek, which feeds Castle Creek, which in turn meets the Roaring Fork River at Aspen.

Count on a lengthy hike and an eventual elevation of 11,000 feet. Nail down clear directions from the Forest Service before setting out.

By the time you arrive, your muscles will thank you for a long, leisurely soak in one of the two rock and sand pools. Conundrum's hot mineral water leaves the ground at body temperature and flows at about 45 gallons a minute.

4UR GUEST RANCH

P.O. Box 340, Creede, CO 81130

(719) 658-2202

- Outdoor warm swimming pool, indoor soaking pool, lodging, restaurant, horseback riding, tennis.
- Bathing suits required.
- Deluxe.
- Two miles south of Wagon Wheel Gap off Highway 149.

This high-country guest ranch offers rooms, meals and other services for a flat weekly rate. It entertains registered guests alone, and only from June and September. You'll need to make reservations well in advance.

The outdoor pool maintains a swimming

temperature of 80°F. The indoor pool, with jets, promises a good hot soak at 105°F to 110°F. Guests also enjoy tennis, horseback riding, good fishing and hiking on the premises.

GLENWOOD HOT SPRINGS LODGE
P.O. Box 308, Glenwood Springs, CO 81601 (303) 945-6571
- Outdoor hot swimming pool, therapy pool, wading pool, steambath, sauna, Jacuzzi, health club, racquetball, miniature golf, lodging, restaurant, bar.
- Bathing suits required.
- Deluxe.
- Right in town.

The Ute Indians called Glenwood Springs *Yampah*, or "Big Medicine." Today its 2,900 gallon-per-minute flow fills the largest outdoor hot mineral water swimming pool in the world.

Open to the public year-round, the two-block-long, 90°F pool comes with everything from Olympic diving facilities to a wading pool for children. A hot therapy pool measures about 104°F. The lodge's athletic club adds steambath, sauna, Jacuzzi, weight training, racquetball and more.

Overnight guests choose from 37 modest rooms in the Main Lodge near the pool and 36 deluxe versions in annex buildings close by. Skiers appreciate the convenient driving distance from Snowmass, Aspen and Vail.

HOT SULPHUR SPRINGS
Hot Sulphur Springs, CO 80451 (303) 725-3306
- Outdoor hot swimming pool, indoor and outdoor soaking pools, lodging, restaurant.
- Bathing suits required outside.

- Reasonable.
- On Highway 40 just north of town, 11 miles west of Granby.

Views of Rocky Mountain splendor surround Hot Sulphur Springs, situated in a high valley bounded by the Continental Divide, Rabbit Ears and Gore ranges. For centuries about two dozen hot springs have been gushing here from the granite, gneiss and sandstone banks of the Colorado River.

Visitors take in the sights from a large chlorinated pool at about 85°F and two untreated flow-through soaking pools at about 115°F. Indoor facilities, drawing from the same 110°F to 120°F springs, include private pools available by the hour and men's and women's pools in separate bathhouses.

The town rests at an elevation of 7,600 feet, about 100 miles west of Denver. Visitors travel over Berthoud Pass and through the Winter Park Ski and Recreational areas. Hot soaks, food and lodging, camping and picnicking in Pioneer Park, a fascinating historical museum at the east end of town and limitless outdoor recreation enhance a region of great natural beauty.

INDIAN SPRINGS RESORT
P.O. Box 1990, Idaho Springs, CO 80452 (303) 623-2050
- Indoor hot swimming pool, seven cave pools, 12 indoor and outdoor hot tubs, massage, lodging, restaurant, RV park, campground, picnic area.
- Bathing suits required in the swimming pool; nude bathing mandatory in the caves.
- Deluxe.
- On Soda Springs Road, just south of Idaho Springs.

GLENWOOD HOT SPRINGS LODGE

HOT SULPHUR SPRINGS

INDIAN SPRINGS RESORT

MOUNT PRINCETON HOT SPRINGS RESORT

A little more than a half-hour's drive from Denver, Idaho Springs has been a popular spa town since the 1880s. The state lists the 32-room lodge at Indian Springs on its inventory of historic sites. Soda Creek tumbles and splashes just in front of the lodge. Additions since the resort's opening in 1905 include a 20-room annex (1980), a campground and an RV park.

Hot-water fans have several unique choices. The most intriguing hide in two natural caves designated men's and women's. The men's cave offers three walk-in pools, the women's four. Soaking temperatures range from 104°F to 112°F, and both caves require nude bathing.

Above-ground features drawing on the 124°F springs include a dozen private baths and a large indoor swimming pool. Landscaped in tropical flora and enclosed by an arc of translucent roof, the main pool perfectly captures the Crystal Palace fashion of the gold-mining spa town's first heyday.

MOUNT PRINCETON HOT SPRINGS RESORT

15870 County Road 162, Nathrop, CO 81236
(719) 395-2361
- Hot outdoor swimming, wading and soaking pools; indoor baths; lodging; bar and restaurant; picnic ground.
- Bathing suits required.
- Deluxe.
- On County Road 162, five miles west of Nathrop.

The Ute Indians attended this spot at the base of Mount Princeton for centuries, until white settlers launched a gold and silver mining boom in the area. In those days, the springs spawned a four-story hotel complete with towering spires, huge ballroom, elevator,

speaking tubes and all the other extravagances of the late nineteenth century. Like so many of the grand resort hotels of yesteryear, Mount Princeton eventually lost favor with the elite. It fell to the wrecking ball in 1950.

Now back in business and doing quite well under new ownership, the hot mineral springs fill indoor soaking tubs and three outdoor pools (one Olympic sized for swimming). The resort welcomes the public to use its pools and tubs.

The hotel accommodates overnighters with 29 reasonably priced units, including 3 with two bedrooms. The dining room serves three meals a day. Skiing, fishing, rafting, hiking and horseback riding benefit from 700 miles of trails in surrounding San Isabel National Forest.

PAGOSA / THE SPRING INN

165 Hot Springs Blvd., Pagosa Springs, CO 81147
(800) 225-0934 (toll free)
- Five outdoor hot pools, three hot tubs, lodging, snack bar.
- Bathing suits required.
- Reasonable
- Right in town.

Outdoor Jacuzzis and 22 rooms complement a naturalistic setting of five rock and sand pools which hold up to 10 and 20 bathers.

SALIDA HOT SPRINGS

410 Rainbow Blvd., Salida, CO 82101
(719) 539-6738
- Indoor warm swimming pool, soaking pool, hot tubs, picnic grounds.
- Bathing suits required.
- Reasonable.
- Right in town.

Salida operates a big splashy family-style park with a huge indoor pool kept at about 90°F and a soaking pool at about 100°F. Private-tub bathers adjust the water to their own satisfaction. The facility stays open year-round Tuesday, Wednesday and Thursday from 4 to 9 p.m. and Friday, Saturday and Sunday from 1 to 9 p.m. Salida pipes the water from Poncha Springs, five miles to the southwest.

THE SPA MOTEL

P.O. Box 37, Pagosa Springs, CO 81147
(303) 264-5910

- Outdoor warm swimming pool, indoor hot pools, steam baths, lodging.
- Bathing suits required.
- Reasonable.
- Right in town.

One of several Colorado towns named after its springs, Pagosa ("Healing Water") has been around for many years making people relaxed and happy. The water bursts from the earth at 153°F and heats some of the community's buildings.

The Spa Motel provides lodgings and a large outdoor pool at a comfortable 80°F to 90°F. Two indoor pools, at 108°F, cater to men and women separately. Enjoy the restaurants in town, take a walk along the San Juan River, then head off for the vast recreation lands of surrounding San Juan National Forest.

SPLASHLAND

P.O. Box J, Alamosa, CO 81101
(719) 589-5151 and 589-5772

- Outdoor warm swimming pool, snack bar.
- Bathing suits required.
- Reasonable.

- On Highway 17, 1.5 miles north of Highway 160 in Alamosa.

Splashland lives up to its name with a big outdoor swimming pool filled with 99 percent pure mineral water. It operates from Memorial Day through Labor Day, just north of the Alamosa city limits.

Alamosa, the hub of transportation and trading for the San Luis Valley, nestles on the Rio Grande at an elevation of 7,500 feet. It provides one night's complimentary stay for RVs in Cole Park as well as two commercial RV parks, numerous lodgings and restaurants.

STEAMBOAT SPRINGS
HEALTH & RECREATION

P.O. Box 1211, Steamboat Springs, CO 80477
(303) 879-1828

- Outdoor warm swimming pool, water slide, hot soaking pools, sauna, massage, exercise classes, gym, tennis, snack bar, picnic area.
- Bathing suits required.
- Reasonable.
- Right in town.

Steamboat Springs invites hot-water fun and relaxation the year around. Some of the area's 157 outflows feed public baths and an indoor municipal plunge. The spring that gave the town its name no longer exists, however. It made a chugging sound, like a steamboat, as it surfaced from the earth.

This friendly facility provides an Olympic-sized swimming pool, a 350-foot water slide, three hot soaking pools (one with jets) and a sauna. Child care paves the way for tennis, weight room workouts, exercise classes and massage. With the family reunited, you can picnic with a magnificent view of Routt National Forest—and still be within walking distance of everything in town.

STRAWBERRY PARK HOT SPRINGS

P.O. Box 773332, Steamboat Springs, CO 80477

(303) 879-0342

- Hot and warm pools, sauna, lodging, campgrounds.
- Bathing suits required during the day.
- Reasonable.
- At the end of County Road 36, about seven miles north of Steamboat Springs.

Cabins and campgrounds accommodate visitors these days at Strawberry Park Hot Springs. Under private management since 1982, the facility invites day use as well as overnight stays.

Hot mineral water leaves the ground through numerous cracks in the hillside. Below, cement and rock dams create a series of idyllic flow-through pools. In several places, bathers can adjust the mixture of creek and 165°F spring water to their personal liking.

In snow time, the spot makes a popular destination for cross-country skiers, who may need four-wheel drive to reach the springs. If you lack an appropriate vehicle, contact one of several tour companies in Steamboat Springs who offer transportation.

In warmer weather, mountain bikers know Strawberry Park as a launching pad to some of the world's best mountain biking. Direct access to Forest Service trails also affords superb hiking in Routt National Forest.

TRIMBLE HOT SPRINGS

6475 County Rd. 203, Durango, CO 81301

(303) 247-0111

- Outdoor swimming and soaking pools, indoor tubs, apartment, massage, beauty treatments, exercise classes, snack bar, picnic area.
- Bathing suits required.
- Reasonable.
- On Trimble Lane off Highway 550, six miles north of Durango.

The late 1980s brought all new facilities to Trimble Hot Springs, a popular resort since the late 1800s. Two outdoor soaking pools and several indoor tubs draw on Trimble's natural springs (102°F to 109°F). An Olympic-size outdoor swimming pool uses heated city water.

Trimble employs a full-time massage therapist, offers salt-glo rubs and herbal wraps and rents out an exercise studio for karate, yoga and aerobics classes.

An apartment with its own garden Jacuzzi accommodates private parties and overnight guests. If you call to reserve the apartment, ask about the schedule of special events. The outdoor stage hosts the Trimble Hot Springs Jazz Festival in July.

VALLEY VIEW HOT SPRINGS

P.O. Box 175, Villa Grove, CO 81155

(719) 256-4315

- Outdoor warm swimming pool, four warm ponds, indoor pool, sauna, lodging, RV space, campground.
- Clothing optional.
- Reasonable.
- On the western slope of the Sangre de Cristo mountains, about four miles

SALIDA HOT SPRINGS

WAUNITA HOT SPRINGS

south of Villa Grove on Highway 17 then eight miles east of the intersection with Highway 285.

Here's one of my personal favorites—a paradise of warm water, grand scenery and peaceful cooperation.

The land received its original resort features—a swimming pool and cabins—in the early part of the century. In the 1970s, a couple bought it with plans to offer a natural alternative to the jet set atmosphere of Aspen and Vail.

The facilities remain charmingly rustic and primitive. Four natural ponds scatter on the hillside for leisurely soaking. They range in temperature from 80°F to 98°F. Spring water also flows through a large cement swimming pool, kept at 85°F and entirely free of sulphurous odor or chemical treatment. Additional hot-spring amenities include a small indoor pool and a wood-burning sauna.

Members and guests bring everything they need, from bedding, towels, food and rain gear to warm clothing for the chilly nights at 8,700 feet. People who stay overnight camp under the stars or use the communal lodge, rooms or cabins. Reservations require a deposit. Some accommodations prohibit pets and smoking. Everyone cheerfully cleans up his or her own trash.

There are a couple of things you need to know before you drop in. Valley View operates on a membership system. Nonmembers may visit only as members' guests or "exceptions." When space permits, the resort welcomes the public on weekdays alone. No one comes or goes between 11 p.m. and 9 a.m.

Two suggestions: First, plan to visit early in the week and arrive early in the day. Second, write or call to inquire about membership. The $150 per individual or $250 per couple costs less that you'd spend for a weekend at some of the other places in this book. Members enjoy up to 30 nights a year and unlimited day use—while contributing to the livelihood of this highly worthy place.

WAUNITA HOT SPRINGS RANCH
**8007 County Rd. 887, Gunnison, CO 81230
(303) 641-1266**
- Outdoor hot swimming pool, lodging, meals, horseback riding.
- Bathing suits required.
- Deluxe.
- Nineteen miles southeast of Gunnison via Highway 50, then eight miles northeast of Doyleville.

The charm of the old West meets neogeothermal comfort at Waunita. The dude ranch heats its spacious guest rooms with water from 175°F springs. The source also fills a 35- by 90-foot swimming pool, maintained at about 98.6°F.

Waunita entertains only registered guests, who enjoy a minimum week of soaking and dude-ranch activities from June through August and a minimum three days in September. A no-alcohol policy contributes to the wholesome atmosphere.

The full American plan covers lodgings, meals, four-by-four trips, fishing, horseback riding, hayrides, cookouts and square dancing. Gunnison Nation Forest lands surround the ranch, perched at a lofty 9,000 feet above sea level.

WIESBADEN HOT SPRINGS

P.O. Box 349, Ouray, CO 81427
(303) 325-4347

- Outdoor hot swimming pool, indoor soaking pool, private hot tub with hot waterfall, sauna, massage, lodging, picnic ground.
- Bathing suits required.
- Deluxe.
- Right in town.

Indians came to Ouray in the old days for the hot springs that flow from the valley floor. Then came the first silver strike in 1875. Today most of the water feeds the town's municipal swimming pool. Sheer peaks all around give Ouray the title Switzerland of America.

Skiers find their sport at its best. Those who stay at Wiesbaden can look forward to a good warming soak afterwards in the hotel's swimming pool, its hot-spring vapor cave or its private Jacuzzi with hot waterfall. Geothermally heated rooms feature various old-world styles—one sports a piano and wood-burning stove.

Wiesbaden welcomes visitors the year around. Ouray's warm-weather attractions include Jeeping, hiking, horseback riding, rock hounding and viewing the wild flowers. Special events highlight Ouray's calendar each year. For a current schedule, write to the Ouray County Chamber of Commerce, P.O. Box 145A, Ouray, CO 81427.

Distribution of hot springs in the state of

U   T   A   H

(Locations are approximate. Consult text and road maps for directions.)

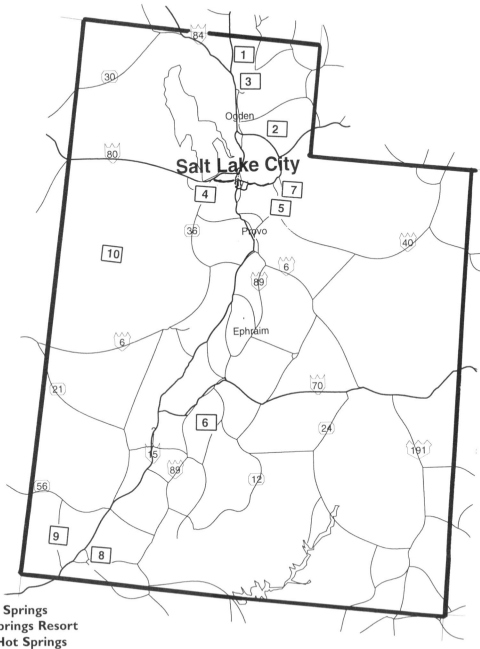

1. Belmont Springs
2. Corno Springs Resort
3. Crystal Hot Springs
4. Grantsville Warm Springs
5. The Homestead
6. Monroe Hot Springs
7. Mountain Spaa Resort
8. Pah Tempe Hot Springs
9. Veyo Resort
10. Wilson Health Springs

UTAH

*T*O ME UTAH MEANS moonlike desert landscapes, lush, fertile valleys and a generous sprinkling of hot springs—most of them beautifully developed for commercial use. Utah also means one-seventh of all the national parks in the country within a 200-mile circle. In the south you have the spectacular gorge of Zion, Bryce Canyon's weather-sculpted pillars and Glen Canyon National Recreation Area with its watery paradise, Lake Powell.

Salt Lake City absorbs a sizable number of Utah's 1,770,212 residents, leaving the rest of the state blissfully uncrowded. You can proceed on your way without concern for throngs of natives or visitors; 84,899 square miles gives everyone plenty of elbow room.

BELMONT SPRINGS

BELMONT SPRINGS

Box 36, Fielding, UT 84311
(801) 458-3200
- Outdoor hot swimming pool,
  soaking pool, two jetted pools, RV park,
  picnic grounds, golf.
- Bathing suits required.
- Reasonable.
- On Highway 15, a mile south of Plymouth.

A tropical fish farm adds an exotic touch to this modern family-style resort. Guests relax with mineral-water jet pools, a gravel-bottomed soaking pool and a large hot swimming pool.

The facility operates from April through September, providing RV parking space and hookups, picnic grounds and a nine-hole golf course.

COMO SPRINGS RESORT

P.O. Box 386, Morgan, UT 84050
(801) 829-3489
- Outdoor swimming pool, lodging, RV
  park, restaurant, picnic ground.
- Bathing suits required.
- Reasonable.
- In Morgan, about 35 miles north of Salt
  Lake City on Highway 66.

Como's springs rise along a concealed fault that crosses the Weber River Valley about a mile east of Morgan. The fault cuts limestone of Middle Paleozoic age, and the springs appear near the base of carbonate rocks of Mississippian age. The water's source remains unknown. But the relatively low temperature, low amount of dissolved solids and point of discharge suggest water of meteoric origin brought to the surface along a conduit formed by the fault.

With this technical data out of the way, you'll probably be more interested to know that this mysterious water fills two swimming pools—one with a thrilling slide attached.

Because Como operates only between Memorial Day and Labor Day, the 77°F temperature suits most of its patrons just fine. You'll find space for your RV, cabins to rent, a restaurant and a lovely place for a picnic. Who could ask for anything more on a sunny day in Utah?

CRYSTAL HOT SPRINGS

8215 N. Hwy. 69, Honeyville, UT 84314
(801) 279-8104
- Outdoor swimming pool, two soaking
  pools, three jetted hot pools, water slides,
  RV park, picnic area, snack bar.
- Bathing suits required.
- Reasonable.
- On Highway 69, about three miles north
  of Honeyville.

This resort boasts the largest adjacent hot and cold springs in the world. Harnessed both in tandem and separately, the sources lend a wide range of temperatures to a variety of pools—from stone cold to 106°F.

The main Olympic-sized pool uses cold spring water alone. The 135°F source warms five soaking pools (three with jets) and the pool at the base of two large water slides.

Crystal Hot Springs operates the year around. It provides travelers with a snack bar, RV hookups, camping and picnic grounds in the midst of tree-studded slopes and beautifully tended lawns.

GRANTSVILLE WARM SPRINGS
Tooele County, UT
No phone.
- Hot pool.
- No clothing requirements.
- Free.
- Off Highway 112 northwest of Grantsville.

Here's a warm spring that would be at home on a planet circling a distant star. It's just about as hard to get to. You'll find no holistic healing, telephones or freeway noises—just the whisper of the wind as it sighs across the lonely desert.

Grantsville's water rises along a fault line from about 5,000 feet below. It's quite salty, around 2.5 percent. But that's nothing compared to its giant cousin nearby. The Great Salt Lake averages 15 to 25 percent salt.

THE HOMESTEAD
700 N. Homestead Dr., P.O. Box 99,
Midway, UT 84049
(801) 654-1102
(800) 327-7220 (toll-free)

- Indoor and outdoor swimming pools, outdoor soaking pool, indoor jetted spa, sauna, lodging, restaurants, lounges, golf, tennis, horseback riding.
- Bathing suits required.
- Deluxe.
- In Midway, 19 miles south of Park City

Established in 1886, the Homestead began as the farm of Swiss-born Simon Schneitter. When the hot springs that foiled his farming efforts became popular with local residents, he turned the place into a bathing retreat. His wife cooked chicken dinners.

These days the classic retreat—now remodeled and updated—specializes in family vacations and meetings for up to 250. It has only one mineral spring pool, with untreated water at about 90°F. The other pools—from 82°F for swimming to 98°F for soaking—draw water from the tap and use chlorine.

Visitors stay in guest rooms, condominiums and a bed-and-breakfast inn. Sports at the Homestead range from cross-country skiing and snowmobiling to lawn games, horseback riding, tennis and 18-hole golf. Nearby attractions include Wasatch Mountain State Park and several major ski slopes.

MONROE HOT SPRINGS
575 E. First N., Monroe, UT 84754
(801) 527-4014
- Outdoor swimming pool, hydrojet pool, soaking pool, restaurant, RV park, picnic area.
- Bathing suits required.
- Reasonable.
- Right in town.

BLUE LAKE SPRING

PAH TEMPE HOT SPRINGS

PAH TEMPE HOT SPRINGS

WILSON HEALTH SPRINGS

From Memorial Day to Labor Day, travelers find good soaking and swimming, picnicking, RV camping and a restaurant at Monroe Hot Springs.

A heat exchanger tempers scalding spring water to just over 100°F for a mineral soaking pool. A swimming pool and whirlpool use the springs' heat alone, which elevates chlorinated tap water to about 90°F.

Hot baths often top off days of sightseeing, fishing or hunting on nearby Fishlake National Forest lands.

MOUNTAIN SPAA RESORT

800 N. Mountain Spaa Lane, Midway, UT 84049

(801) 654-0721 and 654-0807

- Outdoor hot to warm swimming pool, indoor hot swimming pool, soaking pool, lodging, RV hookups, restaurants, horseback riding.
- Bathing suits required.
- Reasonable.
- On Mountain Spaa Lane in Midway, 19 miles south of Park City.

The mineral water at Mountain Spaa Resort bubbles up into "hot pots," a colloquial term for the cone-shaped structures created by lime deposits. The resort maintains its indoor swimming pools *inside* one of these craters. It measures 20 by 66 feet, and the constant flow of five springs eliminates any need for chemicals. A pool nearby soaks up to eight at a time.

First-day readings of water in the outdoor pool register 98°F to 104°F. By day four, just before draining, it measures between 80°F and 85°F. When not swimming or soaking, guests

ride the resort's horses, visit the old-fashioned ice-cream parlor, attend the dance hall or eat in the cafe or dining room.

They might also drive to Park City, just 15 minutes away, or a mile northwest to Wasatch Mountain State Park.

Back home, Mountain Spaa accommodates up to 16 guests in cabins and the remainder in an RV park. Historic buildings erected in the late nineteenth century recall the days when the place was known as Luke's Hot Pots. Still friendly and ideal for families, it opens in mid-April and closes in mid-October.

PAH TEMPE HOT SPRINGS

825 N. 800 E., P.O. Box 1033, Hurricane, UT 84737

(801) 635-2879

- Outdoor hot swimming pool, soaking pools, massage, lodging, some meals, RV park, campground.
- Bathing suits required.
- Deluxe.
- On Highway 9, two miles north of Hurricane.

The September 1992 earthquake that cracked the riverbed at Pah Tempe severely limited the hot springs flow. These days it's nothing like the former rate of 5,000 gallons a minute—but you'll still find plenty of hot mineral-rich water for bathing.

The springs, though diminished, continue to warm this portion of the Virgin River. Folks love to wade and bathe in the shallow, gentle current. Two sandy-bottom ponds and various other small pools use the hot spring water as well. Finally, a shaded outdoor swimming pool steeps at 98°F to 100°F.

Pah Tempe welcomes day visitors as well as

overnight guests, who have the choice of RV park, campground, four rooms and two cabins. A retreat house, with kitchen and wood-burning stove, entertains groups. It sleeps ten in beds or more with sleeping bags. Guests opting for bed-and-breakfast enjoy the morning meal on a deck overlooking the river. With prior arrangement, the resort will prepare a vegetarian dinner.

Pah Tempe lies just a half-hour southwest of Zion National Park. Its 400 acres mix land-scaped portions and natural beauty threaded with hiking trails. A reservation requirement and the absence of alcohol and smoking pre-serve the peaceful and healthful atmosphere.

VEYO RESORT

750 E. Veyo Resort Rd., Veyo, UT 84782
(801) 574-2744

- Outdoor warm swimming pool, picnic area, snack bar.
- Bathing suits required.
- Reasonable.
- In Veyo, via Highway 18 about 18 miles north of St. George.

Like a lot of public swimming pools in Utah, Veyo's is a good place to relax if you like rock 'n' roll music on the loudspeaker.

It opens at the end of March and closes after Labor Day, maintaining its natural miner-al water at about 85°F. The grounds include a small creek, picnic sites and a volleyball court.

WILSON HEALTH SPRINGS

Tooele County, UT
No phone.
- Hot spring.
- No clothing requirements.
- Free.
- Off the old Pony Express Road north of Fish Springs.

You have to be nuts to visit Wilson Health Springs—or at least very careful. "Keep out," warns a sign. "Dangerous hot springs area. Surface may break through at any time or place." Not only is the ground unreliable, but the water is scalding (141°F) and the site rests at the edge of a U.S. government bombing and gunnery range.

If you're still game, drive west from Faust to Fish Springs on the old Pony Express Road. Then, as the road loops north, look for the dirt road to Wilson. Good luck!

NEVADA

*M*OST OF NEVADA'S ROADS follow valley routes, avoiding mountainous regions as much as possible. This makes for great gas economy. It also leaves most people unaware that Nevada offers more than endless miles of desert relieved by occasional views of distant mountains. Many of those mountains shield delightful hot springs from ready view.

Take the lofty Toquima and Monitor ranges in central Nevada, for example. They guard the Monitor Valley, wherein lies the unearthly Diana's Punchbowl. In structure it resembles a miniature volcano, but inside waits a bountiful spring with the most heavenly blue color. Too hot for bathing at its source, the outflow creates a generous stream that cools as it flows downhill.

Nevada's extremes of high and low, hot and cold challenged even the bravest prospectors of yesteryear. Today it's the seventh largest state with the sixth smallest population. This proves ideal for the hot springs lover. You'll find springs of every stripe, from the wilds of Diana's Punchbowl to the luxury of Walley's and Warm Springs Camping Resort. Whether you like them primitive and rough or tamed and polished, or something in between, you'll be glad you got off the beaten track and settled into the hot waters of Nevada.

Distribution of hot springs in the state of

N E V A D A
(Locations are approximate. Consult text and road maps for directions.)

1. **Ash Springs**
2. **Baily's Hot Springs Ranch**
3. **Beowawe Geysers**
4. **Bog Hot Springs**
5. **Bowers Mansion Park**
6. **Caliente Hot Springs Motel**
7. **Carson Hot Springs**
8. **Crystal Springs**
9. **Darrough Hot Springs**
10. **Kyle Hot Springs**
11. **Locke's Spring**
12. **New Gerlach Hot Springs**
13. **Panaca Hot Springs**
14. **Rogers Warm Springs**
15. **Spencer Hot Springs**
16. **Wabuska Hot Springs**
17. **Walley's Hot Springs Resort**
18. **Warm Springs Camping Resort**

ASH SPRINGS

Alamo, NV

(702) 726-3141 (information)

• Hot pool and channels.
• Bathing suits required.
• Free.
• Off Highway 93 north of Alamo.

Ash Springs presents a divinely inspired creation from the air. Its numerous hot springs emerge from rocky grottos, flow through sandy-bottomed channels and fill a shallow rock and concrete pool. A large warm lake completes the picture, lined with giant willows, poplars and cottonwoods.

The shallow soaking pool rests on Bureau of Land Management property, so it's free to the public. RVs find plenty of level parking. A commercial area across the street provides gas, groceries, a restaurant and campground.

The lake, however, occupies private property heavily posted with no-trespassing signs. A popular resort until recently, it's now closed and up for sale for a hefty sum.

Though part of the picture is out of bounds, be sure to visit Ash Springs the next time you're in southern Nevada. It's one of my favorites—especially fantastic in winter. But even the hot summer is pleasant thanks to cooling breezes and the effect of all that lovely water.

ASH SPRINGS

BAILY'S HOT SPRINGS RANCH

P.O. Box 387, Beatty, NV 89003
(702) 553-2395

- Three indoor soaking pools, RV park, campsites, picnic ground, restaurant, bar.
- Clothing optional in bathhouses.
- Reasonable.
- On Highway 95, east of Death Valley National Monument, about three miles north of Beatty.

This typically laid-back Nevada resort offers RV hookups, a cafe, bar and plenty of slot machines to absorb your loose change. The indoor pools are nice, too, with gravel bottoms and a strong flow that makes chlorine unnecessary. The temperatures range from 101°F to 108°F.

If you stay more than a day, take time to drive down to the Amargosa Valley south of Beatty. Here you can explore hot springs to your heart's content. The springs have names like Ash Tree, Fairbanks, Soda, Davis Ranch, Indian Rock, King and Jack Rabbit.

I recall one that makes the ground look like an inverted sieve; the cottonwoods love every drop. Nearby, a fenced spring called Devil's Hole contains rare fish adapted to some mighty hot water.

Then there's Ash Meadows, a former fly-in brothel complete with warm water ablutions. They had to close it, though. Too many pilots with too much alcohol in their bloodstreams turned the adjoining hill into an airplane junkyard.

BEOWAWE GEYSERS

Eureka County, NV
No phone.

- Possible hot pools.
- No clothing requirements.
- Free.
- Seven miles west of Beowawe via gravel road.

A plume makes a tremendous gesture of geothermal power as it shoots out of the ground west of Beowawe.

Various plans in the past aimed to harness the geysers' energy, so you may find the place unusable when you get there. If it's still free, dig yourself a water hole and let a hot pool collect. Go see it in any case. It will give you some idea of the enormous resource we have in the earth's stored heat.

BOG HOT SPRINGS

Humboldt County, NV
No phone.

- Hot stream, warm pond.
- No clothing requirements.
- Free.
- About 12.5 miles northwest of Denio Junction.

Several hot springs fill an irrigation pond between Denio and the Charles Sheldon National Wildlife Refuge. The ditch that channels water to the reservoir provides the best place for a good hot soak.

Bog Hot Springs flanks a gravel road about three and a half miles north of Highway 140 and nine miles west of Denio Junction. You can park your vehicle overnight, or make camp at Onion Reservoir or Sheldon's Virgin Valley Campground.

BOWERS MANSION PARK

4005 U.S. 395 N., Carson City, NV
(702) 849-1825

- Outdoor warm swimming pool, wading

pool, picnic area, playground.
- Bathing suits required.
- Reasonable.
- Off Highway 395, ten miles north of Carson City.

A mansion built in 1864 centers this county park overlooking Washoe Lake. If you visit between mid-May and the end of October, you can tour the restored home of a Comstock Lode millionaire.

The grounds include a large swimming pool and wading pool at about 80°F. Though the county cools the 116°F spring water before you can get to it, the pools, picnic facilities and playground make a great place to take the kids.

CALIENTE HOT SPRINGS MOTEL
P.O. Box 216, Caliente, NV 89008
(702) 726-3777
- Three indoor soaking tubs, lodging (some with hot-spring Jacuzzi tubs), RV park, picnic area.
- Bathing suits required.
- Reasonable.
- Right in town.

This friendly hot-spring motel rests in an interesting old railroad town. Don't miss a tour of the once-elegant old depot that still dominates Caliente. It contains a mural that shows all the points of interest in Lincoln and Clark Counties. State parks nearby include Beaver Dam, Cathedral Gorge, Echo Canyon, Kershaw-Ryan and Spring Valley.

In Caliente, the public can rent the motel's three soaking tubs by the hour. Registered guests have unlimited free use of the tubs.

Lined in ceramic tile, they measure five by six by three feet deep. The lodgings include five rooms with oversized Jacuzzi tubs that call on the same 115°F spring.

RV travelers especially will appreciate the motel's laundry room. They can park the vehicle, do the wash, enjoy a picnic and finish up with a relaxing hot tub soak.

CARSON HOT SPRINGS
1500 Hot Springs Rd., Carson City, NV 89701
(702) 882-9863
- Outdoor hot swimming pool, ten indoor baths, massage, lodging, RV park, restaurant, bar.
- Bathing suits required outside.
- Reasonable.
- On Hot Springs Road, half a mile north of town.

Once a rollicking casino, Carson Hot Springs still entertains fun lovers in the state capital— though the chips are now silent and all you hear is the lapping of warm waters.

The soft odor-free water, estimated at more than 12,000 years old, fills a large outdoor pool and ten Roman baths. Carson maintains its swimming pool at 98°F in summer and 102°F in winter. The private baths hold up to eight people, who adjust the temperatures up to 110°F.

Amenities include licensed massage therapists, a turn-of-the-century restaurant and saloon, 18 motel units and an RV park. The central location puts guests a half-hour's drive from Reno, Virginia City and Lake Tahoe.

CRYSTAL SPRINGS

Lincoln County, NV
No phone.
- Hot pools.
- No clothing requirements.
- Free.
- Just west of the intersection of Highway 93 and Highway 375.

The Cessna 150 circled high over the sleepy railroad town of Caliente, Nevada. I gave it a bit of throttle, and we began the climb west over the pass toward Crystal Springs. Sparse traffic below droned along the Pan-Am Highway. Once past the summit, I eased forward on the controls and began the long, lovely glide toward Pahranagat Valley straight ahead.

Suddenly the stark desert landscape gave way to brilliant green splotches of corn and alfalfa fields. What made the difference? Crystal Springs, of course. And there it was— the first pool, the stream and then the white foam of the miniature Niagara that pours into a splendid whirlpool.

At first sight of Crystal, I'd never seen such a flow of warm water—thousands of gallons per hour. We swiftly discarded our clothes— Crystal is quite secluded despite the proximity to Highways 93 and 375—and leaped into a deep pool fed by a section of conduit. Tons of comfortable water cascaded onto our delighted bodies. The torrent provides a continuous massage that can't help washing all cares and worries away downstream.

DARROUGH HOT SPRINGS

HC 60, Box 56202
Round Mountain, NV 89045-9801
(702) 377-2253

- Outdoor hot swimming pool, indoor soaking tubs, campsites, picnic ground.
- Bathing suits required.
- Reasonable.
- On Highway 376, about ten miles north of Round Mountain.

Once a stage stop, Darrough now operates as an out-of-the-way hot springs resort. It attracts people all the way from Reno who come to sober up in the outdoor pool, about 100°F. If they've really hung one on, they head for the hotter indoor tubs.

You can park your RV, take a soak and enjoy a picnic with a view that goes on for hundreds of miles.

KYLE HOT SPRINGS

Pershing County, NV
No phone.
- Possible hot pool and steam bath.
- No clothing requirements.
- Free.
- About 27 miles southeast of Mill City.

Be careful as you explore the dilapidated buildings of this ghost development. It's a mess and quite remote. Over the years, visitors have used old lumber and other trash to build various enclosures to trap the hot sulphur water and steam from a nearby vent. The water issues from the mountainside at about 106°F.

To reach Kyle from Highway 80, drive 16 miles south of Mill City on Highway 400. Turn left on the gravel road (there's a sign) and follow it east about 11 miles.

PANACA HOT SPRINGS

STEAMBOAT SPRINGS

ROGERS WARM SPRING

WARM SPRINGS CAMPING RESORT

LOCKE'S SPRING
Nye County, NV
No phone.
- Hot stream.
- No clothing requirements.
- Free.
- On Highway 6, 22 miles southwest of Currant.

Next time you find yourself driving Highway 6 between the Grant and Pancake ranges, plan to pull off at the rest stop 22 miles southwest of Currant. Locke's Spring is nothing more than an irrigation ditch, but the water is perfect body temperature.

NEW GERLACH HOT SPRINGS
Gerlach, NV
(702) 557-2220
- Hot swimming pool, campground.
- Bathing suits required.
- Reasonable.
- On Highway 447 at the north end of Gerlach.

For many years people from all over Nevada and beyond would drive to the Gerlach area and spend the winter enjoying the clear desert air and hot waters. They would camp on the desert and live in their RVs. This created some problems with private property owners.

Today the spring closest to town has a large community-owned soaking pool, men's and women's dressing rooms and spaces for overnight camping. Tap water cools the extremely hot spring water to a lovely 100°F.

PANACA HOT SPRINGS
Lincoln County, NV
No phone.
- Warm swimming hole.
- No clothing requirements.
- Free.
- Just east of Panaca.

The whole town seems to enjoy this hot-water swimming hole. As you drive east from Panaca, turn left onto a dirt road just before you leave the settled area. Now follow it to the end.

The 88°F spring flows at 6,000 gallons a minute. Surrounded by tules, the pond provides a fine, relaxing place for natives and tourists to soak and socialize.

ROGERS WARM SPRINGS
Clark County, NV
No phone.
- Two warm pools, picnic area, rest rooms.
- Bathing suits required.
- Free.
- On Northshore Road, about 15 miles south of Overton.

Rogers has long been one of my personal favorites. Located in Lake Mead National Recreation Area, it's a real beauty: rugged mountains as a backdrop, a view of cerulean waters in the distance, beige sand studded with olive brush and two shimmering pools of warm spring water.

Smooth pebbles line the large, shallow 80°F pool. Lacy tamarisks filter the hot sun. A natural cave adds a grand view of the surroundings.

You can picnic and soak till after dark, but there's no parking after 10 p.m. Other areas nearby provide plenty of places to park overnight, however.

WALLEY'S HOT SPRINGS RESORT

WHITE SULPHUR HOT SPRINGS

SPENCER HOT SPRINGS

P.O. Box 212, Austin, NV 89310-0212
(702) 964-2200 (information)
• Soaking pools and tub.
• No clothing requirements.
• Free.
• About six miles southeast of the
  intersection of Highway 50 and 376.

This is the type of hot springs true outdoor
lovers appreciate. Nothing fancy, just hot
water, the desert and big sky. A hill, adorned
with a tub and natural and visitor-improved
hot soaking pools, offers a view you'll find
only in Nevada.

To reach the spot, take the gravel road off
Highway 376 about 100 yards south of the
intersection with Highway 50. Follow it five
and a half miles, then turn left onto the dirt
road heading up the hot springs hill. For more
information, contact the Austin Chamber of
Commerce at the address or number above.

WABUSKA HOT SPRINGS

Lyon County, NV
No phone.
• Soaking pool.
• No clothing requirements.
• Free.
• Off Highway 95, 1.5 miles northeast
  of Wabuska.

The basement ruins of an old building form a
big primitive soaking pool outside Wabuska.
To find the spring, turn right onto a dirt road
a mile north of the Wabuska railroad crossing
on Highway 95, and drive another half-mile.

WALLEY'S HOT SPRINGS RESORT

P.O. Box 26, Genoa, NV 89411
(702) 782-8155
• Outdoor swimming pool, indoor and outdoor hot soaking pools, sauna, steam bath,
  massage, fitness rooms, lodging, restaurant, bar.
• Bathing suits required.
• Deluxe.
• A mile and a half south of Genoa, about
  50 miles south of Reno.

This hot springs resort first opened in 1862.
Early guest lists included luminaries like Mark
Twain, President U.S. Grant and Clark Gable.
While its history lends a certain charm and a
depth of character, Walley's also reflects a
modern trend in upscale spas. It caters to folks
with both good health and a budget allowing
for those little extras in life.

In addition to six flow-through hot-spring
pools and a freshwater swimming pool,
Walley's provides complete men's and women's
fitness centers. Workout fans find weight-
training rooms, saunas, steam baths and massage facilities in the main two-story building,

Walley's will serve breakfast in bed if you

WALLEY'S HOT SPRINGS RESORT

overdo it in the exercise department. But regular meals take place in a multilevel dining room with a spectacular view of the Carson Valley and Sierras.

Walley's operates as a membership club but welcomes the public on a fee basis. If you love the Carson Valley as much as I do, you'll do yourself a favor by visiting this prime example of a great hot spring resort.

WARM SPRINGS CAMPING RESORT
P.O. Box 41, Moapa, NV 89025
(702) 865-2780

- Outdoor hot swimming pool, whirlpool, soaking pools, hot channels, RV park, campsites, picnic ground.
- Bathing suits required.
- Deluxe.
- On Highway 168, nine miles northwest of Highway 15 at Glendale.

In 1978, *Esquire* magazine rated Desert Oasis the number one hot springs resort in America.

Now called Warm Springs, it still presents a fairyland of blue warm-water pools, waterfalls, streams and waterways.

There is something ethereal about Warm Springs and something improbable too. The surrounding desert, dry as the moon, makes the three-million-gallon-per-day spring seem delightfully out of place. Palms and other tropical plants line channels connecting a series of warm gravel-bottom soaking pools. While the resort heats the water to just over 100°F for the hydrotherapy pool, a huge flow-through swimming pool maintains the 90°F temperature of the springs.

A walk around the grounds reveals green lawns and 18 ponds full of ornamental koi and more than 30 varieties of water lilies. Hikes lead to a neighboring warm spring for variety and picturesque meadows with grazing cattle and quaint old farmhouses.

The resort operated as a private club for a while, but no longer. You can stop by unannounced to spend the day, but call ahead to reserve an RV hookup or camping space.

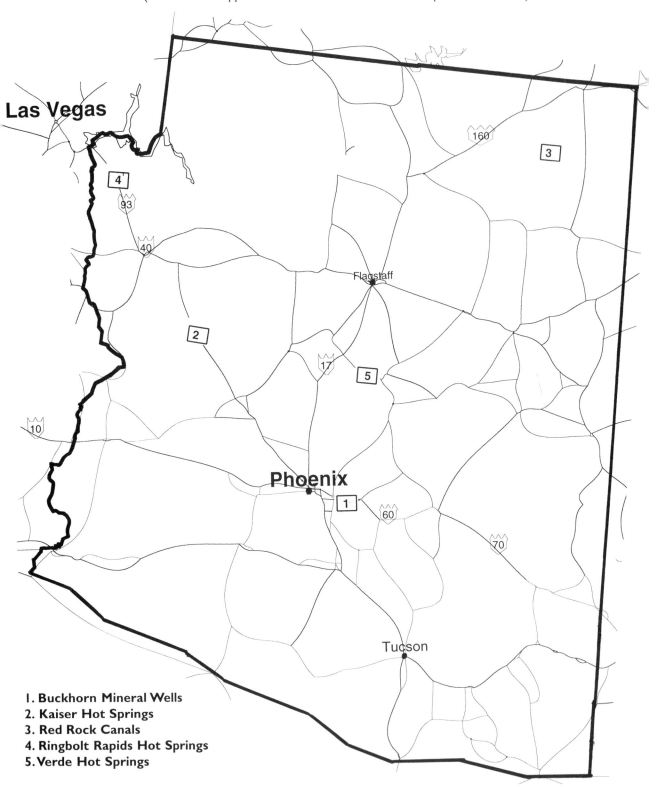

Distribution of hot springs in the state of
A R I Z O N A
(Locations are approximate. Consult text and road maps for directions.)

Las Vegas

Flagstaff

Phoenix

Tucson

1. Buckhorn Mineral Wells
2. Kaiser Hot Springs
3. Red Rock Canals
4. Ringbolt Rapids Hot Springs
5. Verde Hot Springs

ARIZONA

*A*RIZONA PRESENTS a twentieth-century paradox: thousands of square miles of lovely open desert with crystal-clear air and, in contrast, cities jammed with people and pollution. You make a choice when you live in Arizona. Earn a modest living in tiny towns like Wickieup or Sonoita, or make big bucks in Phoenix and choke on smog.

Fortunately, open spaces far exceed urban sprawl. So if you're a traveler, you don't have to bother with civilization.

We found a predominance of thermal wells over hot springs in Arizona—and that the hot springs are hard to find. We enjoyed the traveling and searching—and fixed a lot of flat tires along the way—but many of the springs we looked for still wait to be found. Wild winter weather, impossible terrain and a lack of information hung us up. But along the way we met some friendly people and saw some beautiful scenery.

We did find a few fine hot springs, however. So do check out Arizona. You'll have a good time exploring. If you happen to stumble upon Tom Brown Canyon or Monkey Spring, write and let us know what they're like. We never could find them.

BUCKHORN MINERAL WELLS MOTEL & SPA

5900 E. Main St., Mesa, AZ 85205
(602) 832-1111
- Private indoor hot tubs, massage, lodging, restaurant.
- Bathing suits optional.
- Reasonable.
- On Highway 60 just east of Mesa.

When the sights of Phoenix pall, drive due east until you see the red, red mountains of Mesa. Here Buckhorn Motel presents the obvious choice of lodging for hot mineral water lovers.

Built in 1936, the motel became a spa catering to the New York Giants in the mid-'50s. The team stayed at Buckhorn for 25 consecutive training seasons. Today's facilities include more than two dozen men's and women's private tubs with whirlpool pumps.

Drop-in visitors and motel guests alike enjoy Buckhorn's waters, Swedish massage and sweat wraps. Rustic lodgings include kitchens and black-and-white TVs but no phones. A restaurant serves meals across the street.

KAISER HOT SPRINGS

Mojave County, AZ
No phone.
- Soaking pool.
- No clothing requirements.
- Free.
- On Highway 93, about 12 miles south of Wickieup.

The waters of this magnificent thermal area flow beneath towering bluffs of sedimentary and volcanic rock. Watercress and maidenhair ferns grow lush amid the crystal-clear flows.

Some springs sport tiny waterfalls; others simply seep from cracks in the colorful rocks. All join a tributary to the Big Sandy River, one of west-central Arizona's major waterways.

A search of the little-known canyon reveals two outstanding features: lovely trees drawing sustenance from the springs and a sandy-bottomed bathing pool filled with inviting warm water.

Incidentally, we discovered that some of the residents of the nearby campground were unaware that the waters they saw issuing from the cliff side were warm—and they'd been visiting the area for years. A good rule of thumb: Never pass up an inviting pool without testing the waters. You might miss a great soak!

KAISER HOT SPRINGS

RED ROCK CANALS

Pinal County, AZ
No phone.
- Warm canals.
- No clothing requirements.
- Free.
- In and around the town of Red Rock.

While driving from Phoenix to Tucson, we happened to stop for the night at a tiny village

RINGBOLT RAPIDS HOT SPRING

VERDE HOT SPRINGS

called Red Rock. No stores, no gas stations, just a small school and a post office. In the chilly morning, I took my usual walk and was astounded to see wisps of steam rising from a wide irrigation ditch. I dipped a finger in and found, to my delight, a most comfortable temperature, around 80°F.

To my further delight, I discovered similar warm canals all around the area, dug by local ranchers and filled with water from warm mineral wells. Naturally, I advise you to get permission from the local owner before stripping down and diving in. But I can tell you that I found the people of Red Rock as warm and friendly as the water.

RINGBOLT RAPIDS HOT SPRING
Mojave County, AZ
No phone.
- Soaking pools, hot waterfall.
- No clothing requirements.
- Free.
- About three miles south of Hoover Dam in Lake Mead National Recreation Area.

As you probably gathered, I have a special affection for springs in the desert. Partly, it's the dramatic contrast between the water and the arid setting. Partly, it's the solitude of most desert hot springs. Then, there are the delightful surprises. It's not often, for example, that one finds hot water cascading for 25 feet in a spectacular thermal waterfall.

This phenomenon waits between Hoover Dam and Kingman, about a three-mile hike off Highway 93. From Hoover Dam, drive about four miles southeast and park in the dirt lot at the head of White Rock Canyon. Follow the canyon down to the river. Hike a quarter-mile south, then upstream to the springs. If you have a boat, just sail on up from Willow Beach.

You'll find two artificial pools with temperatures around 100°F—just perfect for those cool desert evenings. The water proceeds from the pools and over the falls to create a better shower than you'll ever find in a hotel room. Two cautions: Take care on the rickety ladder, and watch out for venomous snakes.

VERDE HOT SPRINGS
Camp Verde, AZ
(602) 567-4501 (information)
- Indoor and outdoor cement pools, river bank pools.
- Clothing optional.
- Free.
- On the west bank of the Verde River, bordering the Tonto and Coconino national forests about 25 miles southeast of Camp Verde.

It's a mile-and-a-half hike to this well-pre-served remnant of a hot spring resort. Lovely hot water and high desert scenery make the trip well worth it.

Several indoor and outdoor cement pools remain from the resort's heyday in the 1920s—including one in a riverside cave. More primitive rock and sand pools adjoin the river. Temperatures range up to 104°F.

To reach the spot, drive south from Camp Verde to the end of Forest Service Road 708. Ford the river and follow the trail to the springs. Before setting out, call the Camp Verde Forest Station at the number above for information on road and river conditions.

UNLISTED ARIZONA HOT SPRING

NEW MEXICO

*O*NE NOVEMBER NIGHT north of Taos, I stepped outside our trailer and my Levis promptly froze to my legs. I've spent winters in some fairly cold places, including the Mother Lode of California, the shores of Lake Tahoe and the Sheep Range of Nevada. But I don't think I've ever felt such penetrating cold as I did that night in New Mexico.

I was in luck, however. In just a matter of minutes I had my body in the water of a nearby hot spring. The shivering stopped, and I could laugh at the chill of the clear night air.

It's magical contrasts like this—and the blessings of 73 hot springs in the state—that make New Mexico exceptional, truly a land of enchantment.

Distribution of hot springs in the state of
NEW MEXICO

(Locations are approximate. Consult text and road maps for directions.)

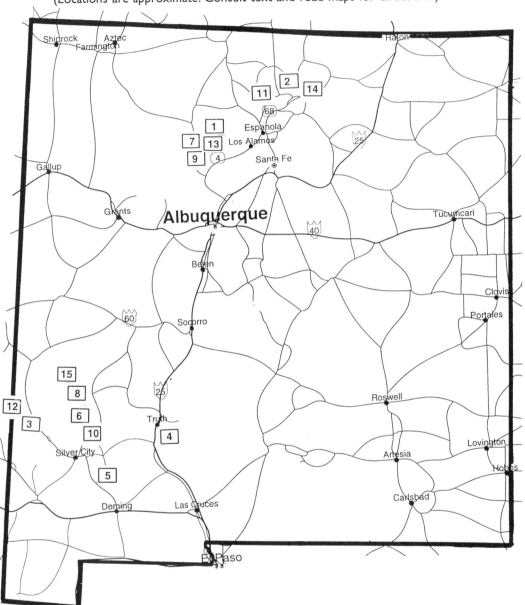

1. **Battleship Rock Hot Springs**
2. **Black Rock Hot Springs**
3. **Bubbles Hot Springs**
4. **Charles Motel & Bathhouse**
5. **Faywood Hot Springs**
6. **Gila Hot Springs**
7. **Jemez Springs Bath House**
8. **Lightfeather Hot Springs**
9. **McCauley Hot Springs**
10. **Melanie Hot Springs**
11. **Ojo Caliente Mineral Spring**
12. **San Francisco Hot Springs**
13. **Spence Hot Springs**
14. **Stagecoach Hot Springs**
15. **Upper Middle Fork Hot Spring**

GILA HOT SPRINGS VACATION CENTER

GILA HOT SPRINGS VACATION CENTER

BATTLESHIP ROCK HOT SPRINGS

Sandoval County, NM

No phone.

- Warm pond.
- No clothing requirements.
- Free.
- Off Highway 4, about five miles north of Jemez Springs.

This natural pond delights the hearts of hikers and hot spring lovers. About 50 feet long, it has water at about 90°F flowing through continuously.

To reach the springs off Highway 4, take the trail at the foot of Battleship Rock and follow it up the canyon.

BLACK ROCK HOT SPRINGS

Taos County, NM

No phone.

- Hot pool.
- No clothing requirements.
- Free.
- On the west bank of the Rio Grande Gorge, northwest of Taos.

Here's another heaven-sent design: a 12-foot long, sand-bottomed pool of near-100°F water—and a spectacular view down the Rio Grande Gorge.

To reach the springs, drive north from Taos on Highway 3. Turn left onto a dirt road at the traffic sign reading "HILL." Go two and a half miles, then right and drive a half-mile. Turn left and drive till you cross the river, where you'll find the parking area. Park and follow the trail downstream.

Conditions at Black Rock depend on the mood of the Rio Grande. As with most riverside pools, check the current status with locals.

BUBBLES HOT SPRING

Catron County, NM

No phone.

- Hot soaking pools.
- No clothing requirements.
- Free.
- On the San Francisco River in Gila National Forest, a few miles southwest of Pleasanton.

Bubbles fills a large sandy-bottomed natural pool about a half-mile hike from San Francisco Hot Springs. Like its sister spring up river, Bubbles can change rapidly due to flooding. The temperature ranges up to 102°F. Smaller springs nearby feed volunteer-built pools.

To reach Bubbles, follow the sign to San Francisco Hot Springs on Highway 180, about two miles south of Pleasanton. Park—and camp, if you like—at San Francisco and follow the river downstream. You can also pitch a tent for up to a week on a flat area alongside the main Bubbles pool.

CHARLES MOTEL & BATHHOUSE

701 Broadway, Truth or Consequences, NM 87901

(505) 894-7154

- Eight indoor tubs, massage, sauna, lodging, RV park.
- Bathing suits optional.
- Reasonable.
- Right in town.

Truth or Consequences (it got the name from an old TV show) offers several hot water facilities. Used exclusively by the Apache Indians until the late 1800s, the springs—at 110°F—inspired a flush of "modern" bathhouses in the early 1900s.

BATTLESHIP ROCK HOT SPRINGS

OJO CALIENTE MINERAL SPRING

OJO CALIENTE MINERAL SPRING

Like the Charles Motel & Bathhouse, most of today's facilities provide lodgings with a good soak. Nearly all offer massage plus additional therapeutic services like acupressure, reflexology, diathermy and sweat wraps. Numerous restaurants in town suit every taste and pocketbook.

FAYWOOD HOT SPRING
Grant County, NM
No phone.
- Soaking pool.
- No clothing requirements.
- Free.
- Off Highway 61, a few miles south of Sherman.

A rock-lined pool about 60 square feet by 3 feet deep allows Faywood's hot mineral water to linger. You control the temperature by diverting the flow and allowing the pool to cool.

To reach the spring, drive south from Sherman on Highway 61 and turn right onto a dirt road about a mile past the City of Rocks State Park. Stay overnight if you wish.

GILA HOT SPRINGS VACATION CENTER
88061 Gila Hot Springs, Rt. 11, Box 80, Silver City, NM 88061
(505) 536-9551 or 536-9314
- Outdoor soaking pools, indoor Jacuzzi tub, lodging, RV park, campground, picnic area, grocery store, snack bar.
- Bathing suits required outdoors.
- Reasonable.
- On Highway 15, 40 miles north of Silver City and 4 miles south of Gila Cliff Dwellings National Monument.

This is the place for folks who want to live the good life outdoors at little expense. You can park your trailer for just $100 a month and use the hot riverside pools and indoor Jacuzzi as much as you want. Try that in Smogville or Fog City!

The 100-acre facility welcomes shorter stays as well, entertaining with homemade ice cream in the general store, a museum of dolls and miniatures, rental apartments, horseback riding, guided fishing and hunting trips—plus all the spectacular desert and mountain scenery you can handle.

JEMEZ SPRINGS BATH HOUSE
P.O. Box 87, Jemez Springs, NM 87025
(505) 829-3303
- Eight indoor tubs.
- Bathing suits optional.
- Reasonable.
- Near Jemez Springs, between mile markers 16 and 17 on Highway 4.

The Jemez Springs Bath House once served as the hub of life in San Diego Canyon. People came from miles around to take advantage of the water's healing power. Located in scenic red-rock country, the facility now rests on the state's list of registered historic sites.

Hot mineral water comes out of the earth at between 154°F and 189°F. Holding tanks cool it so you can mix the temperature to your liking. Men's and women's sections each contain four individual tubs. The modest fee includes soap and towel. Therapeutic massage is extra, by appointment only.

Relax with a bath and massage after a day of cross-country skiing, then enjoy a meal at one of the local restaurants. The area also provides lodging, RV hookups and campgrounds.

LIGHTFEATHER HOT SPRING
Catron County, NM
(505) 536-9461 (information)
- Hot pool.
- No clothing requirements.
- Free.
- A half-mile from the visitors center at Gila Cliff Dwellings National Monument.

Lightfeather's 40-foot natural rock and sand pool provides a range of temperatures for bathing. Spring water that enters at 150°F cools gradually as it flows to the far end of the pool.

The trail to Lightfeather begins outside the Gila Cliff Dwellings National Monument Visitors Center. Inside you'll find wonderful exhibits on ancient dwellings and the natural history of the area.

McCAULEY HOT SPRING
Jemez Springs, NM
No phone.
- Warm pool.
- No clothing requirements.
- Free.
- One and a quarter miles from the Battleship Rock picnic grounds on Highway 4, about five miles north of Jemez Springs.

McCauley's waters fill a shallow man-made pool in a leafy forest glade. The pool reminds me of Rogers Hot Springs near Las Vegas, Nevada. Both have lovely settings and temperatures of about 85°F.

To reach the spring, take Forest Service Trail 137 from the picnic grounds at Battleship Rock.

MELANIE HOT SPRING
Grant County, NM
No phone.
- Hot pools.
- No clothing requirements.
- Free.
- On the Gila River in Gila National Forest, off Highway 15 about halfway between Silver City and Gila Cliff Dwellings National Monument.

Here's a challenge for the hot spring lover—a hike down the Gila with a collection of fine pools at the end of the line. Several hot basins and the cold, cold river give you a variety of choices.

As you drive north from Silver City on Highway 15, watch for where the river runs under the highway. Park and take the trail south. Be prepared for several river crossings.

OJO CALIENTE MINERAL SPRING
P.O. Box 468, Ojo Caliente, NM 87549
(505) 583-2233
- Outdoor warm swimming pool, indoor hot soaking pools, private tubs, massage, lodging, RV park, campground, picnic ground, restaurant.
- Bathing suits required.
- Reasonable.
- On Highway 285, 35 miles southwest of Taos.

One of the oldest, if not *the* oldest hot springs facility in North America caters to a steady flow of satisfied customers. Many believe the waters benefit their ailments. While there we observed a considerable number of people "taking the cure."

Management makes no claims for it, but customers often bring containers to take home a supply of the mineral-rich water. They believe it's good for washing the inside of the body as well as the outside.

Pools range from a large one outdoors for swimming to indoor men's and women's soaking pools to coed and individual tubs. An indoor grotto features the sight of the water emerging from its source, a fissure in a sandstone boulder. Pool and tub temperatures range from 80°F to 113°F.

Visitors find massage services, sweat wraps, food, lodging and an RV park on the premises. Alongside a small river, the adjoining Mexican-style village and park complete an idyllic tableau.

SAN FRANCISCO HOT SPRINGS
Catron County, NM
No phone.
- Soaking pools.
- No clothing requirements.
- Free.
- On the San Francisco River in Gila National Forest, a few miles southwest of Pleasanton.

The fortunes of the river determine what you'll find at San Francisco Hot Springs. Often, the main spring's flow fills a large shallow pool, inviting a most comfortable bath the year around.

About two miles south of Pleasanton, a sign on Highway 180 directs you to the spot. The Forest Service allows overnight camping in designated areas.

SPENCE HOT SPRINGS
Sandoval County, NM
No phone.
- Hot soaking pool.
- Bathing suits optional.
- Free.
- Off Highway 4, about seven miles north of Jemez Springs.

With its pristine surroundings, Spence typifies New Mexico's many undeveloped hot springs. The sand-bottomed, rock-sided pool rests up a steep slope beside the Jemez River, in the midst of Santa Fe National Forest lands. After you've soaked in the 102°F water and taken in the views, drift down below to sample the tiny waterfalls, each cooler than the last.

Natives informed us that Spence can be especially delightful in winter. A log laid across the Jemez River augments a short trail leading from the generous parking area just off the highway.

STAGECOACH HOT SPRINGS
Taos County, NM
No phone.
- Two soaking pools.
- No clothing requirements.
- Free.
- In the Rio Grande Gorge, northwest of Taos.

Stagecoach has two modest-sized pools, the upper at around 100°F and the lower at about 90°F. For contrast, try a quick leap into the Rio Grande!

You can reach the springs by driving north from Taos on Highway 3. Turn left onto a dirt road at the traffic sign reading "HILL." Go two and a half miles, then left and another two miles. Park and hike downhill a short distance to the springs.

UPPER MIDDLE FORK HOT SPRING

Catron County, NM

No phone.

- Hot pool.
- No clothing requirements.
- Free.
- About nine miles from the visitors center at Gila Cliff Dwellings National Monument.

Get a party together and you can make a memorable adventure out of this geothermal wonder.

First, prepare for a round-trip hike of about 18 miles. Start at the trail beside Gila Cliff Dwellings National Monument Visitor Center and follow the Gila River, crossing it many times. You'll need good boots or, better yet, a horse.

For the intrepid, the reward is well worth the effort. The hot springs feed a large natural rock pool tucked in a leafy glade.

UNLISTED NEW MEXICO HOT SPRING

APPENDIX

*T*he previous section describes some of our favorite hot springs around the West. We hope you'll visit many of these fine places and share our enthusiasm for their hot water.

However, the first section only begins your hot springs adventure. The Western United States teems with geothermal springs—hundreds of them—too numerous to describe in full. Therefore, we've created this appendix of maps and tables to lead you to additional hot springs. They're out there waiting for you right now!

Turn to the overall map key on pages TK and TK to find which part of each state the detailed maps explore. Arranged by state, then roughly by ascending latitude, the tables list the springs' names, latitudes, longitudes and water temperatures (when known).

To use the detailed maps to plan a journey, simply transfer the locations to your road map. You can also approach the appendix another way. If you happen upon a hot spring and want more data, turn to the map key to determine which detailed map holds the information you seek.

The tables list all hot springs known to the government, but not all thermal wells. Throughout the 11 Western states, dozens of springs share generic names like Hot Spring, Warm Spring, Sulphur Spring and so on. If you've heard of one of these, to find the temperature you must rely on the latitude and longitude.

A scale of 1:625,000 applies to all but two of the states' detailed maps. California's scale is 1:937,500; Montana's, 1:1,250,000.

Finally, we wish to thank the National Oceanic and Atmospheric Administration of the U.S. Department of Commerce for providing the data for the tables. For the maps, we thank the U.S. Geological Survey and the Division of Mines and Geology of the U.S. Department of Energy.

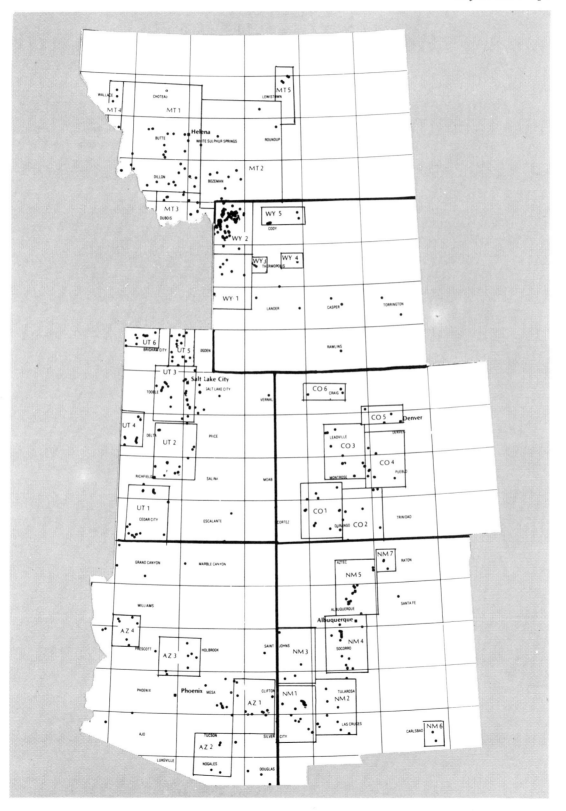

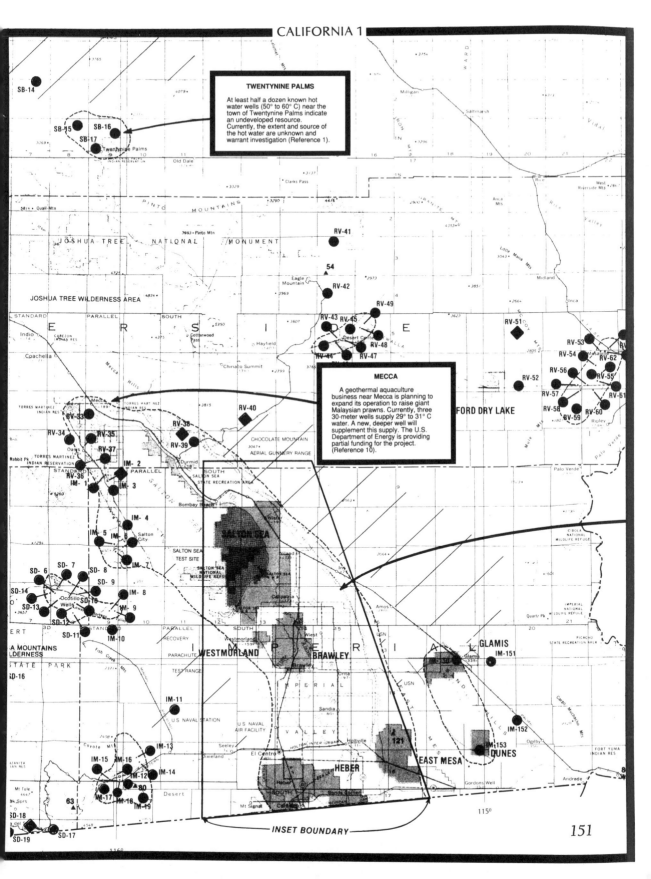

TWENTYNINE PALMS

At least half a dozen known hot water wells (50° to 60° C) near the town of Twentynine Palms indicate an undeveloped resource. Currently, the extent and source of the hot water are unknown and warrant investigation (Reference 1).

MECCA

A geothermal aquaculture business near Mecca is planning to expand its operation to raise giant Malaysian prawns. Currently, three 30-meter wells supply 29° to 31° C water. A new, deeper well will supplement this supply. The U.S. Department of Energy is providing partial funding for the project. (Reference 10).

INSET BOUNDARY

151

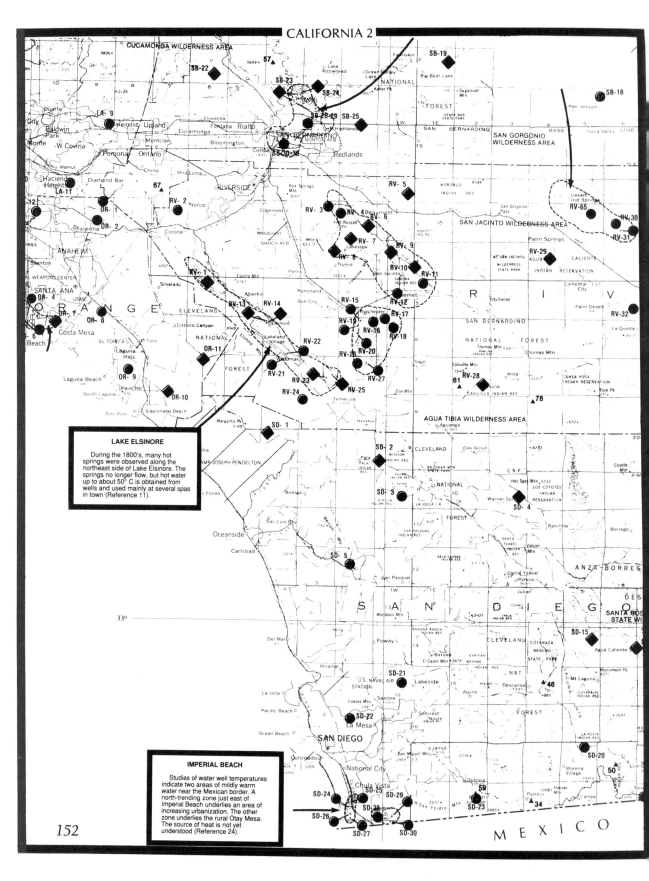

LAKE ELSINORE

During the 1800's, many hot springs were observed along the northeast side of Lake Elsinore. The springs no longer flow, but hot water up to about 50° C is obtained from wells and used mainly at several spas in town (Reference 11).

IMPERIAL BEACH

Studies of water well temperatures indicate two areas of mildly warm water near the Mexican border. A north-trending zone just east of Imperial Beach underlies an area of increasing urbanization. The other zone underlies the rural Otay Mesa. The source of heat is not yet understood (Reference 24).

152

MEXICO

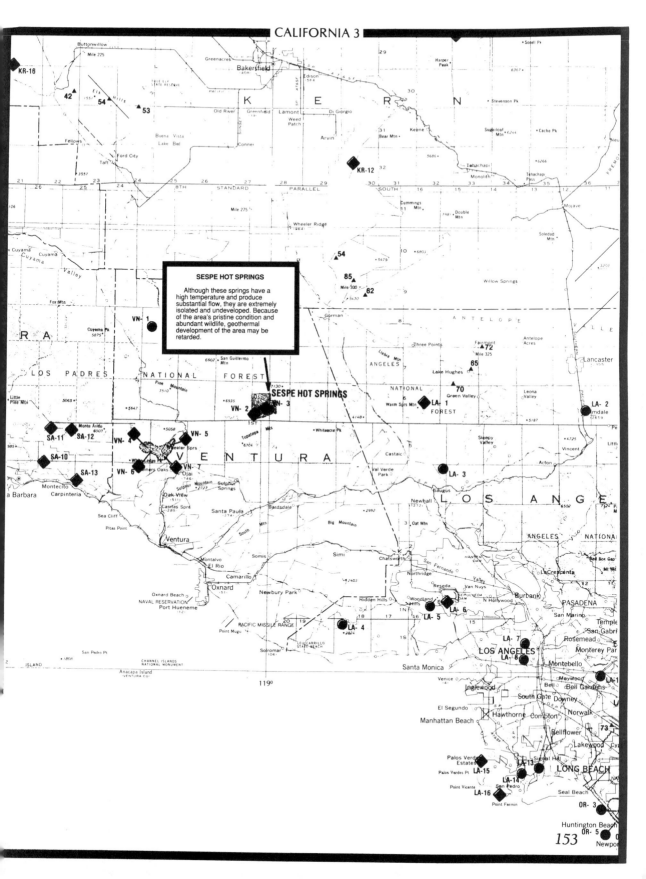

SESPE HOT SPRINGS

Although these springs have a high temperature and produce substantial flow, they are extremely isolated and undeveloped. Because of the area's pristine condition and abundant wildlife, geothermal development of the area may be retarded.

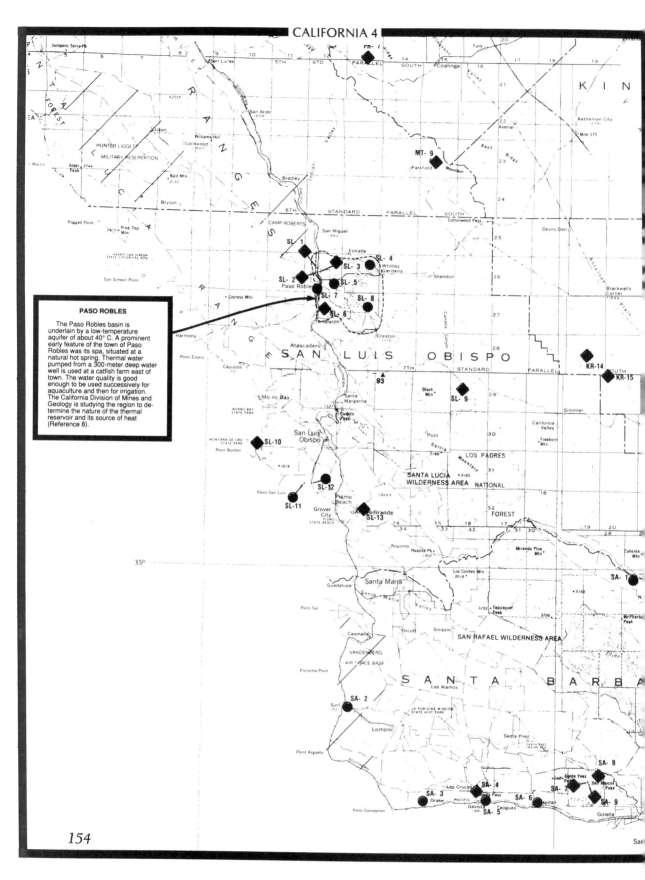

PASO ROBLES

The Paso Robles basin is underlain by a low-temperature aquifer of about 40° C. A prominent early feature of the town of Paso Robles was its spa, situated at a natural hot spring. Thermal water pumped from a 300-meter deep water well is used at a catfish farm east of town. The water quality is good enough to be used successively for aquaculture and then for irrigation. The California Division of Mines and Geology is studying the region to determine the nature of the thermal reservoir and its source of heat (Reference 8).

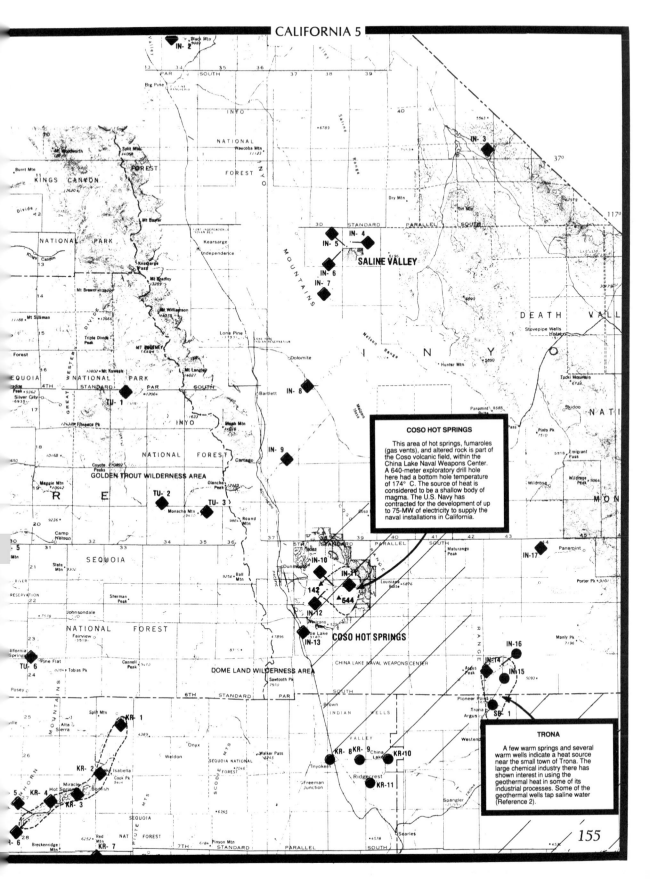

COSO HOT SPRINGS

This area of hot springs, fumaroles (gas vents), and altered rock is part of the Coso volcanic field, within the China Lake Naval Weapons Center. A 640-meter exploratory drill hole here had a bottom hole temperature of 174° C. The source of heat is considered to be a shallow body of magma. The U.S. Navy has contracted for the development of up to 75-MW of electricity to supply the naval installations in California.

TRONA

A few warm springs and several warm wells indicate a heat source near the small town of Trona. The large chemical industry there has shown interest in using the geothermal heat in some of its industrial processes. Some of the geothermal wells tap saline water (Reference 2).

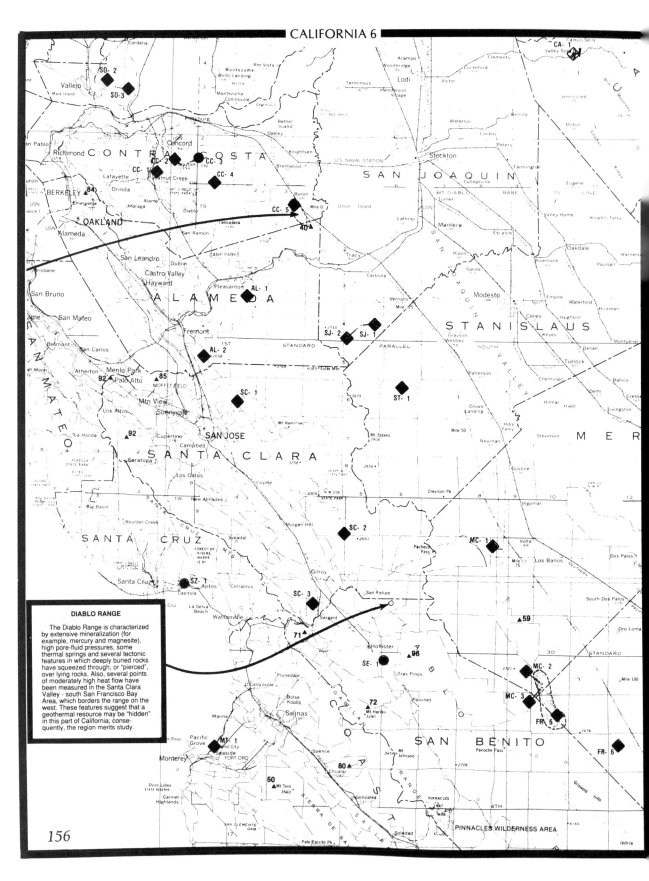

DIABLO RANGE

The Diablo Range is characterized by extensive mineralization (for example, mercury and magnesite), high pore-fluid pressures, some thermal springs and several tectonic features in which deeply buried rocks have squeezed through, or "pierced", over lying rocks. Also, several points of moderately high heat flow have been measured in the Santa Clara Valley - south San Francisco Bay Area, which borders the range on the west. These features suggest that a geothermal resource may be "hidden" in this part of California; consequently, the region merits study.

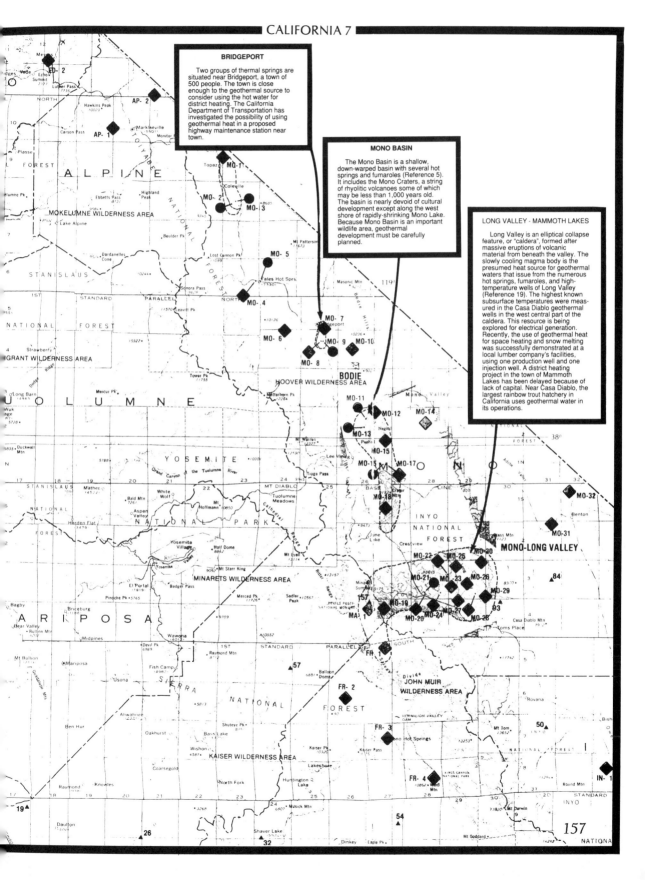

BRIDGEPORT

Two groups of thermal springs are situated near Bridgeport, a town of 500 people. The town is close enough to the geothermal source to consider using the hot water for district heating. The California Department of Transportation has investigated the possibility of using geothermal heat in a proposed highway maintenance station near town.

MONO BASIN

The Mono Basin is a shallow, down-warped basin with several hot springs and fumaroles (Reference 5). It includes the Mono Craters, a string of rhyolitic volcanoes some of which may be less than 1,000 years old. The basin is nearly devoid of cultural development except along the west shore of rapidly-shrinking Mono Lake. Because Mono Basin is an important wildlife area, geothermal development must be carefully planned.

LONG VALLEY - MAMMOTH LAKES

Long Valley is an elliptical collapse feature, or "caldera", formed after massive eruptions of volcanic material from beneath the valley. The slowly cooling magma body is the presumed heat source for geothermal waters that issue from the numerous hot springs, fumaroles, and high-temperature wells of Long Valley (Reference 19). The highest known subsurface temperatures were measured in the Casa Diablo geothermal wells in the west central part of the caldera. This resource is being explored for electrical generation. Recently, the use of geothermal heat for space heating and snow melting was successfully demonstrated at a local lumber company's facilities, using one production well and one injection well. A district heating project in the town of Mammoth Lakes has been delayed because of lack of capital. Near Casa Diablo, the largest rainbow trout hatchery in California uses geothermal water in its operations.

157

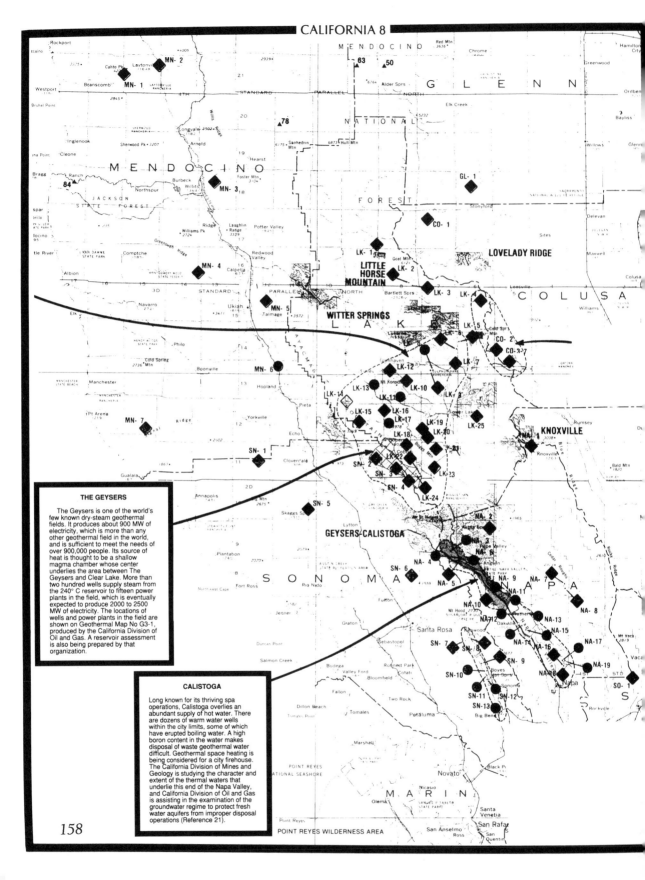

THE GEYSERS

The Geysers is one of the world's few known dry-steam geothermal fields. It produces about 900 MW of electricity, which is more than any other geothermal field in the world, and is sufficient to meet the needs of over 900,000 people. Its source of heat is thought to be a shallow magma chamber whose center underlies the area between The Geysers and Clear Lake. More than two hundred wells supply steam from the 240° C reservoir to fifteen power plants in the field, which is eventually expected to produce 2000 to 2500 MW of electricity. The locations of wells and power plants in the field are shown on Geothermal Map No G3-1, produced by the California Division of Oil and Gas. A reservoir assessment is also being prepared by that organization.

CALISTOGA

Long known for its thriving spa operations, Calistoga overlies an abundant supply of hot water. There are dozens of warm water wells within the city limits, some of which have erupted boiling water. A high boron content in the water makes disposal of waste geothermal water difficult. Geothermal space heating is being considered for a city firehouse. The California Division of Mines and Geology is studying the character and extent of the thermal waters that underlie this end of the Napa Valley, and California Division of Oil and Gas is assisting in the examination of the groundwater regime to protect fresh water aquifers from improper disposal operations (Reference 21).

SURPRISE VALLEY

The Fort Bidwell Indian Reservation has proposed a study for the use of geothermal fluids for space heating, agriculture, and greenhouse operations (Reference 7). Abundant hot water rises along the Surprise Valley fault and associated faults. Several exploratory geothermal wells were drilled in the vicinity of Lake City and Cedarville, but because of temperature and permeability problems, development has not proceeded. Because of the area's isolation and small population, direct heat applications will probably be used first in agriculture.

KELLY HOT SPRING

The U.S. Department of Energy is partially funding a project here that will use geothermal fluids from an existing well to supply heat to a pork feedlot operation. Fluids will be disposed of through an injection well. The area has been studied using several geophysical and geochemical techniques (Reference 4). Reportedly, hot water of about 115° C extends under an area of several square kilometers.

LITTLE HOT SPRING VALLEY

Only one hot spring is known in this remote valley, but there are reports of nearby warm water wells. South of the spring, warm water is suspected along a fault zone bounding the east side of the valley. On the west side of the valley are abundant volcanic rocks probably less than 10,000 years old.

SUSANVILLE

The south part of Susanville is underlain by hot water approaching 75° C. The U.S. Department of Energy is partially funding a project that will heat 17 government buildings. Three production wells and two injection wells are planned for this operation. Thermal waters may also be distributed to a commercial park for use in industrial processes. Eventually, geothermal water may be used to heat all residences and commercial buildings in the town (Reference 23).

CALIFORNIA 10

CALIFORNIA 11

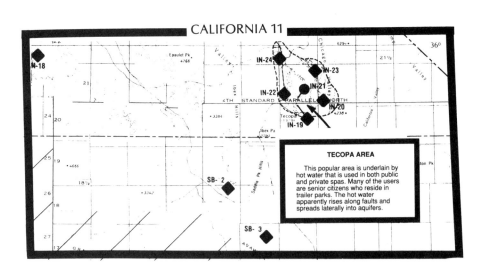

TECOPA AREA

This popular area is underlain by hot water that is used in both public and private spas. Many of the users are senior citizens who reside in trailer parks. The hot water apparently rises along faults and spreads laterally into aquifers.

CALIFORNIA 12

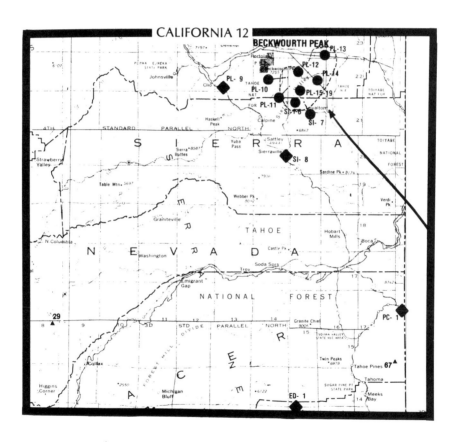

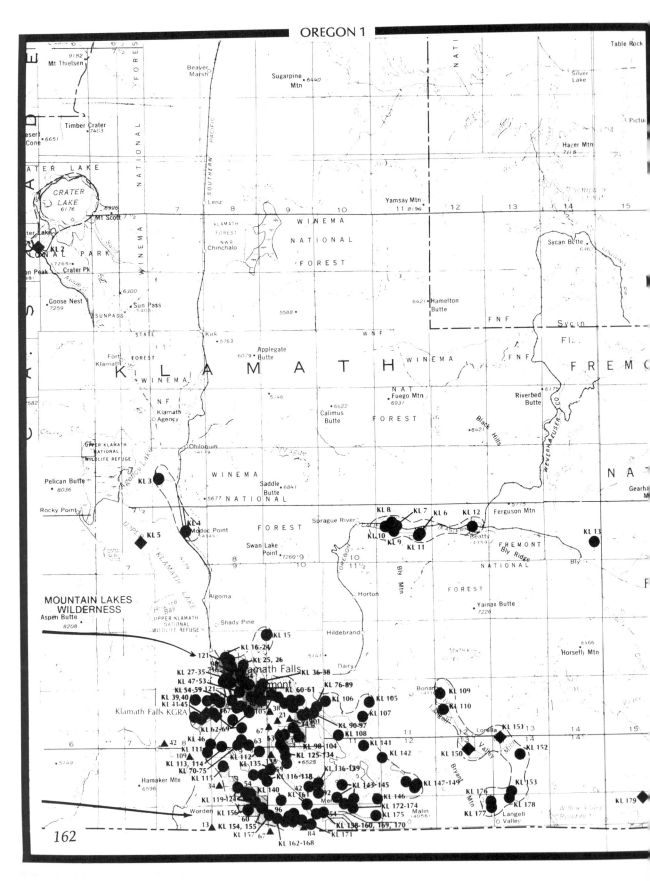

LAKEVIEW

Lakeview is one of the most promising geothermal areas in Oregon. The city and geothermal area are at the foot of a major fault scarp on the west side of the Warner Range. Hunters Hot Springs (LK-45) (96° C), Leithead Hot Spring (LK-62) (72° C), Barry Ranch Hot Springs (LK-64) (92° C), and more than 40 shallow thermal wells, 3 to 549 m deep, are in the area. Well water temperatures are 20° to 113° C. In a deep geothermal exploration well (LK-59) the temperature was 116° C at 1,658 m. Chemical geothermometers indicate that a minimum reservoir temperature of 150° C may exist in the Lakeview geothermal reservoir. The system is probably maintained by deep circulation of meteoric water in a Basin and Range environment of high heat flow, with convective upwelling along and adjacent to the major fault zone. In the Hunters Hot Springs area thermal water is used for space heat at a motel, eight residences, and commercial greenhouses, where the growing of tomatoes, bedding plants, and cut flowers is being expanded. A thermal well (LK-53) is used for Lakeview's municipal swimming pool. South of Lakeview, recently drilled shallow (73 to 415 m) wells (LK-75-77) yield 78° C water for use in commercial production of shrimp. Following an Oregon Department of Geology and Mineral Industries study and drilling program funded by the U.S. Department of Energy, Northwest Geothermal Corp. drilled a production well (LK-37) to total depth of 209 m which produced on pump 3,750 L/min of 101° C water. Northwest Geothermal Corp. has a franchise from the City of Lakeview for a geothermal district heating system. (Reference: Peterson, Brown, and McLean, 1980).

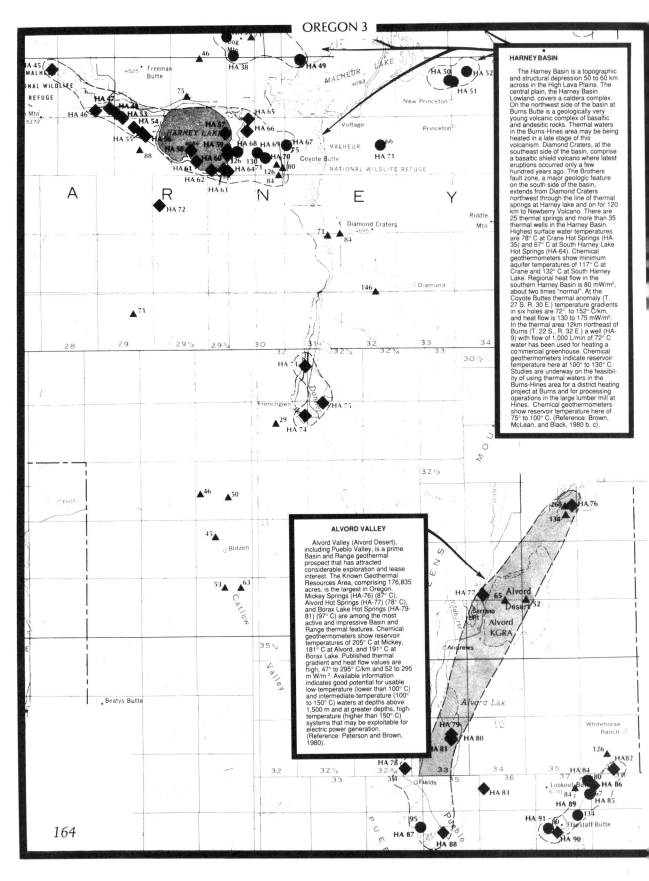

HARNEY BASIN

The Harney Basin is a topographic and structural depression 50 to 60 km across in the High Lava Plains. The central plain, the Harney Basin Lowland, covers a caldera complex. On the northwest side of the basin at Burns Butte is a geologically very young volcanic complex of basaltic and andesitic rocks. Thermal waters in the Burns-Hines area may be being heated in a late stage of this volcanism. Diamond Craters, at the southeast side of the basin, comprise a basaltic shield volcano where latest eruptions occurred only a few hundred years ago. The Brothers fault zone, a major geologic feature on the south side of the basin, extends from Diamond Craters northwest through the line of thermal springs at Harney lake and on for 120 km to Newberry Volcano. There are 25 thermal springs and more than 35 thermal wells in the Harney Basin. Highest surface water temperatures are 78° C at Crane Hot Springs (HA-35) and 67° C at South Harney Lake Hot Springs (HA-64). Chemical geothermometers show minimum aquifer temperatures of 117° C at Crane and 132° C at South Harney Lake. Regional heat flow in the southern Harney Basin is 80 mW/m², about two times "normal". At the Coyote Buttes thermal anomaly (T. 27 S. R. 30 E.) temperature gradients in six holes are 72° to 152° C/km, and heat flow is 130 to 175 mW/m². In the thermal area 12km northeast of Burns (T. 22 S., R. 32 E.) a well (HA-9) with flow of 1,000 L/min of 72° C water has been used for heating a commercial greenhouse. Chemical geothermometers indicate reservoir temperature here at 100° to 130° C. Studies are underway on the feasibility of using thermal waters in the Burns-Hines area for a district heating project at Burns and for processing operations in the large lumber mill at Hines. Chemical geothermometers show reservoir temperature here of 75° to 100° C. (Reference: Brown, McLean, and Black, 1980 b, c).

ALVORD VALLEY

Alvord Valley (Alvord Desert), including Pueblo Valley, is a prime Basin and Range geothermal prospect that has attracted considerable exploration and lease interest. The Known Geothermal Resources Area, comprising 176,835 acres, is the largest in Oregon. Mickey Springs (HA-76) (87° C), Alvord Hot Springs (HA-77) (78° C), and Borax Lake Hot Springs (HA-79-81) (97° C) are among the most active and impressive Basin and Range thermal features. Chemical geothermometers show reservoir temperatures of 205° C at Mickey, 181° C at Alvord, and 191° C at Borax Lake. Published thermal gradient and heat flow values are high, 47° to 295° C/km and 52 to 295 m W/m². Available information indicates good potential for usable low-temperature (lower than 100° C) and intermediate-temperature (100° to 150° C) waters at depths above 1,500 m and at greater depths, high-temperature (higher than 150° C) systems that may be exploitable for electric power generation. (Reference: Peterson and Brown, 1980).

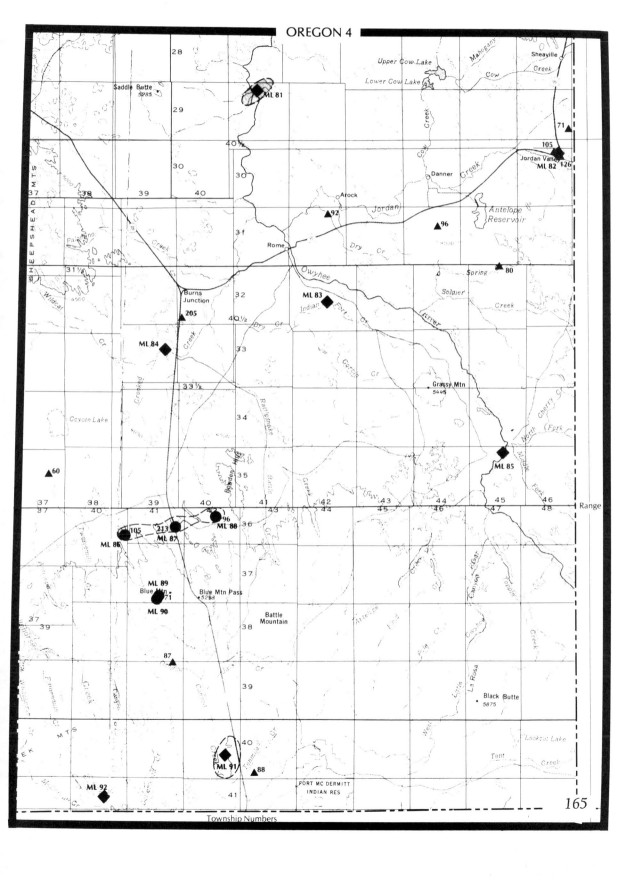

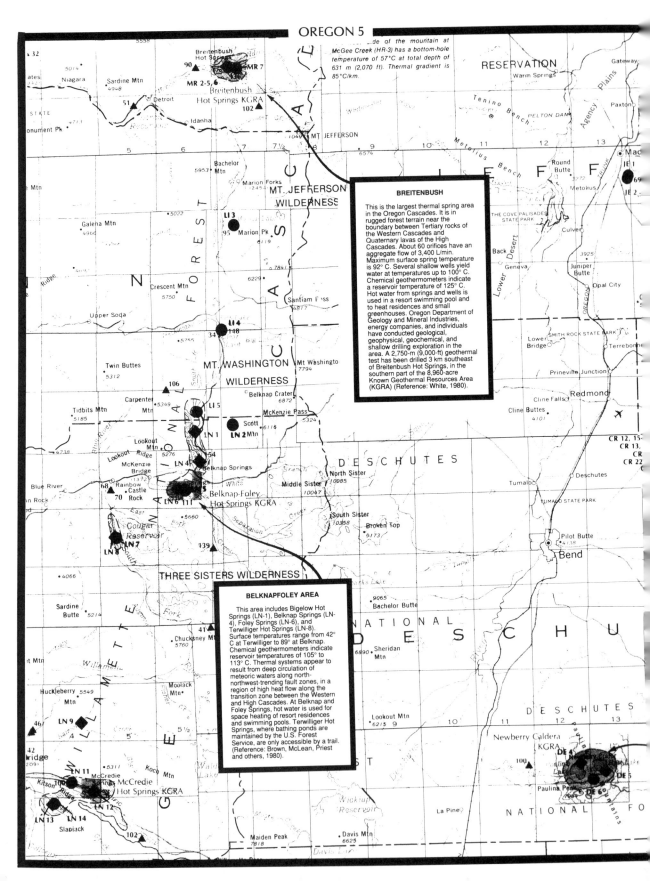

...de of the mountain at McGee Creek (HR-3) has a bottom-hole temperature of 57°C at total depth of 631 m (2,070 ft). Thermal gradient is 85°C/km.

BREITENBUSH

This is the largest thermal spring area in the Oregon Cascades. It is in rugged forest terrain near the boundary between Tertiary rocks of the Western Cascades and Quaternary lavas of the High Cascades. About 60 orifices have an aggregate flow of 3,400 L/min. Maximum surface spring temperature is 92° C. Several shallow wells yield water at temperatures up to 100° C. Chemical geothermometers indicate a reservoir temperature of 125° C. Hot water from springs and wells is used in a resort swimming pool and to heat residences and small greenhouses. Oregon Department of Geology and Mineral Industries, energy companies, and individuals have conducted geological, geophysical, geochemical, and shallow drilling exploration in the area. A 2,750-m (9,000-ft) geothermal test has been drilled 3 km southeast of Breitenbush Hot Springs, in the southern part of the 8,960-acre Known Geothermal Resources Area (KGRA) (Reference: White, 1980).

BELKNAPFOLEY AREA

This area includes Bigelow Hot Springs (LN-1), Belknap Springs (LN-4), Foley Springs (LN-6), and Terwilliger Hot Springs (LN-8). Surface temperatures range from 42° C at Terwilliger to 89° at Belknap. Chemical geothermometers indicate reservoir temperatures of 105° to 113° C. Thermal systems appear to result from deep circulation of meteoric waters along north-northwest-trending fault zones, in a region of high heat flow along the transition zone between the Western and High Cascades. At Belknap and Foley Springs, hot water is used for space heating of resort residences and swimming pools. Terwilliger Hot Springs, where bathing ponds are maintained by the U.S. Forest Service, are only accessible by a trail. (Reference: Brown, McLean, Priest and others, 1980).

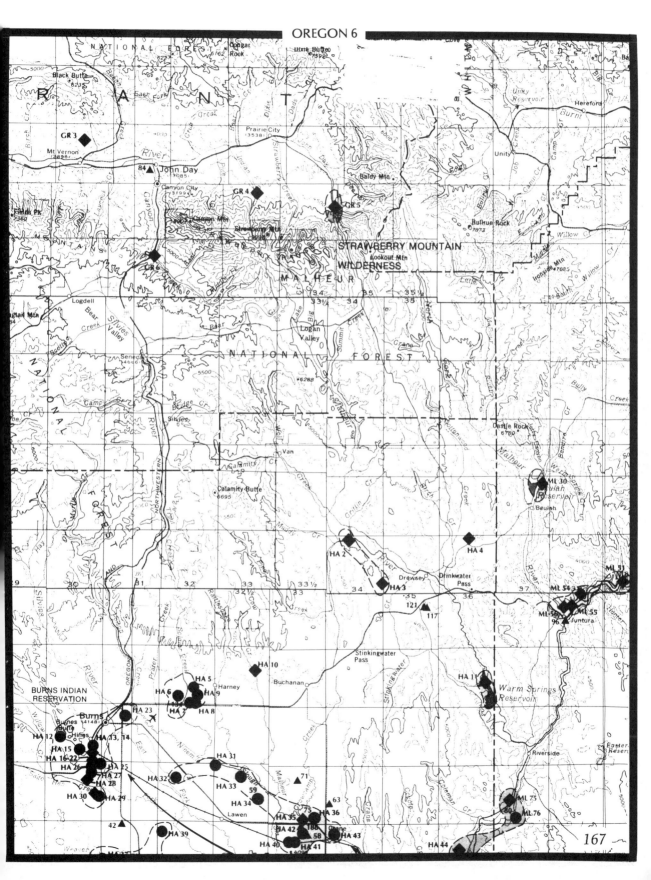

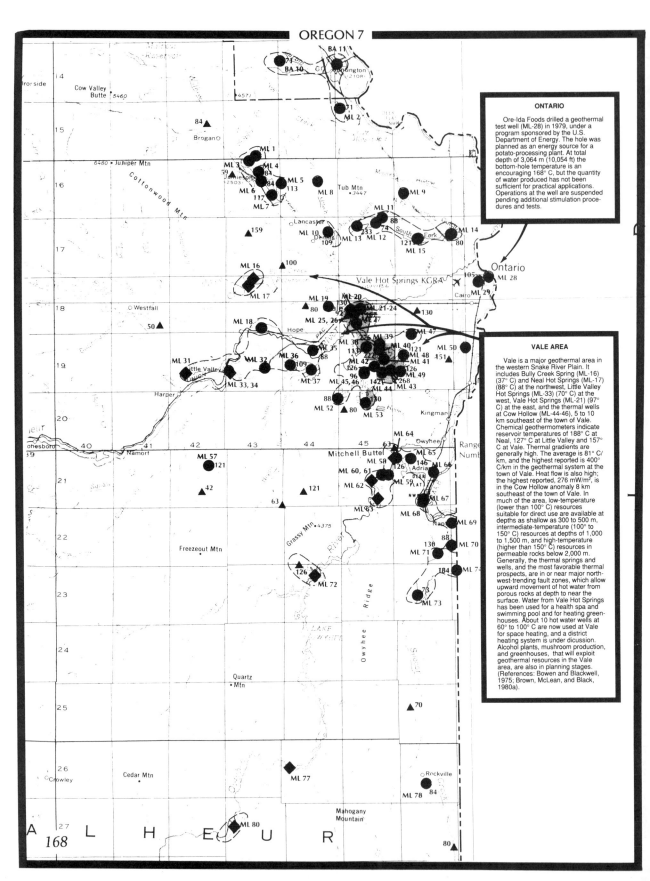

ONTARIO

Ore-Ida Foods drilled a geothermal test well (ML-28) in 1979, under a program sponsored by the U.S. Department of Energy. The hole was planned as an energy source for a potato-processing plant. At total depth of 3,064 m (10,054 ft) the bottom-hole temperature is an encouraging 168° C, but the quantity of water produced has not been sufficient for practical applications. Operations at the well are suspended pending additional stimulation procedures and tests.

VALE AREA

Vale is a major geothermal area in the western Snake River Plain. It includes Bully Creek Spring (ML-16) (37° C) and Neal Hot Springs (ML-17) (88° C) at the northwest, Little Valley Hot Springs (ML-33) (70° C) at the west, Vale Hot Springs (ML-21) (97° C) at the east, and the thermal wells at Cow Hollow (ML-44-46), 5 to 10 km southeast of the town of Vale. Chemical geothermometers indicate reservoir temperatures of 188° C at Neal, 127° C at Little Valley and 157° C at Vale. Thermal gradients are generally high. The average is 81° C/km, and the highest reported is 400° C/km in the geothermal system at the town of Vale. Heat flow is also high; the highest reported, 276 mW/m², is in the Cow Hollow anomaly 8 km southeast of the town of Vale. In much of the area, low-temperature (lower than 100° C) resources suitable for direct use are available at depths as shallow as 300 to 500 m, intermediate-temperature (100° to 150° C) resources at depths of 1,000 to 1,500 m, and high-temperature (higher than 150° C) resources in permeable rocks below 2,000 m. Generally, the thermal springs and wells, and the most favorable thermal prospects, are in or near major northwest-trending fault zones, which allow upward movement of hot water from porous rocks at depth to near the surface. Water from Vale Hot Springs has been used for a health spa and swimming pool and for heating greenhouses. About 10 hot water wells at 60° to 100° C are now used at Vale for space heating, and a district heating system is under discussion. Alcohol plants, mushroom production, and greenhouses, that will exploit geothermal resources in the Vale area, are also in planning stages. (References: Bowen and Blackwell, 1975; Brown, McLean, and Black, 1980a).

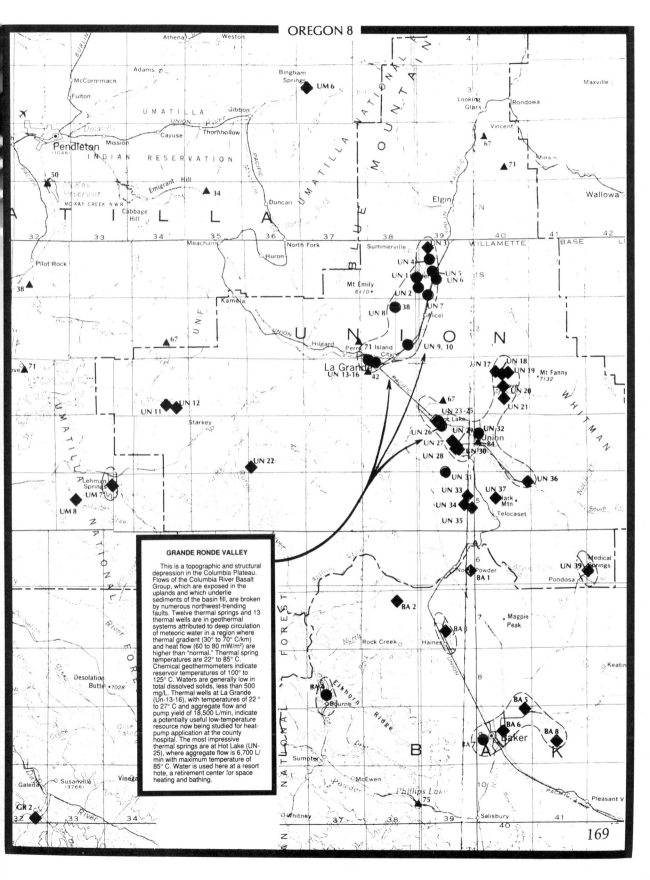

GRANDE RONDE VALLEY

This is a topographic and structural depression in the Columbia Plateau. Flows of the Columbia River Basalt Group, which are exposed in the uplands and which underlie sediments of the basin fill, are broken by numerous northwest-trending faults. Twelve thermal springs and 13 thermal wells are in geothermal systems attributed to deep circulation of meteoric water in a region where thermal gradient (30° to 70° C/km) and heat flow (60 to 80 mW/m²) are higher than "normal." Thermal spring temperatures are 22° to 85° C. Chemical geothermometers indicate reservoir temperatures of 100° to 125° C. Waters are generally low in total dissolved solids, less than 500 mg/L. Thermal wells at La Grande (Un-13-16), with temperatures of 22° to 27° C and aggregate flow and pump yield of 18,500 L/min, indicate a potentially useful low-temperature resource now being studied for heat-pump application at the county hospital. The most impressive thermal springs are at Hot Lake (UN-25), where aggregate flow is 6,700 L/min with maximum temperature of 85° C. Water is used here at a resort hote, a retirement center for space heating and bathing.

ASHLAND AREA

Two warm springs and several warm wells indicate an attractive low-temperature geothermal resource at Ashland. Water from Jackson Hot Springs (JA-2) (44° C) is used for a swimming pool and for space heating a resort. Helman Hot Spring (JA-4) (32° C) and White Sulfur Well (JA-5) (29° C) are sites of former resorts and swimming pools. An Ashland greenhouse operator has recently drilled a 137-m well (JA-3) that produces 375 L/min of 22° C water. Feasibility of heating the greenhouse is being studied.

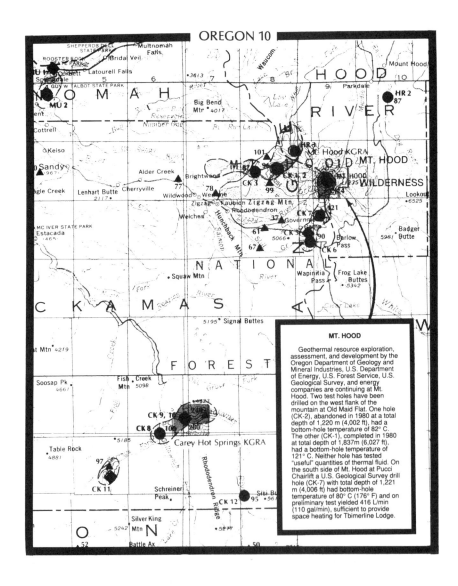

MT. HOOD

Geothermal resource exploration, assessment, and development by the Oregon Department of Geology and Mineral Industries, U.S. Department of Energy, U.S. Forest Service, U.S. Geological Survey, and energy companies are continuing at Mt. Hood. Two test holes have been drilled on the west flank of the mountain at Old Maid Flat. One hole (CK-2), abandoned in 1980 at a total depth of 1,220 m (4,002 ft), had a bottom-hole temperature of 82° C. The other (CK-1), completed in 1980 at total depth of 1,837m (6,027 ft), had a bottom-hole temperature of 121° C. Neither hole has tested "useful" quantities of thermal fluid. On the south side of Mt. Hood at Pucci Chairlift a U.S. Geological Survey drill hole (CK-7) with total depth of 1,221 m (4,006 ft) had bottom-hole temperature of 80° C (176° F) and on preliminary test yielded 416 L/min (110 gal/min), sufficient to provide space heating for Tbimerline Lodge.

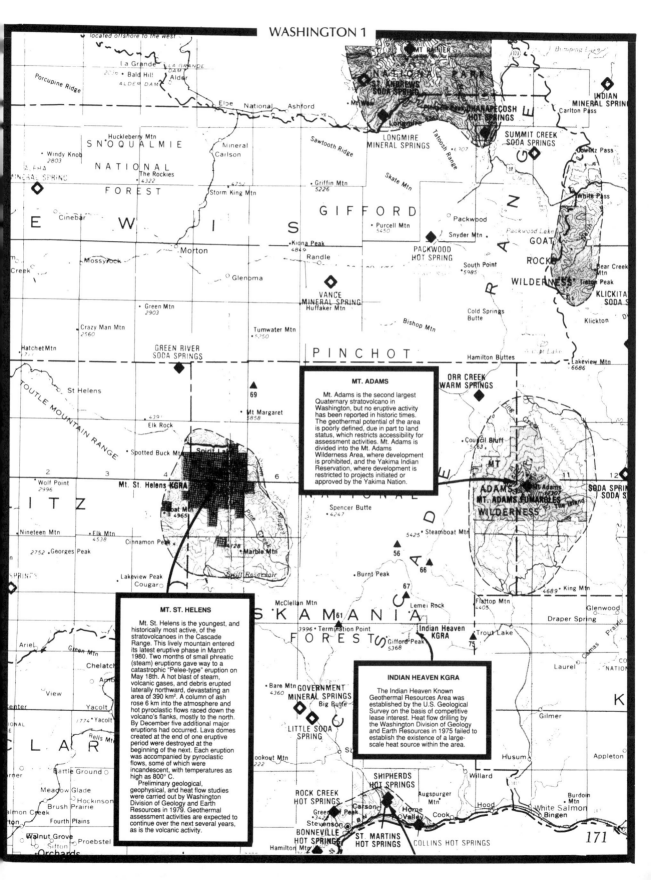

MT. ADAMS

Mt. Adams is the second largest Quaternary stratovolcano in Washington, but no eruptive activity has been reported in historic times. The geothermal potential of the area is poorly defined, due in part to land status, which restricts accessibility for assessment activities. Mt. Adams is divided into the Mt. Adams Wilderness Area, where development is prohibited, and the Yakima Indian Reservation, where development is restricted to projects initiated or approved by the Yakima Nation.

MT. ST. HELENS

Mt. St. Helens is the youngest, and historically most active, of the stratovolcanoes in the Cascade Range. This lively mountain entered its latest eruptive phase in March 1980. Two months of small phreatic (steam) eruptions gave way to a catastrophic "Pelee-type" eruption on May 18th. A hot blast of steam, volcanic gases, and debris erupted laterally northward, devastating an area of 390 km². A column of ash rose 6 km into the atmosphere and hot pyroclastic flows raced down the volcano's flanks, mostly to the north. By December five additional major eruptions had occurred. Lava domes created at the end of one eruptive period were destroyed at the beginning of the next. Each eruption was accompanied by pyroclastic flows, some of which were incandescent, with temperatures as high as 800° C.

Preliminary geological, geophysical, and heat flow studies were carried out by Washington Division of Geology and Earth Resources in 1979. Geothermal assessment activities are expected to continue over the next several years, as is the volcanic activity.

INDIAN HEAVEN KGRA

The Indian Heaven Known Geothermal Resources Area was established by the U.S. Geological Survey on the basis of competitive lease interest. Heat flow drilling by the Washington Division of Geology and Earth Resources in 1975 failed to establish the existence of a large-scale heat source within the area.

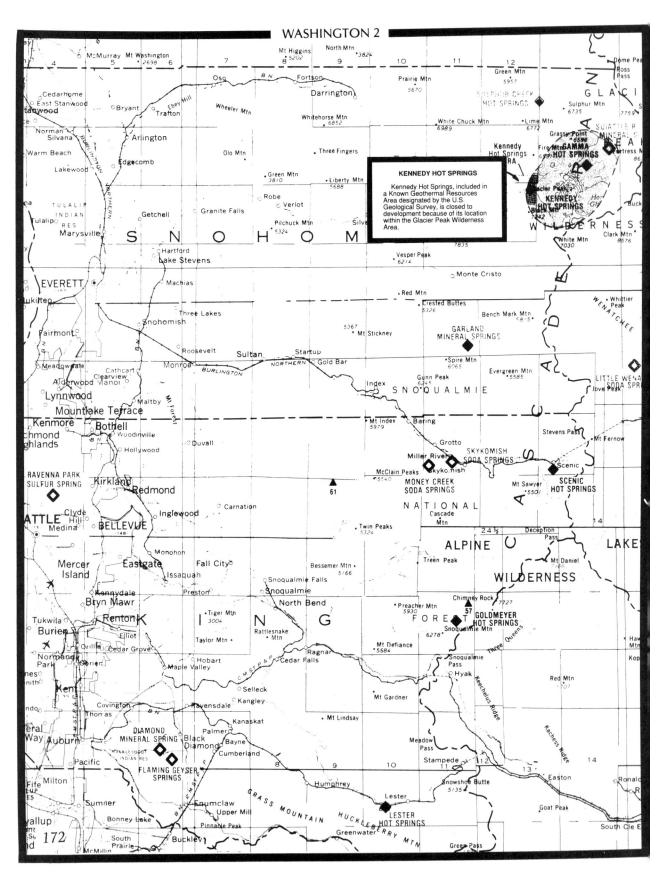

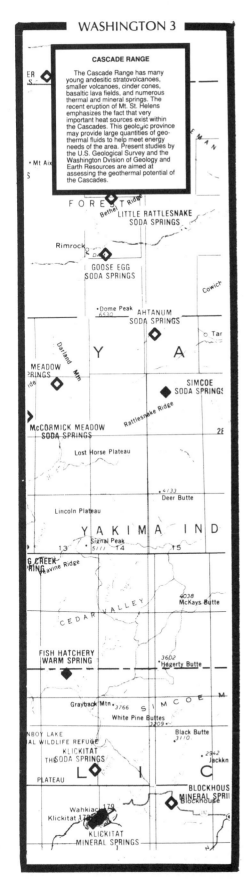

CASCADE RANGE

The Cascade Range has many young andesitic stratovolcanoes, smaller volcanoes, cinder cones, basaltic lava fields, and numerous thermal and mineral springs. The recent eruption of Mt. St. Helens emphasizes the fact that very important heat sources exist within the Cascades. This geologic province may provide large quantities of geothermal fluids to help meet energy needs of the area. Present studies by the U.S. Geological Survey and the Washington Division of Geology and Earth Resources are aimed at assessing the geothermal potential of the Cascades.

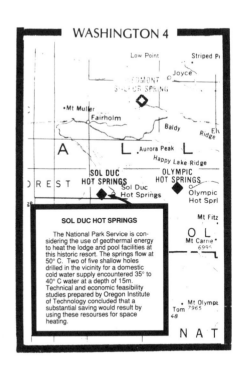

SOL DUC HOT SPRINGS

The National Park Service is considering the use of geothermal energy to heat the lodge and pool facilities at this historic resort. The springs flow at 50° C. Two of five shallow holes drilled in the vicinity for a domestic cold water supply encountered 35° to 40° C water at a depth of 15m. Technical and economic feasibility studies prepared by Oregon Institute of Technology concluded that a substantial saving would result by using these resourses for space heating.

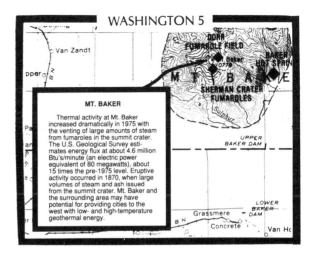

MT. BAKER

Thermal activity at Mt. Baker increased dramatically in 1975 with the venting of large amounts of steam from fumaroles in the summit crater. The U.S. Geological Survey estimates energy flux at about 4.6 million Btu's/minute (an electric power equivalent of 80 megawatts), about 15 times the pre-1975 level. Eruptive activity occurred in 1870, when large volumes of steam and ash issued from the summit crater. Mt. Baker and the surrounding area may have potential for providing cities to the west with low- and high-temperature geothermal energy.

173

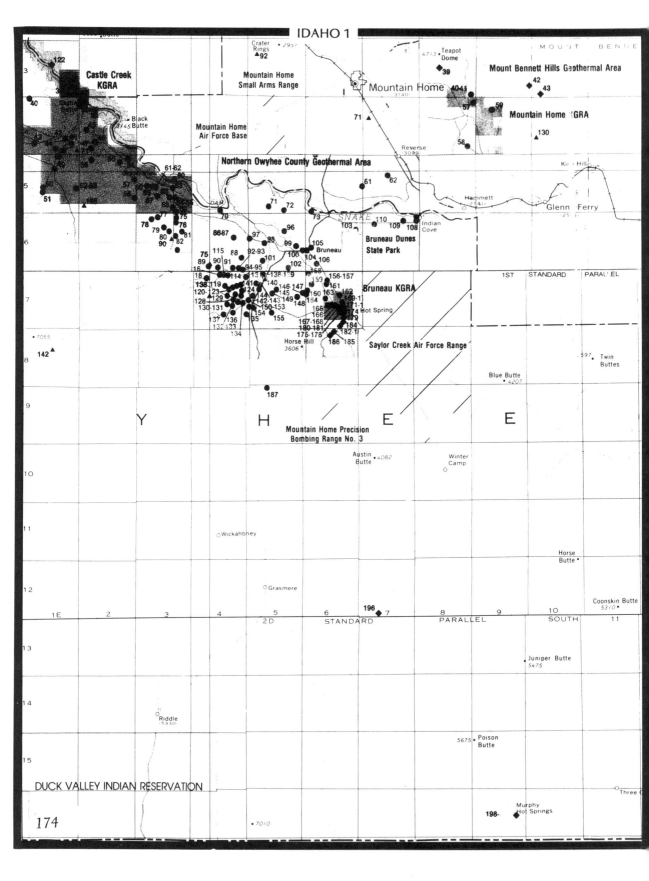

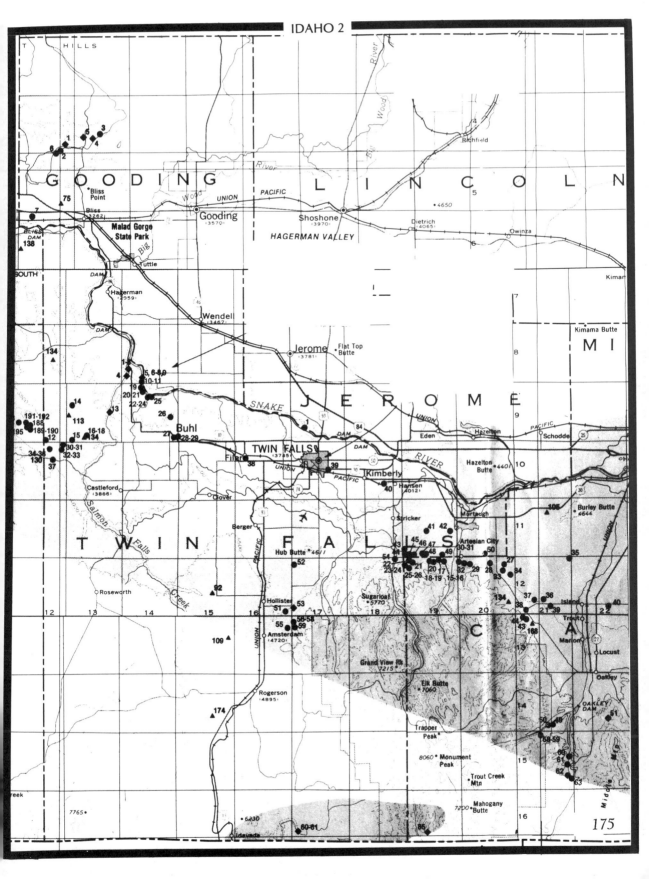

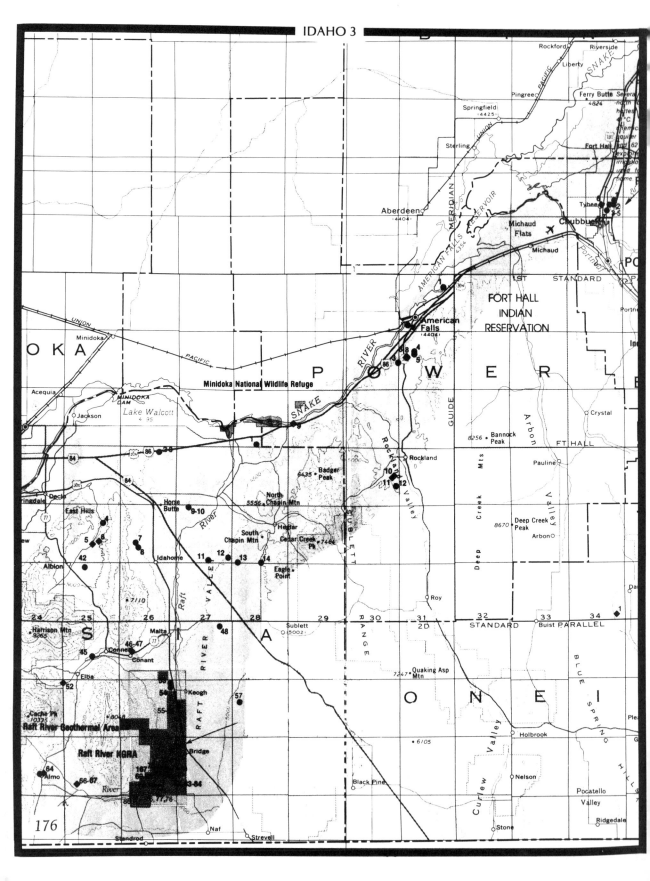

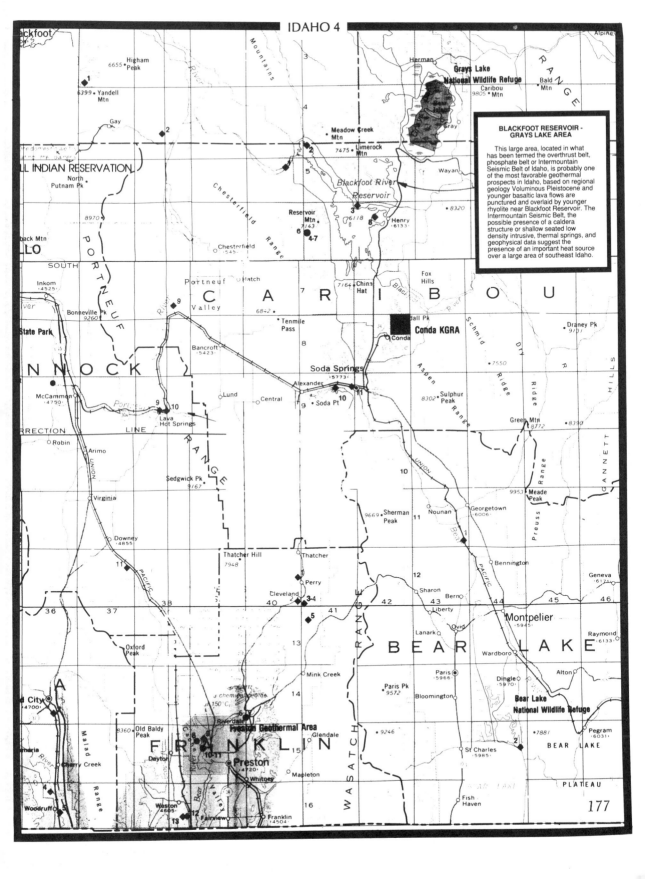

BLACKFOOT RESERVOIR - GRAYS LAKE AREA

This large area, located in what has been termed the overthrust belt, phosphate belt or Intermountain Seismic Belt of Idaho, is probably one of the most favorable geothermal prospects in Idaho, based on regional geology Voluminous Pleistocene and younger basaltic lava flows are punctured and overlaid by younger rhyolite near Blackfoot Reservoir. The Intermountain Seismic Belt, the possible presence of a caldera structure or shallow seated low density intrusive, thermal springs, and geophysical data suggest the presence of an important heat source over a large area of southeast Idaho.

177

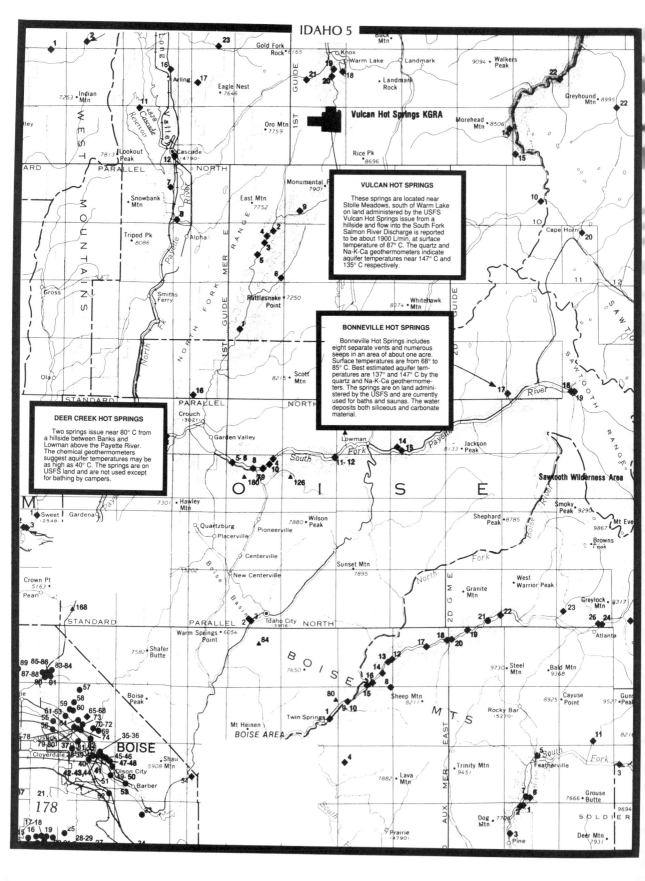

VULCAN HOT SPRINGS KGRA

VULCAN HOT SPRINGS

These springs are located near Stolle Meadows, south of Warm Lake on land administered by the USFS Vulcan Hot Springs issue from a hillside and flow into the South Fork Salmon River Discharge is reported to be about 1900 L/min, at surface temperature of 87° C. The quartz and Na-K-Ca geothermometers indicate aquifer temperatures near 147° C and 135° C respectively.

BONNEVILLE HOT SPRINGS

Bonneville Hot Springs includes eight separate vents and numerous seeps in an area of about one acre. Surface temperatures are from 68° to 85° C. Best estimated aquifer temperatures are 137° and 147° C by the quartz and Na-K-Ca geothermometers. The springs are on land administered by the USFS and are currently used for baths and saunas. The water deposits both siliceous and carbonate material.

DEER CREEK HOT SPRINGS

Two springs issue near 80° C from a hillside between Banks and Lowman above the Payette River. The chemical geothermometers suggest aquifer temperatures may be as high as 40° C. The springs are on USFS land and are not used except for bathing by campers.

178

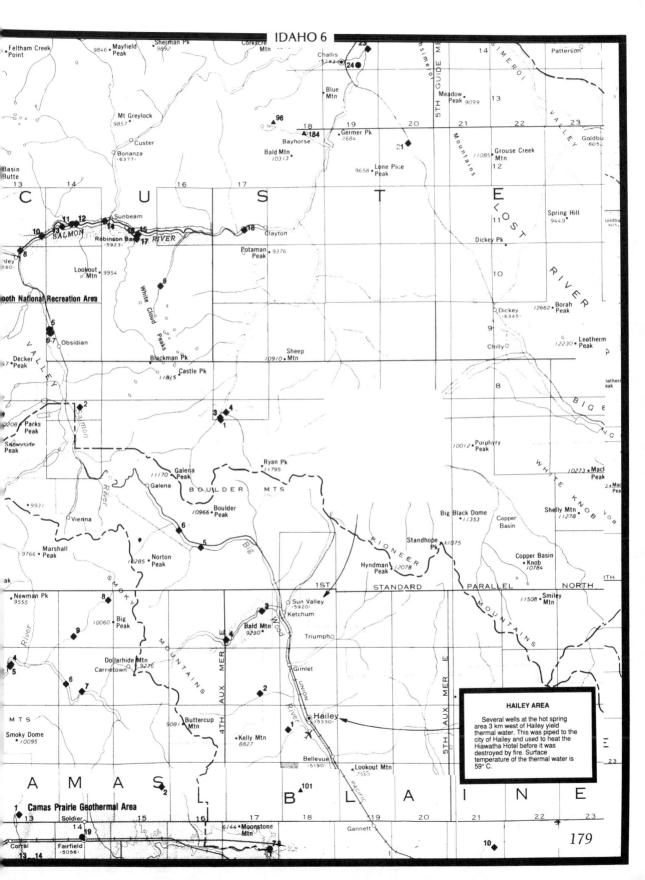

HAILEY AREA

Several wells at the hot spring area 3 km west of Hailey yield thermal water. This was piped to the city of Hailey and used to heat the Hiawatha Hotel before it was destroyed by fire. Surface temperature of the thermal water is 59° C.

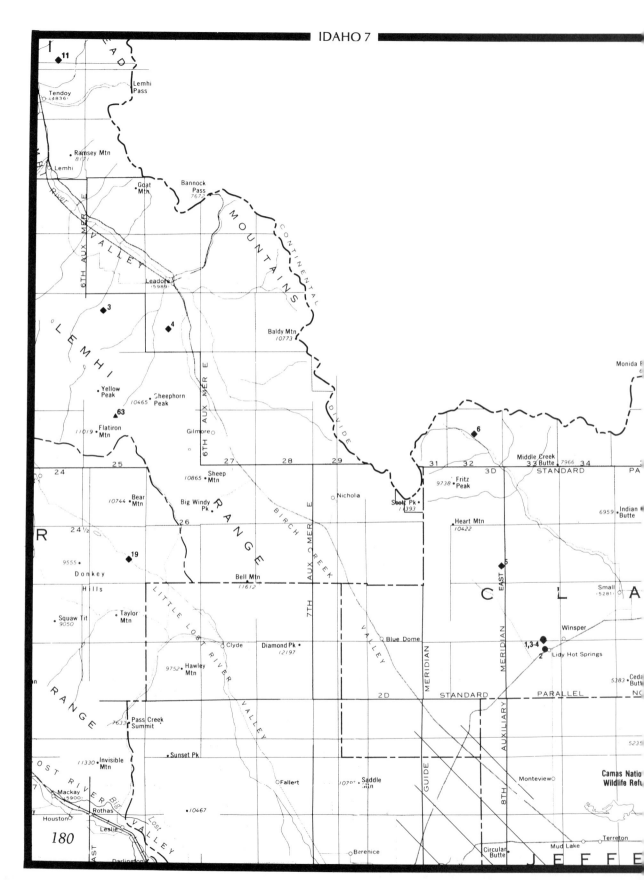

◆11

Lemhi
Pass

Tendoy
(4836)

• Ramsey Mtn
8171

• Lemhi

• Goat
Mtn

Bannock
Pass
7672

MOUNTAINS

CONTINENTAL

Leadore
(5980)

◆3

◆4

Baldy Mtn
10773

DIVIDE

Monida P

6TH AUX MER E

• Yellow
Peak
10465

• Sheephorn
Peak

▲63

Flatiron
11019 • Mtn

Gilmore○

6TH AUX MER E

◆6

Middle Creek
33 Butte 7966 34

25   24   26   27   28   29   31   32   3D   STANDARD   PA

10865 • Sheep
Mtn

Nichola○

Fritz
9738 • Peak

6959 • Indian
Butte

BIRCH

Bear
10744 • Mtn

Big Windy
Pk •

RANGE

Scott Pk •
11393

Heart Mtn
10422

R   24½   26

9555 •

◆19

CREEK

7TH AUX MER E

◆5

EAST

C   L   A

Donkey

Hills

Bell Mtn
11612

LITTLE

Small
(5281)

• Squaw Tit
9050

• Taylor
Mtn

LOST

VALLEY

Winsper○

1,3-4

Clyde○   Diamond Pk •
12197

○ Blue Dome

MERIDIAN

2 •   Lidy Hot Springs

9752 • Hawley
Mtn

RIVER

MERIDIAN

5383 • Ceda
Butt

RANGE

Pass Creek
7633 • Summit

VALLEY

STANDARD   PARALLEL   NO

5235

• Invisible
11330 • Mtn

• Sunset Pk

GUIDE

AUXILIARY

Camas Natio
Wildlife Refu

OST

RIVER   BIG

Mackay
(5900)

Houston○   • Rothas

Leslie

VALLEY

• 10467

○Fallert

10705 • Saddle
Mtn

8TH

Monteview○

2D

Terreton

○ Berenice

Circular
Butte

Mud Lake○

J E F F E

Darlington○

180

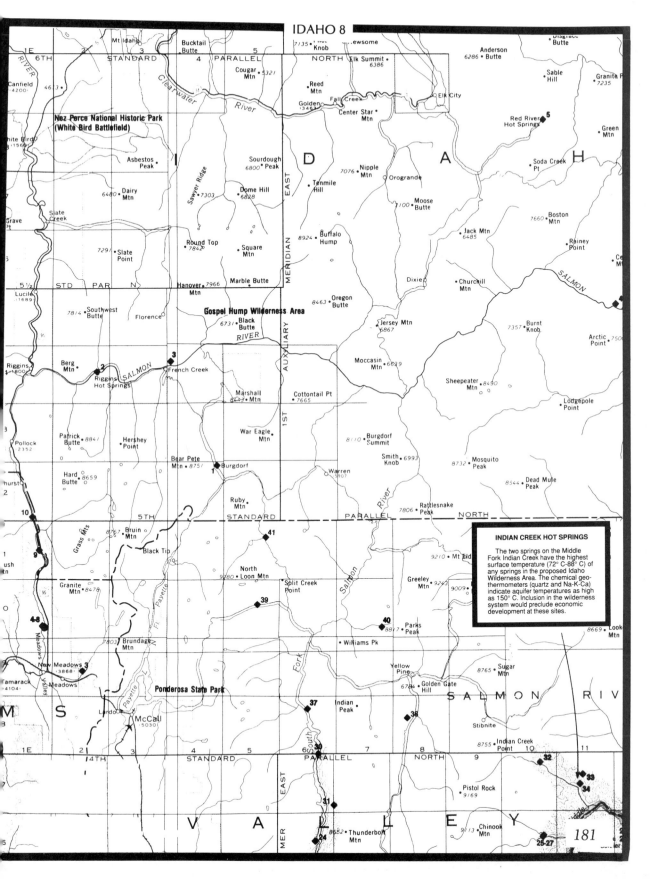

INDIAN CREEK HOT SPRINGS

The two springs on the Middle Fork Indian Creek have the highest surface temperature (72° C-88° C) of any springs in the proposed Idaho Wilderness Area. The chemical geo-thermometers (quartz and Na-K-Ca) indicate aquifer temperatures as high as 150° C. Inclusion in the wilderness system would preclude economic development at these sites.

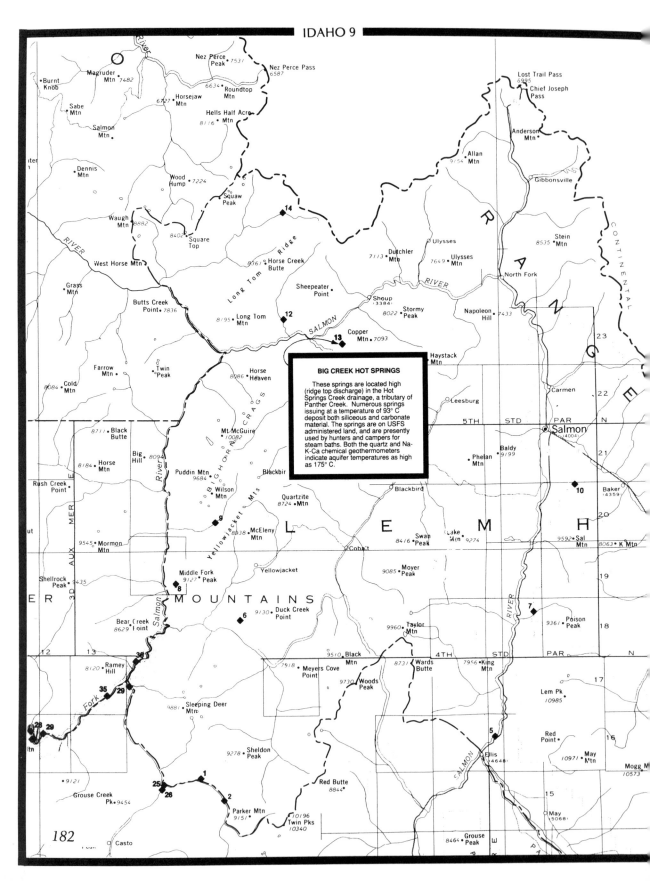

BIG CREEK HOT SPRINGS

These springs are located high (ridge top discharge) in the Hot Springs Creek drainage, a tributary of Panther Creek. Numerous springs issuing at a temperature of 93° C deposit both siliceous and carbonate material. The springs are on USFS administered land, and are presently used by hunters and campers for steam baths. Both the quartz and Na-K-Ca chemical geothermometers indicate aquifer temperatures as high as 175° C.

182

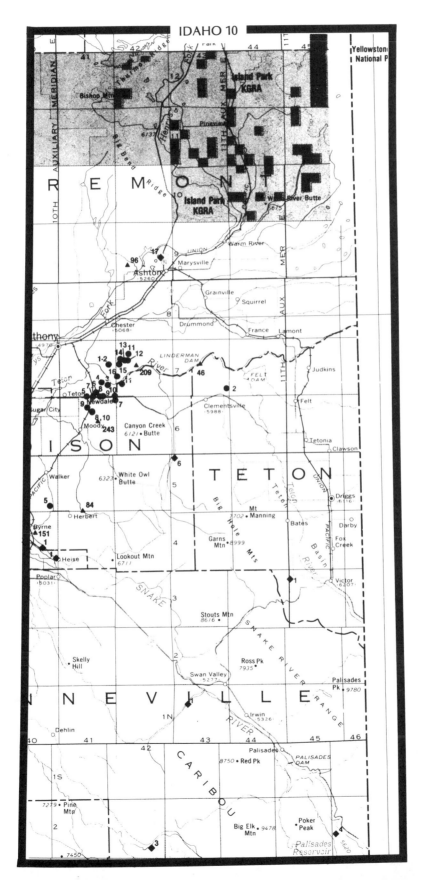

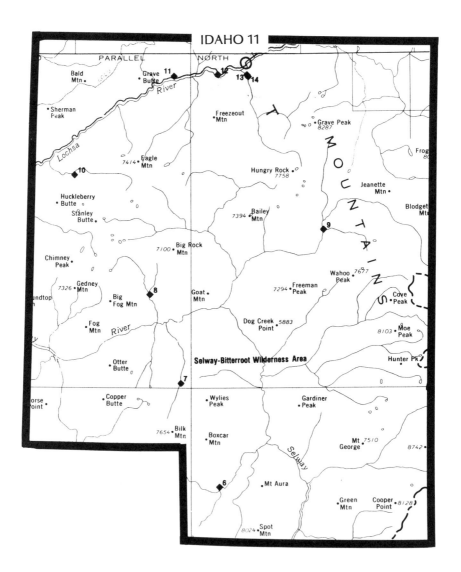

PARALLEL NORTH

Bald Mtn .

Grave Butte • ■ 11

■ 12

13 ■ ■ 14

Sherman Peak

Lochsa River

Freezeout • Mtn

Grave Peak • 8287

Eagle • Mtn 7414

■ 10

Hungry Rock 7758

Jeanette Mtn .

Blodget Mtn

Huckleberry • Butte

Stanley Butte .

Bailey • Mtn 7394

■ 9

Chimney Peak .

Big Rock 7100 • Mtn

Wahoo 7677 • Peak

Gedney 7326 • Mtn

undtop n

Big • Fog Mtn

■ 8

Goat • Mtn

Freeman 7294 • Peak

Cove • Peak

Fog • Mtn

River

Dog Creek Point • 5883

8103 • Moe Peak

Otter • Butte

Selway-Bitterroot Wilderness Area

Hunter Pk

orse oint

Copper • Butte

Wylies • Peak

Gardiner • Peak

Bilk 7654 • Mtn

Boxcar • Mtn

Mt 7510 George •

8742

■ 6

• Mt Aura

Selway

Green • Mtn

Cooper Point • 8128

8024 Spot • Mtn

MOUNTAINS

Frog 80

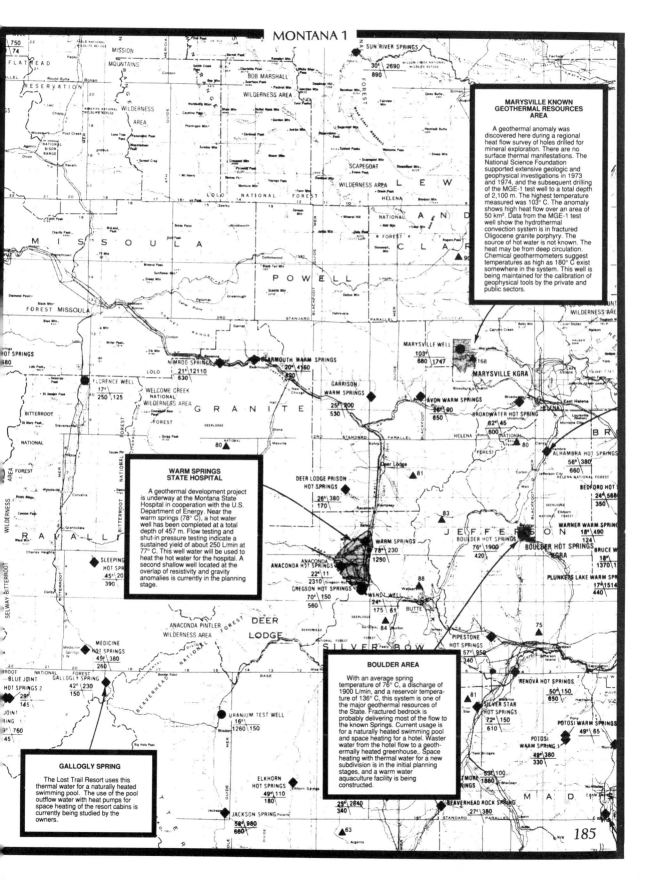

MARYSVILLE KNOWN GEOTHERMAL RESOURCES AREA

A geothermal anomaly was discovered here during a regional heat flow survey of holes drilled for mineral exploration. There are no surface thermal manifestations. The National Science Foundation supported extensive geologic and geophysical investigations in 1973 and 1974, and the subsequent drilling of the MGE-1 test well to a total depth of 2,100 m. The highest temperature measured was 103° C. The anomaly shows high heat flow over an area of 50 km². Data from the MGE-1 test well show the hydrothermal convection system is in fractured Oligocene granite porphyry. The source of hot water is not known. The heat may be from deep circulation. Chemical geothermometers suggest temperatures as high as 180° C exist somewhere in the system. This well is being maintained for the calibration of geophysical tools by the private and public sectors.

WARM SPRINGS STATE HOSPITAL

A geothermal development project is underway at the Montana State Hospital in cooperation with the U.S. Department of Energy. Near the warm springs (78° C), a hot water well has been completed at a total depth of 457 m. Flow testing and shut-in pressure testing indicate a sustained yield of about 250 L/min at 77° C. This well water will be used to heat the hot water for the hospital. A second shallow well located at the overlap of resistivity and gravity anomalies is currently in the planning stage.

BOULDER AREA

With an average spring temperature of 76° C, a discharge of 1900 L/min, and a reservoir temperature of 136° C, this system is one of the major geothermal resources of the State. Fractured bedrock is probably delivering most of the flow to the known Springs. Current usage is for a naturally heated swimming pool and space heating for a hotel. Waster water from the hotel flow to a geothermally heated greenhouse. Space heating with thermal water for a new subdivision is in the initial planning stages, and a warm water aquaculture facility is being constructed.

GALLOGLY SPRING

The Lost Trail Resort uses this thermal water for a naturally heated swimming pool. The use of the pool outflow water with heat pumps for space heating of the resort cabins is currently being studied by the owners.

185

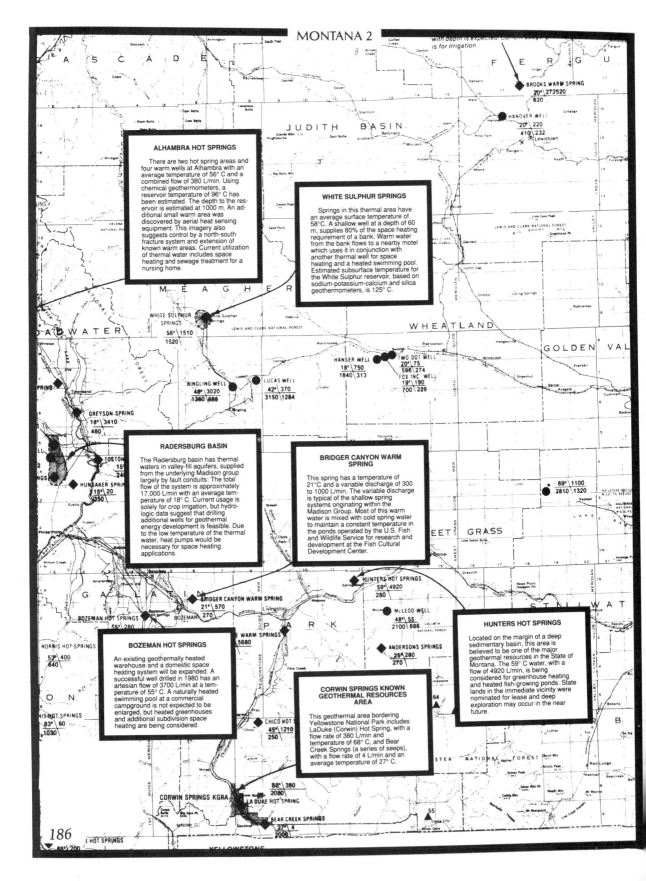

...with depth is expected. Current usage is for irrigation.

BROOKS WARM SPRING
20° 272520
620

HANOVER WELL
20° 220
410 232

ALHAMBRA HOT SPRINGS

There are two hot spring areas and four warm wells at Alhambra with an average temperature of 56° C and a combined flow of 380 L/min. Using chemical geothermometers, a reservoir temperature of 96° C has been estimated. The depth to the reservoir is estimated at 1000 m. An additional small warm area was discovered by aerial heat sensing equipment. This imagery also suggests control by a north-south fracture system and extension of known warm areas. Current utilization of thermal water includes space heating and sewage treatment for a nursing home.

WHITE SULPHUR SPRINGS

Springs in this thermal area have an average surface temperature of 58°C. A shallow well at a depth of 60 m, supplies 80% of the space heating requirement of a bank. Warm water from the bank flows to a nearby motel which uses it in conjunction with another thermal well for space heating and a heated swimming pool. Estimated subsurface temperature for the White Sulphur reservoir, based on sodium-potassium-calcium and silica geothermometers, is 125° C.

WHITE SULPHUR SPRINGS
58° 1510
1520

HANSER WELL
18° 750
1840 313

TWO DOT WELL
20° 75
596 274

FOX INC WELL
19° 190
700 229

RINGLING WELL
48° 3020
1360 686

LUCAS WELL
42° 370
3150 1284

GREYSON SPRING
18° 3410
460

TOSTON
15°

HUNSAKER SPRING
18° 20
350

RADERSBURG BASIN

The Radersburg basin has thermal waters in valley-fill aquifers, supplied from the underlying Madison group largely by fault conduits: The total flow of the system is approximately 17,000 L/min with an average temperature of 18° C. Current usage is solely for crop irrigation, but hydrologic data suggest that drilling additional wells for geothermal energy development is feasible. Due to the low temperature of the thermal water, heat pumps would be necessary for space heating applications.

BRIDGER CANYON WARM SPRING

This spring has a temperature of 21°C and a variable discharge of 300 to 1000 L/min. The variable discharge is typical of the shallow spring systems originating within the Madison Group. Most of this warm water is mixed with cold spring water to maintain a constant temperature in the ponds operated by the U.S. Fish and Wildlife Service for research and development at the Fish Cultural Development Center.

69° 1100
2810 1320

HUNTERS HOT SPRINGS
59° 4920
280

BRIDGER CANYON WARM SPRING
21° 570
270

McLEOD WELL
48° 55
2100 686

ANDERSONS SPRINGS
25° 280
270

BOZEMAN HOT SPRINGS
55° 280

E WARM SPRINGS
5680

NORRIS HOT SPRINGS
53° 400
640

NIS HOT SPRINGS
83° 60
1030

BOZEMAN HOT SPRINGS

An existing geothermally heated warehouse and a domestic space heating system will be expanded. A successful well drilled in 1980 has an artesian flow of 3700 L/min at a temperature of 55° C. A naturally heated swimming pool at a commercial campground is not expected to be enlarged, but heated greenhouses and additional subdivision space heating are being considered.

HUNTERS HOT SPRINGS

Located on the margin of a deep sedimentary basin, this area is believed to be one of the major geothermal resources in the State of Montana. The 59° C water, with a flow of 4920 L/min, is being considered for greenhouse heating and heated fish-growing ponds. State lands in the immediate vicinity were nominated for lease and deep exploration may occur in the near future.

64

CORWIN SPRINGS KNOWN GEOTHERMAL RESOURCES AREA

This geothermal area bordering Yellowstone National Park includes LaDuke (Corwin) Hot Spring, with a flow rate of 380 L/min and temperature of 68° C, and Bear Creek Springs (a series of seeps), with a flow rate of 4 L/min and an average temperature of 27° C.

CHICO HOT S
45° 1210
250

CORWIN SPRINGS KGRA

LA DUKE HOT SPRING
68° 380
2080

BEAR CREEK SPRINGS
27° 4
2008

55

68° 200

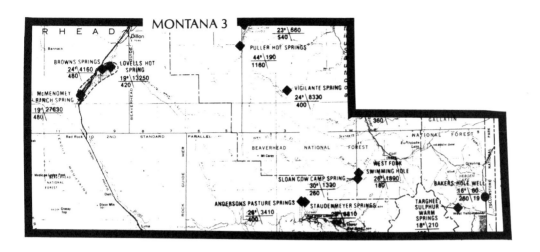

MONTANA 3

R H E A D

Dillon

Bannack

BROWNS SPRINGS
24° 4160
480

LOVELLS HOT SPRING
19° 13250
420

McMENOMEY RANCH SPRING
19° 27630
480

PULLER HOT SPRINGS
23° 660
540
44° 190
1160

VIGILANTE SPRING
24° 8330
400

Red Rock   2ND   STANDARD   PARALLEL

GALLATIN

NATIONAL FOREST

BEAVERHEAD   NATIONAL   FOREST

Mt Carey

SLOAN COW CAMP SPRING
30° 1330
260

WEST FORK SWIMMING HOLE
26° 1890
180

BAKERS HOLE WELL
16° 60
260 19

ANDERSONS PASTURE SPRINGS
26° 3410
400

STAUDENMEYER SPRINGS
28° 4810

TARGHEE SULPHUR WARM SPRINGS
18° 210

MONTANA 4

CAMAS HOT SPRINGS
45° 90
330

I N D I A

Camas Prairie

GREEN SPR
28° 300
280

Paradise   Perma

QUINNS HOT SPRING WE
25°
147 44

Superior

R A L

Lozeau

Stark Mtn

St Patrick Peak   Rivulet Peak

L O L O   NATIONA

Admiral Peak

White Mtn

Pilot Knob   Lolo Hot   LOL
44
20

MONTANA 5

LODGEPOLE WARM

LITTLE WARM
22°
1750

LANDUSKY SPRINGS
21° 11730
1480

LANDUSKY PLUNGE
24° 10980
960

5TH   STANDARD   PARALLEL

S

P E T R O L

Grass Range   Teigen   Winnett

Flatwillow

DURFEE CREEK SPRINGS
21° 8710

187

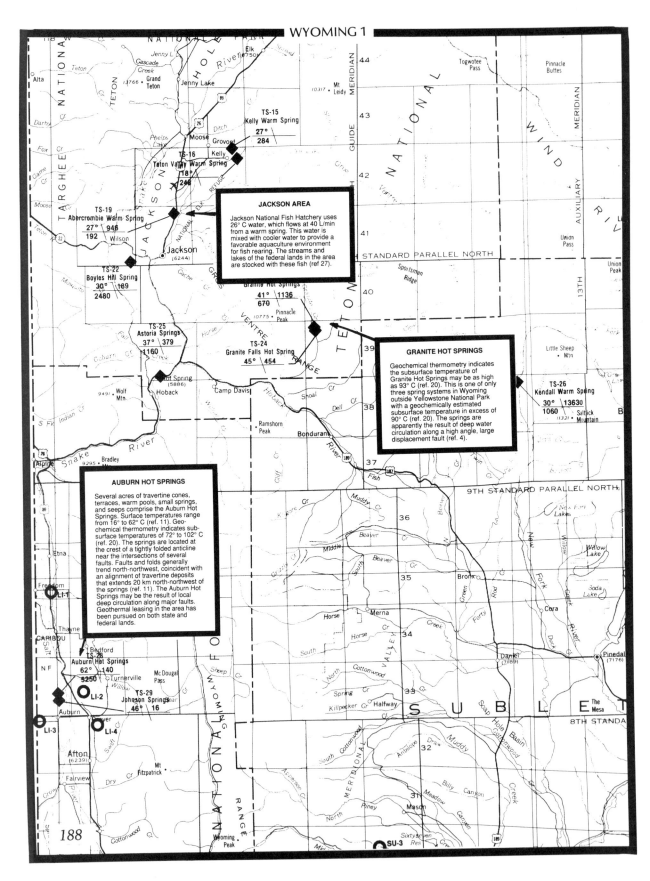

TS-15
Kelly Warm Spring
27° 284

TS-16
Teton Valley Warm Spring
18° 248

TS-19
Abercrombie Warm Spring
27° 946
192

TS-22
Boyles Hill Spring
30° 189
2480

TS-25
Astoria Springs
37° 379
1160

Granite Hot Springs
41° 1136
670

TS-24
Granite Falls Hot Spring
45° 454

TS-26
Kendall Warm Spring
30° 13630
1060

TS-28
Auburn Hot Springs
62° 140
5250

TS-29
Johnson Springs
46° 16

JACKSON AREA

Jackson National Fish Hatchery uses 26° C water, which flows at 40 L/min from a warm spring. This water is mixed with cooler water to provide a favorable aquaculture environment for fish rearing. The streams and lakes of the federal lands in the area are stocked with these fish (ref 27).

GRANITE HOT SPRINGS

Geochemical thermometry indicates the subsurface temperature of Granite Hot Springs may be as high as 93° C (ref. 20). This is one of only three spring systems in Wyoming outside Yellowstone National Park with a geochemically estimated subsurface temperature in excess of 90° C (ref. 20). The springs are apparently the result of deep water circulation along a high angle, large displacement fault (ref. 4).

AUBURN HOT SPRINGS

Several acres of travertine cones, terraces, warm pools, small springs, and seeps comprise the Auburn Hot Springs. Surface temperatures range from 16° to 62° C (ref. 11). Geochemical thermometry indicates subsurface temperatures of 72° to 102° C (ref. 20). The springs are located at the crest of a tightly folded anticline near the intersections of several faults. Faults and folds generally trend north-northwest, coincident with an alignment of travertine deposits that extends 20 km north-northwest of the springs (ref. 11). The Auburn Hot Springs may be the result of local deep circulation along major faults. Geothermal leasing in the area has been pursued on both state and federal lands.

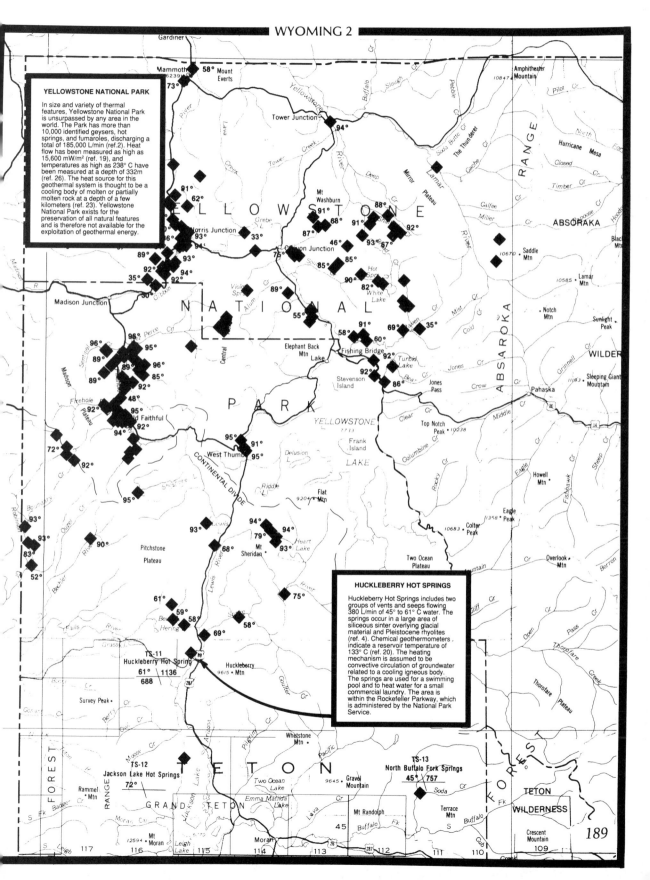

YELLOWSTONE NATIONAL PARK

In size and variety of thermal features, Yellowstone National Park is unsurpassed by any area in the world. The Park has more than 10,000 identified geysers, hot springs, and fumaroles, discharging a total of 185,000 L/min (ref.2). Heat flow has been measured as high as 15,600 mW/m² (ref. 19), and temperatures as high as 238° C have been measured at a depth of 332m (ref. 26). The heat source for this geothermal system is thought to be a cooling body of molten or partially molten rock at a depth of a few kilometers (ref. 23). Yellowstone National Park exists for the preservation of all natural features and is therefore not available for the exploitation of geothermal energy.

HUCKLEBERRY HOT SPRINGS

Huckleberry Hot Springs includes two groups of vents and seeps flowing 380 L/min of 45° to 61° C water. The springs occur in a large area of siliceous sinter overlying glacial material and Pleistocene rhyolites (ref. 4). Chemical geothermometers indicate a reservoir temperature of 133° C (ref. 20). The heating mechanism is assumed to be convective circulation of groundwater related to a cooling igneous body. The springs are used for a swimming pool and to heat water for a small commercial laundry. The area is within the Rockefeller Parkway, which is administered by the National Park Service.

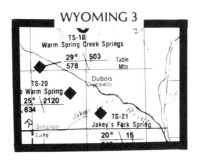

WYOMING 3

TS-18
Warm Spring Creek Springs

29° | 503
578

Table
Mtn

TS-20
Warm Spring
25° | 2120
634

Dubois
(6940)

TS-21
Jakey's Fork Spring

20° | 15

Simpson
Lake

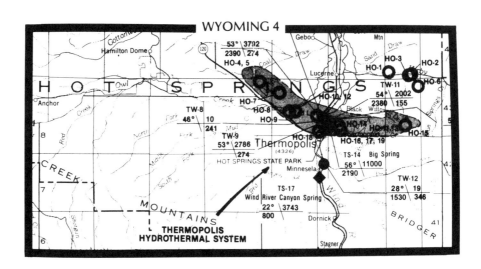

WYOMING 4

Cottont

Hamilton Dome

Gebo

Mtn

53° | 3702
2390 | 274
HO-4, 5

(120)

Lucerne

Sand
Draw

HO-3

HO-2

HO-1

HO-6

HO-7

TW-11
54° | 2002
2380 | 155

HO-10, 12

Anchor

Black
Willo

TW-8
46° | 10
241

HO-8

HO-9

TW-9
53° | 2786
274

HO-18

Thermopolis
(4326)

HO-16, 17, 19

HO-11

HO-15

TS-14 Big Spring
56° | 11000
2190

HOT SPRINGS STATE PARK

Minnesela

Dornick

TW-12
28° | 19
1530 | 346

CREEK

MOUNTAINS

TS-17
Wind River Canyon Spring
22° | 3743
800

Stagner

BRIDGER

41

**THERMOPOLIS
HYDROTHERMAL SYSTEM**

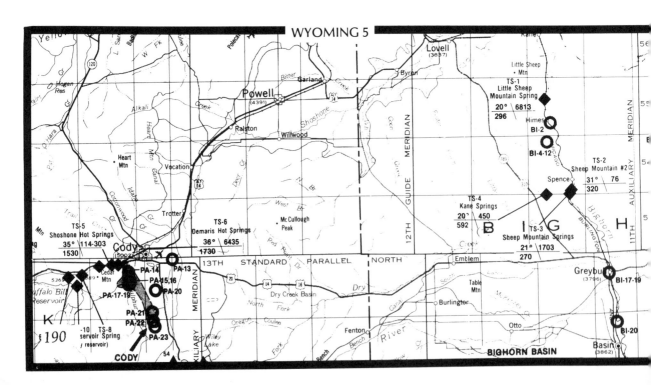

WYOMING 5

Yello

W FK

Polecat

Kane

Lovell
(3887)

Little Sheep
Mtn

Bitter

Garland

Byron

TS-1
Little Sheep
Mountain Spring

20° | 6813
296

Logan
Res

(120)

Powell
(4391)

Shoshone

Himes

BI-2

BI-4-12

Alkali

Ralston

Wilwood

TS-2
Sheep Mountain #2

31° | 76
320

Heart
Mtn

Vocation

Spence

Heart

Trotter

TS-6
Demaris Hot Springs
36° | 6435
1730

McCullough
Peak

TS-4
Kane Springs
20° | 450
592

B I G H

TS-5
Shoshone Hot Springs
35° | 114-303
1530

Cody
(5002)

TS-3
Sheep Mountain Springs
21° | 1703
270

Greybu
(3796)

BI-17-19

Cedar
Mtn

PA-14

PA-13

13TH STANDARD PARALLEL NORTH

Emblem

Table
Mtn

Buffalo Bill
Reservoir

PA-15,16

PA-20

Dry Creek Basin

Burlington

K

-10 TS-8
servoir Spring
reservoir)

PA-17-19

PA-21

PA-22

PA-23

Fenton

Otto

BI-20

§ 190

CODY

54

BIGHORN BASIN

Basin
(3862)

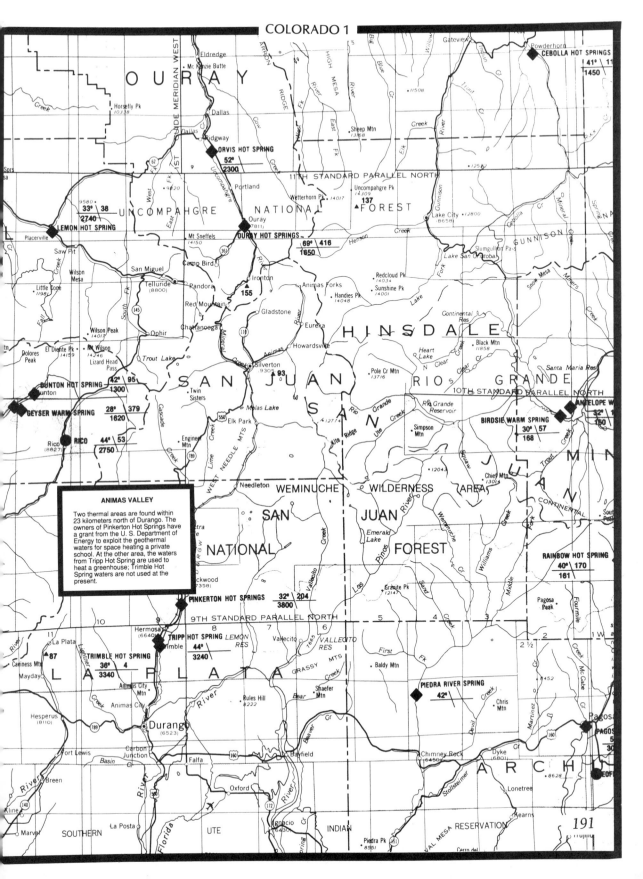

OURAY

Mc Kenzie Butte
Eldredge

Horsefly Pk
10338

Dallas

Dallas
Ridgway

ORVIS HOT SPRING
52°
2300

11TH STANDARD PARALLEL NORTH

Portland

Wetterhorn Pk • 14017

Uncompahgre Pk
14309
▲ 137

UNCOMPAHGRE NATIONAL FOREST

9580
33° \ 38
14246
2740

LEMON HOT SPRING

Placerville

Saw Pit

Ouray
7811

Mt Sneffels
14150

OURAY HOT SPRINGS
69° \ 416
1650

Lake City • 12800
8658

Henson Creek

Slumgullion Pass

GUNNISON

Camp Bird

San Miguel

Telluride
(8800)

Pandora

Ironton
155

Animas Forks

Redcloud Pk
14034
Sunshine Pk
14001

Handies Pk
14048

Lake San Cristobal

Wilson Mesa

Little Cone
1198?

Red Mountain

Chattanooga

Gladstone

Eureka

HINSDALE

Black Mtn
11858

Heart Lake

Santa Maria Res

Dolores Peak

El Diente Pk
14159

Mt Wilson
14246
Wilson Peak
14017

Lizard Head Pass

Ophir

Trout Lake

Silverton
9305

Howardsville

93

Pole Cr Mtn
13716

RIO **GRANDE**

10TH STANDARD PARALLEL NORTH

ANTELOPE W
32° \ 1
160

DUNTON HOT SPRING
42° \ 95
Dunton
1300

SAN **JUAN**

Twin Sisters

Molas Lake

550

Elk Park

Rio Grande Reservoir

Simpson Mtn

BIRDSIE WARM SPRING
30° \ 57
168

GEYSER WARM SPRING
28° \ 379
1620

RICO
44° \ 53
Rico
(8827)
2750

Engineer Mtn
789

Cascade

WEST NEEDLE MTS

Lime Creek

SAN

JUAN

Chief Mtn
13014

12043

M IN

Needleton

WEMINUCHE **WILDERNESS** **AREA**

CONTINENTAL

ANIMAS VALLEY

Two thermal areas are found within 23 kilometers north of Durango. The owners of Pinkerton Hot Springs have a grant from the U. S. Department of Energy to exploit the geothermal waters for space heating a private school. At the other area, the waters from Tripp Hot Spring are used to heat a greenhouse; Trimble Hot Spring waters are not used at the present.

SAN

JUAN

Emerald Lake

FOREST

NATIONAL

Extra

Rockwood
7358)

RAINBOW HOT SPRING
40° \ 170
161

Pagosa Peak

Fourmile

PINKERTON HOT SPRINGS
32° \ 204
3800

9TH STANDARD PARALLEL NORTH

Hermosa
(6640)

Granite Pk
12147

La Plata

TRIPP HOT SPRING
44° \
3240

Trimble

LEMON RES

Vallecito

VALLECITO RES

First

2 ½

1 W

87

TRIMBLE HOT SPRING
36° \ 4
3340

Caviness Mtn

Mayday

Animas City Mtn

GRASSY MTS

Baldy Mtn

LA **PLATA**

Animas City

Rules Hill
8222

Bear

Shaefer Mtn

PIEDRA RIVER SPRING
42° \

Chris Mtn

8452

Pagos

Hesperus
(8110)

Durango
(6523)

PAGOS

Fort Lewis

Carbon Junction

Falfa

Bayfield

Chimney Rock
(6450)

Dyke
(6801)

ARCH

Breen

Oxford

8628

EOF

Kline

140

La Posta

Ignacio
(6430)

INDIAN

AL MESA RESERVATION

191

Marvel

SOUTHERN

UTE

Piedra Pk
8551

Cerro del

Trujillo

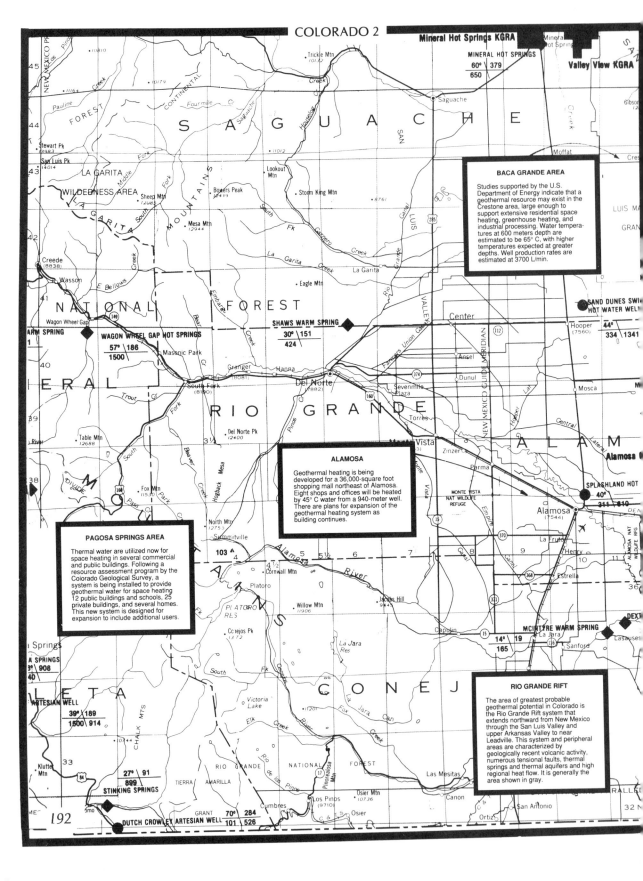

BACA GRANDE AREA

Studies supported by the U.S. Department of Energy indicate that a geothermal resource may exist in the Crestone area, large enough to support extensive residential space heating, greenhouse heating, and industrial processing. Water temperatures at 600 meters depth are estimated to be 65° C, with higher temperatures expected at greater depths. Well production rates are estimated at 3700 L/min.

ALAMOSA

Geothermal heating is being developed for a 36,000-square foot shopping mall northeast of Alamosa. Eight shops and offices will be heated by 45° C water from a 940-meter well. There are plans for expansion of the geothermal heating system as building continues.

PAGOSA SPRINGS AREA

Thermal water are utilized now for space heating in several commercial and public buildings. Following a resource assessment program by the Colorado Geological Survey, a system is being installed to provide geothermal water for space heating 12 public buildings and schools, 25 private buildings, and several homes. This new system is designed for expansion to include additional users.

RIO GRANDE RIFT

The area of greatest probable geothermal potential in Colorado is the Rio Grande Rift system that extends northward from New Mexico through the San Luis Valley and upper Arkansas Valley to near Leadville. This system and peripheral areas are characterized by geologically recent volcanic activity, numerous tensional faults, thermal springs and thermal aquifers and high regional heat flow. It is generally the area shown in gray.

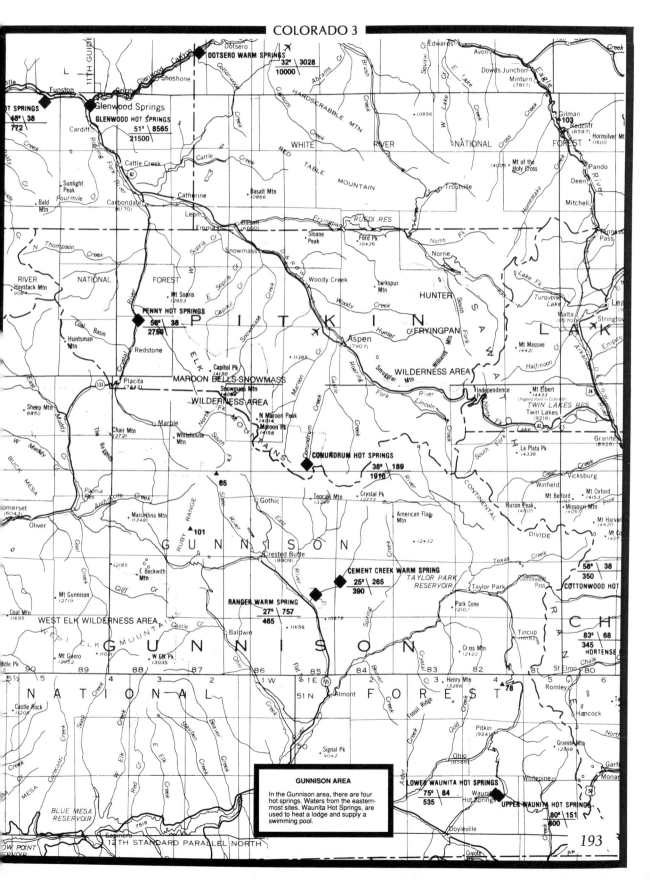

GUNNISON AREA

In the Gunnison area, there are four hot springs. Waters from the easternmost sites, Waunita Hot Springs, are used to heat a lodge and supply a swimming pool.

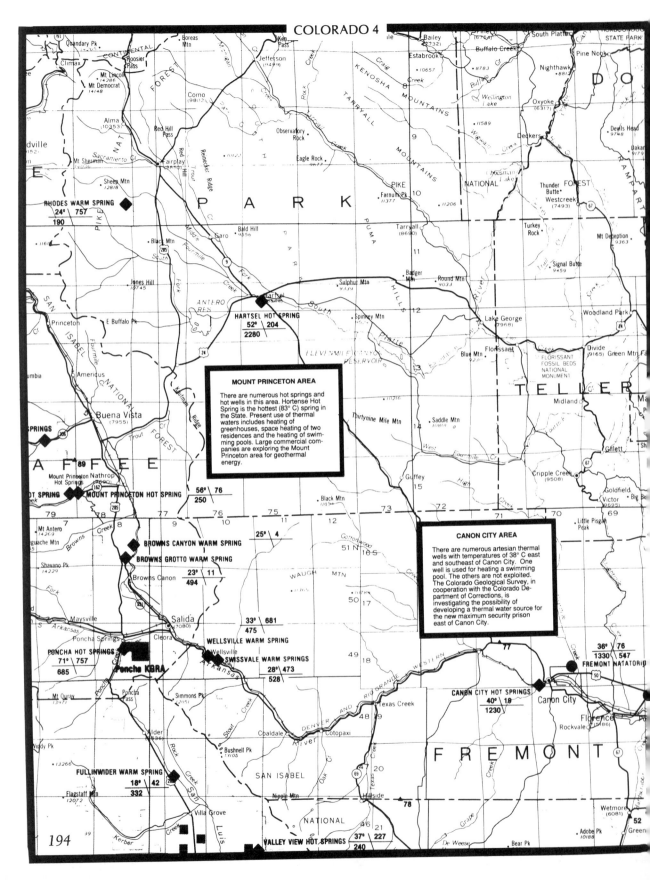

MOUNT PRINCETON AREA

There are numerous hot springs and hot wells in this area. Hortense Hot Spring is the hottest (83° C) spring in the State. Present use of thermal waters includes heating of greenhouses, space heating of two residences and the heating of swimming pools. Large commercial companies are exploring the Mount Princeton area for geothermal energy.

CANON CITY AREA

There are numerous artesian thermal wells with temperatures of 38° C east and southeast of Canon City. One well is used for heating a swimming pool. The others are not exploited. The Colorado Geological Survey, in cooperation with the Colorado Department of Corrections, is investigating the possibility of developing a thermal water source for the new maximum security prison east of Canon City.

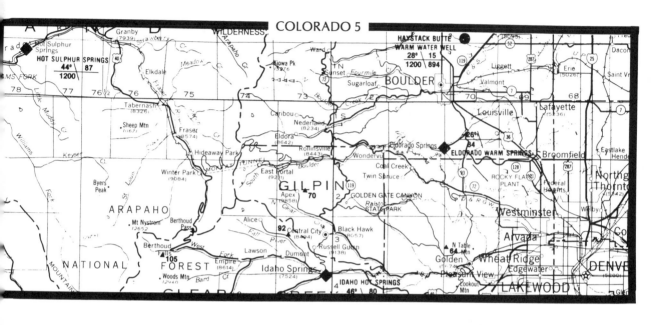

COLORADO 5

HAYSTACK BUTTE
WARM WATER WELL
28°   15
1200 \ 894

HOT SULPHUR SPRINGS
44°   87
1200

ELDORADO WARM SPRINGS
26°
84

GILPIN   70

92 Central City

105

IDAHO HOT SPRINGS
46°   80

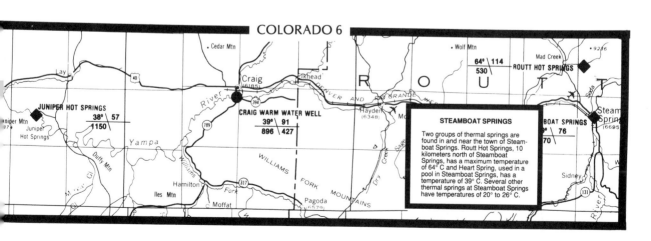

COLORADO 6

ROUTT HOT SPRINGS
64°   114
530

JUNIPER HOT SPRINGS
38°   57
1150

CRAIG WARM WATER WELL
39°   91
896 \ 427

STEAMBOAT SPRINGS
9°   76
70

STEAMBOAT SPRINGS

Two groups of thermal springs are
found in and near the town of Steamboat Springs. Routt Hot Springs, 10
kilometers north of Steamboat
Springs, has a maximum temperature
of 64° C and Heart Spring, used in a
pool in Steamboat Springs, has a
temperature of 39° C. Several other
thermal springs at Steamboat Springs
have temperatures of 20° to 26° C.

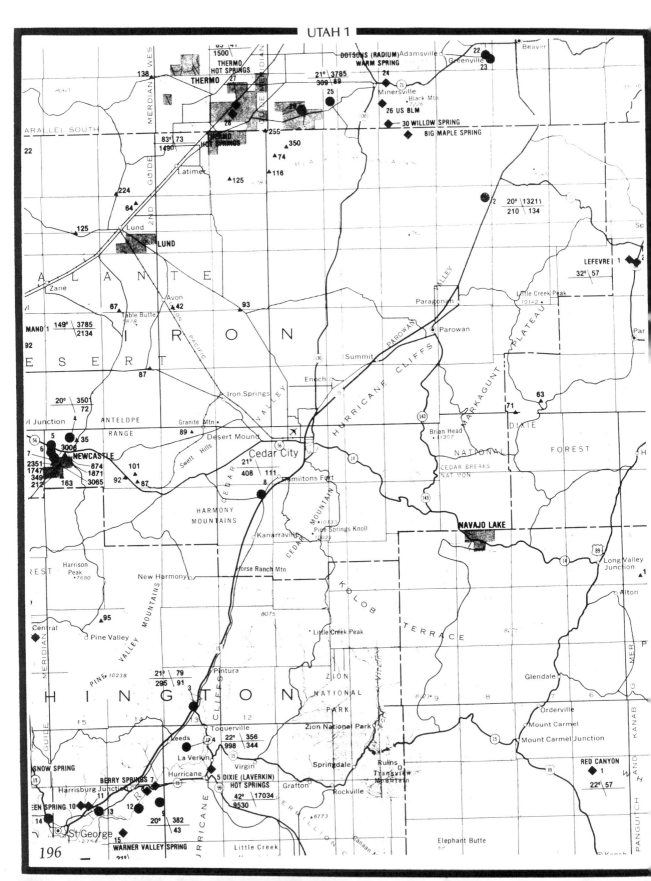

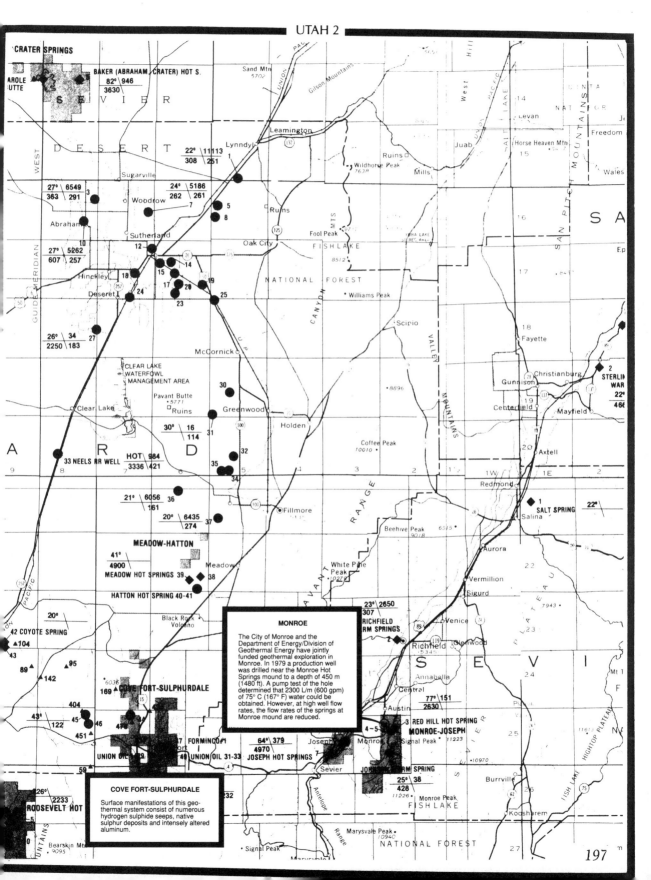

MONROE

The City of Monroe and the Department of Energy/Division of Geothermal Energy have jointly funded geothermal exploration in Monroe. In 1979 a production well was drilled near the Monroe Hot Springs mound to a depth of 450 m (1480 ft). A pump test of the hole determined that 2300 L/m (600 gpm) of 75° C (167° F) water could be obtained. However, at high well flow rates, the flow rates of the springs at Monroe mound are reduced.

COVE FORT-SULPHURDALE

Surface manifestations of this geothermal system consist of numerous hydrogen sulphide seeps, native sulphur deposits and intensely altered aluminum.

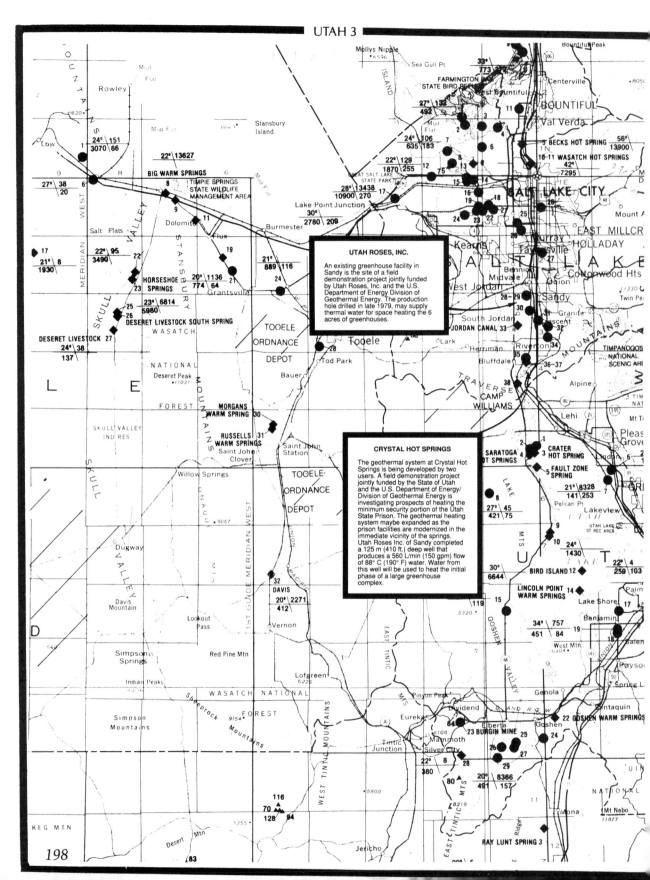

UTAH ROSES, INC.

An existing greenhouse facility in Sandy is the site of a field demonstration project jointly funded by Utah Roses, Inc. and the U.S. Department of Energy Division of Geothermal Energy. The production hole drilled in late 1979, may supply thermal water for space heating the 6 acres of greenhouses.

CRYSTAL HOT SPRINGS

The geothermal system at Crystal Hot Springs is being developed by two users. A field demonstration project jointly funded by the State of Utah and the U.S. Department of Energy/ Division of Geothermal Energy is investigating prospects of heating the minimum security portion of the Utah State Prison. The geothermal heating system maybe expanded as the prison facilities are modernized in the immediate vicinity of the springs. Utah Roses Inc. of Sandy completed a 125 m (410 ft.) deep well that produces a 560 L/min (150 gpm) flow of 88° C (190° F) water. Water from this well will be used to heat the initial phase of a large greenhouse complex.

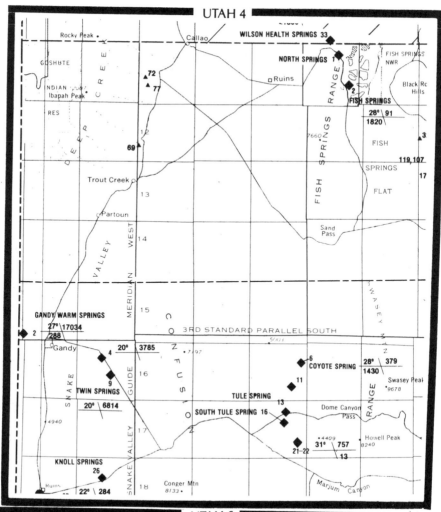

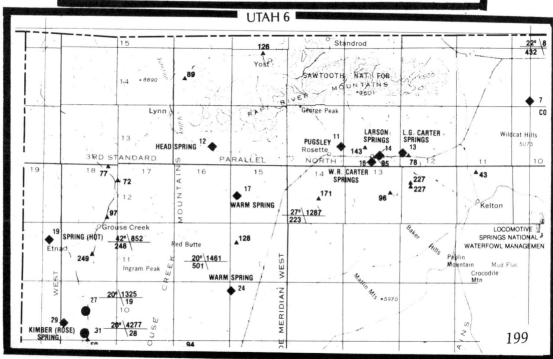

199

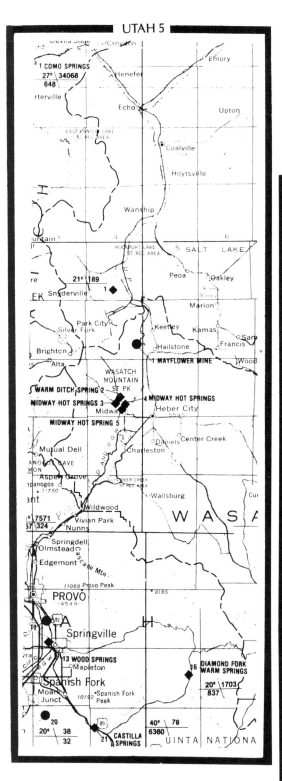

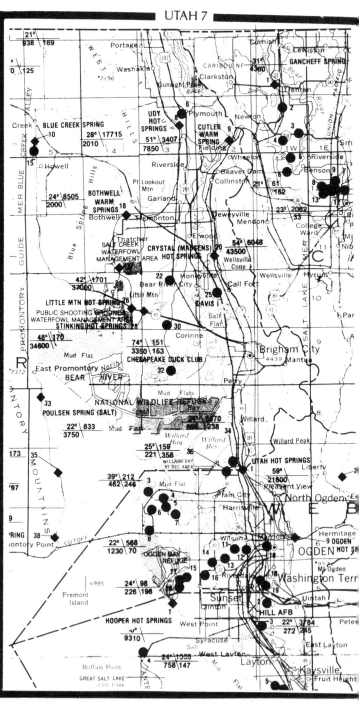

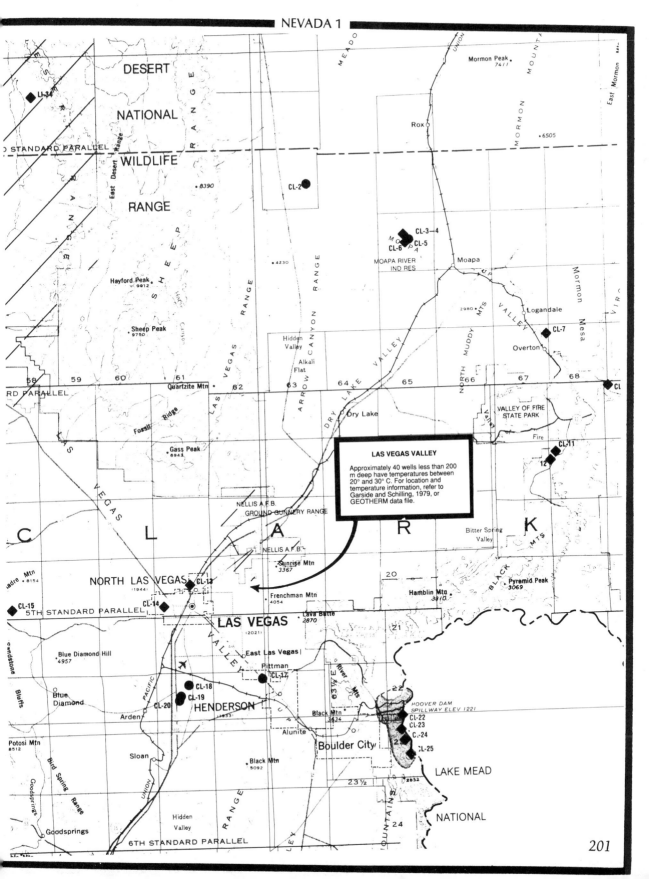

DESERT

NATIONAL

WILDLIFE

RANGE

LL-34

D STANDARD PARALLEL

East Desert Range

SHEEP RANGE

Hayford Peak
9912

Sheep Peak
9750

• 8390

• 4230

CL-2

Hidden
Valley

Alkali
Flat

MOAPA RIVER
IND RES

CL-3—4
CL-6 CL-5
Moapa

Mormon Peak
7411

MORMON MOUNTAIN

East Mormon

Rox

• 6505

MORMON MTS

2980

Logandale

CL-7

Overton

Mormon Mesa

VIRG

RD PARALLEL

Quartzite Mtn

ARROW CANYON RANGE

DRY LAKE VALLEY

NORTH MUDDY MTS

MUDDY VALLEY

58   59   60   61   62   63   64   65   66   67   68

CL

Fossil Ridge

Gass Peak
6943

Dry Lake

VALLEY OF FIRE
STATE PARK

Fire

CL-11
12

LAS VEGAS VALLEY

Approximately 40 wells less than 200
m deep have temperatures between
20° and 30° C. For location and
temperature information, refer to
Garside and Schilling, 1979, or
GEOTHERM data file.

Bitter Spring
Valley

BLACK MTS

Pyramid Peak
3069

C   L   A   R   K

NELLIS A.F.B.
GROUND GUNNERY RANGE

NELLIS A.F.B.

Sunrise Mtn
3367

20

Hamblin Mtn
3810

adre Mtn
• 8154

CL-15

NORTH LAS VEGAS
11944

CL-13

CL-14

5TH STANDARD PARALLEL

LAS VEGAS
(2021)

Frenchman Mtn
4054

Lava Butte
2870

21

LAS VEGAS

Blue Diamond Hill
4957

Blue
Diamond

Bluffs

sandstone

East Las Vegas

Pittman

CL-17

PACIFIC

CL-18
CL-19
CL-20

Arden

HENDERSON
1633

Alunite

River MTS

63½

22

Black Mtn
3634

HOOVER DAM
SPILLWAY ELEV 1221

CL-22
CL-23
C-24
CL-25

LAKE MEAD

Potosi Mtn
8512

Sloan

Black Mtn
5092

Boulder City

2

2832

Bird Spring Range

Goodsprings

Goodsprings

UNION

Hidden
Valley

RANGE

VLEY

MOUNTAIN

23½

LAKE MEAD

02

24

NATIONAL

6TH STANDARD PARALLEL

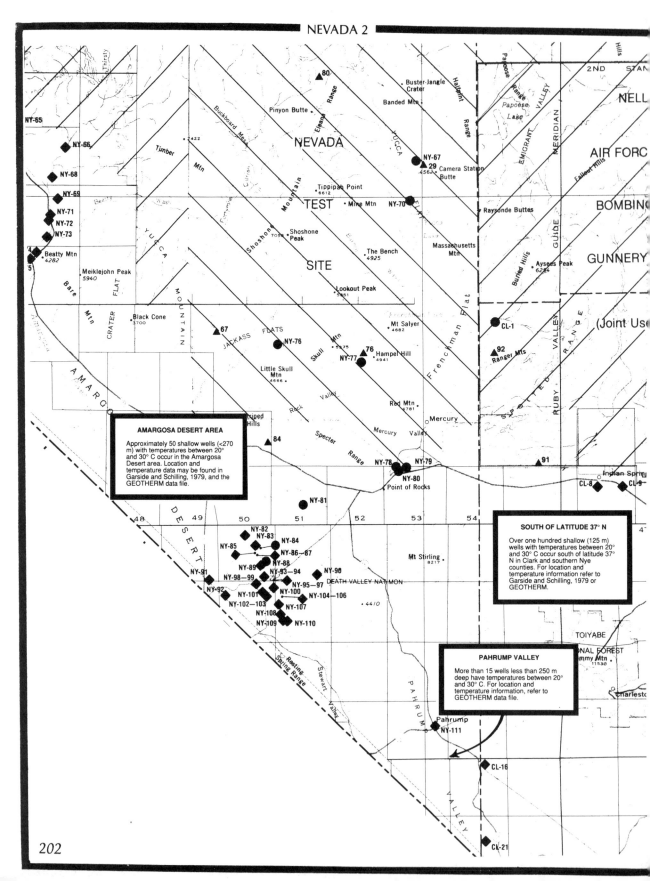

AMARGOSA DESERT AREA

Approximately 50 shallow wells (<270 m) with temperatures between 20° and 30° C occur in the Amargosa Desert area. Location and temperature data may be found in Garside and Schilling, 1979, and the GEOTHERM data file.

SOUTH OF LATITUDE 37° N

Over one hundred shallow (125 m) wells with temperatures between 20° and 30° C occur south of latitude 37° N in Clark and southern Nye counties. For location and temperature information refer to Garside and Schilling, 1979 or GEOTHERM.

PAHRUMP VALLEY

More than 15 wells less than 250 m deep have temperatures between 20° and 30° C. For location and temperature information, refer to GEOTHERM data file.

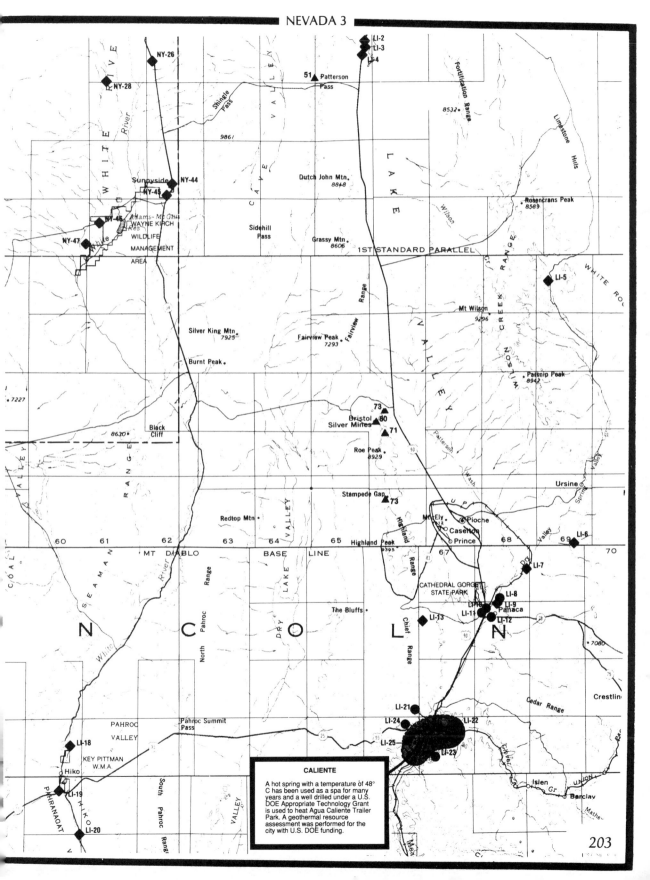

CALIENTE

A hot spring with a temperature of 48° C has been used as a spa for many years and a well drilled under a U.S. DOE Appropriate Technology Grant is used to heat Agua Caliente Trailer Park. A geothermal resource assessment was performed for the city with U.S. DOE funding.

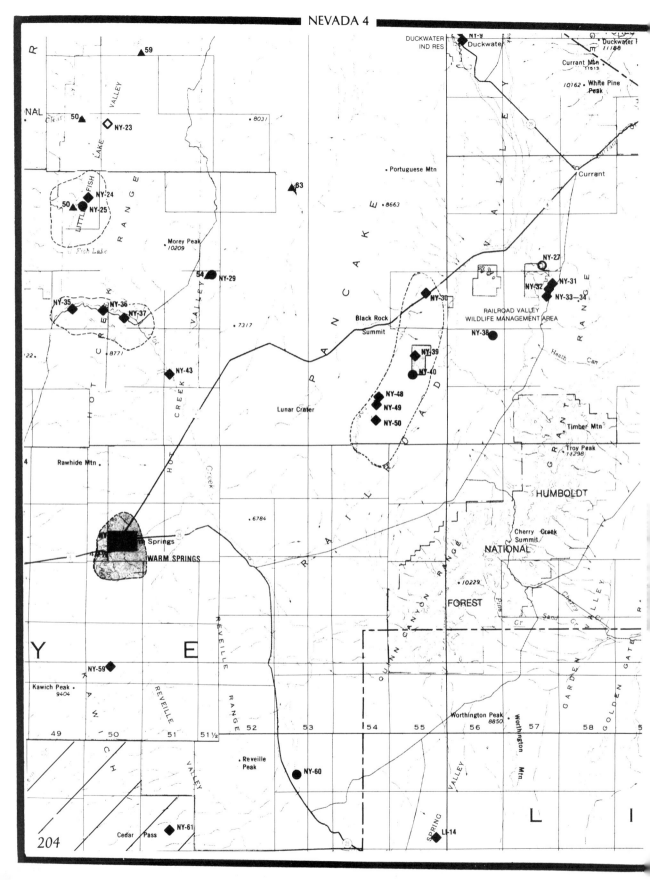

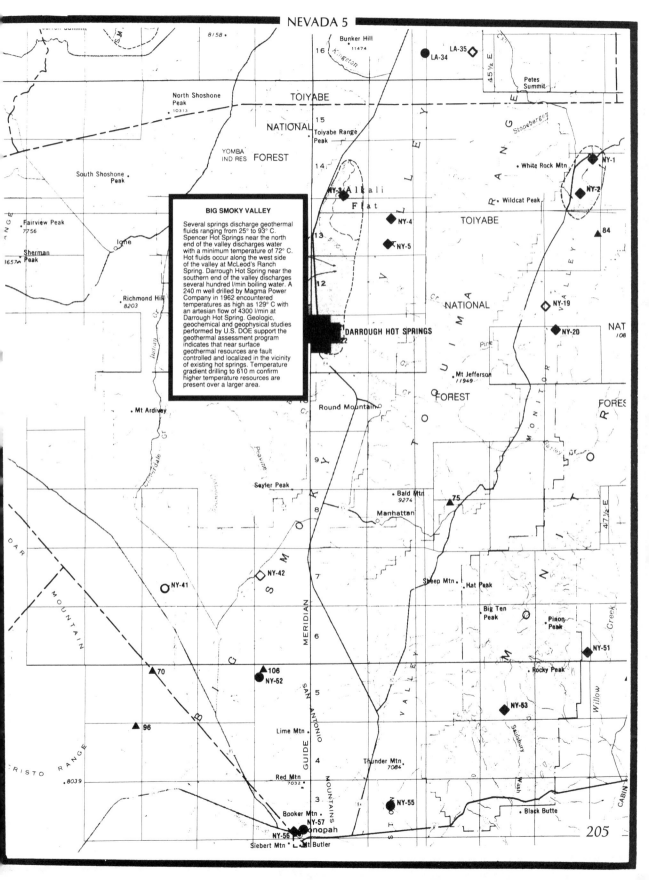

BIG SMOKY VALLEY

Several springs discharge geothermal fluids ranging from 25° to 93° C. Spencer Hot Springs near the north end of the valley discharges water with a minimum temperature of 72° C. Hot fluids occur along the west side of the valley at McLeod's Ranch Spring. Darrough Hot Spring near the southern end of the valley discharges several hundred l/min boiling water. A 240 m well drilled by Magma Power Company in 1962 encountered temperatures as high as 129° C with an artesian flow of 4300 l/min at Darrough Hot Spring. Geologic, geochemical and geophysical studies performed by U.S. DOE support the geothermal assessment program indicates that near surface geothermal resources are fault controlled and localized in the vicinity of existing hot springs. Temperature gradient drilling to 610 m confirm higher temperature resources are present over a larger area.

MOANA AREA
(Refer to inset map)

Located within the city limits of Reno, the known geothermal resource occupies an area of slightly more than 10 square kilometers. Temperatures as high as 98° C have been encountered in wells 300 m deep. More than 150 homes are heated by individual shallow (<100 m) wells. Two motels and two churches also use the resource for heating. A district-wide space heating system heats an additional 60 homes.

STEAMBOAT HOT SPRINGS

The Steamboat Hot Springs area has been extensively studied by several U.S. Geological Survey personnel; D.E. White in particular, has authored or co-authored numerous reports on the area including U.S. Geological Survey Prof. Paper 458 A-C. The hot spring system was formed in the early Pleistocene and probably has been active, possibly intermittently, for the past 2.5 m.y. The source of the energy for the hydrothermal convective system is most probably a rhyolitic magma chamber from which the 1.5 m.y. rhyolitic domes were emplaced. Relatively high concentrations of trace metals and highly soluble elements which have low crustal abundance coupled with the longevity of the systems suggest that a continuing small supply of magmatic waters are mixing with meteoric waters. Oxygen isotope data show that there could be no more than approximately 10 percent magmatic water supplied to the hydrothermal system. Six geothermal exploration wells were drilled by Nevada Thermal Power between 1954 and 1961. Depths ranged from 218 to 558 m. A shallow well of 50 m depth had a reported temperature of 138° C. An extensive thermal gradient drilling program was initiated by Phillips Petroleum in the late 1970's which culminated in the location of two production well sites. The first was drilled to a depth of 920 m and had a reported maximum temperature of 220° C. In 1981 a second well was drilled to a depth of 1058 m; initial results tend to indicate that it was not as successful as the first well. Further production drilling is anticipated.

FALLON

Several shallow water wells with temperatures ranging from 30° to 72° C are located near the Fallon Naval Air Station 5 km south-east of Fallon. In 1978 the U.S. Navy drilled four temperature gradient holes that ranged in depth from 100 to 150 meters and had gradients ranging from 78° to 218° C/km. Four additional gradient holes, 150 meters deep, were drilled in 1979 closer to the operating facilities of the Air Station. These holes had gradients 60° C/km or less. The Navy drilled a 607 m test hole in 1981 which has a bottom hole temperature of 97° C.

WABUSKA

Hot springs occur along a trace of an east-west trending fault. Temperatures range from 59° to 72° C. In 1959 Magma Power Company drilled three exploration wells. Two of the wells were shallow, less than 180 m. A third well was drilled to 677 m and had a reported temperature of 108° C. In 1972 Agri-Technology Corporation attempted to grow vegetables hydroponically. However, this venture failed. Tad's Enterprises has built a ethanol plant which utilizes geothermal energy in the form of hot water (104° C) to distill alcohol from corn.

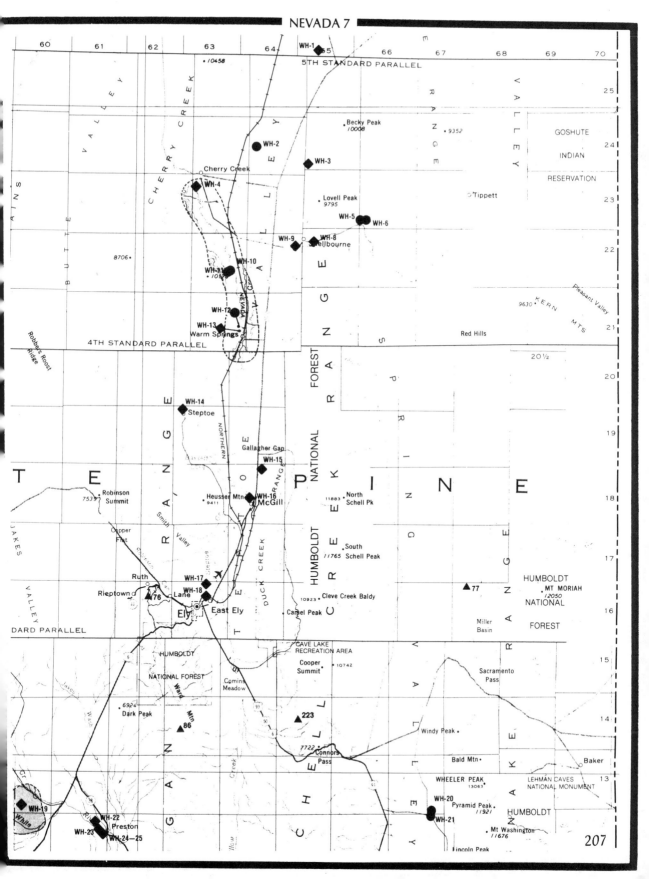

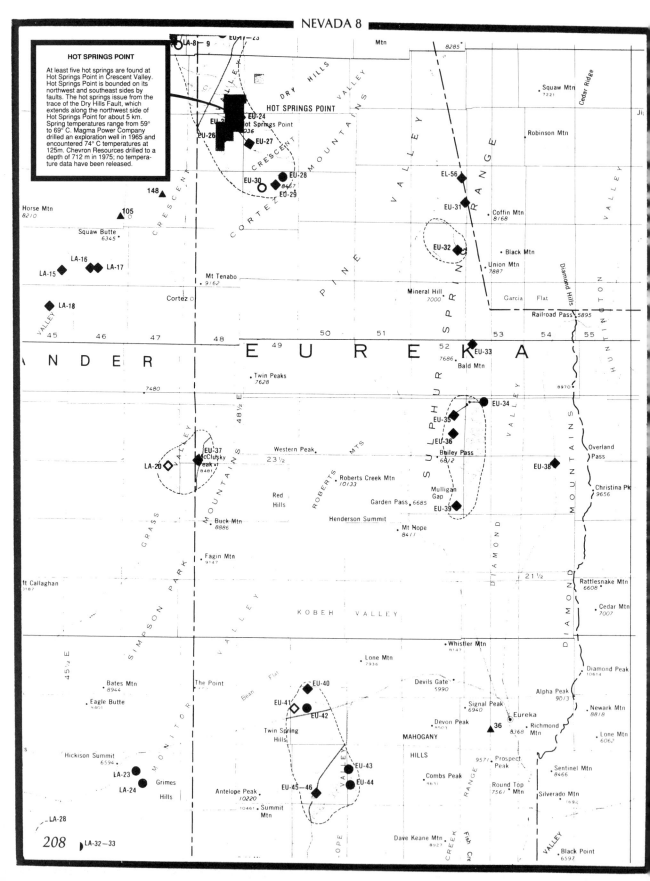

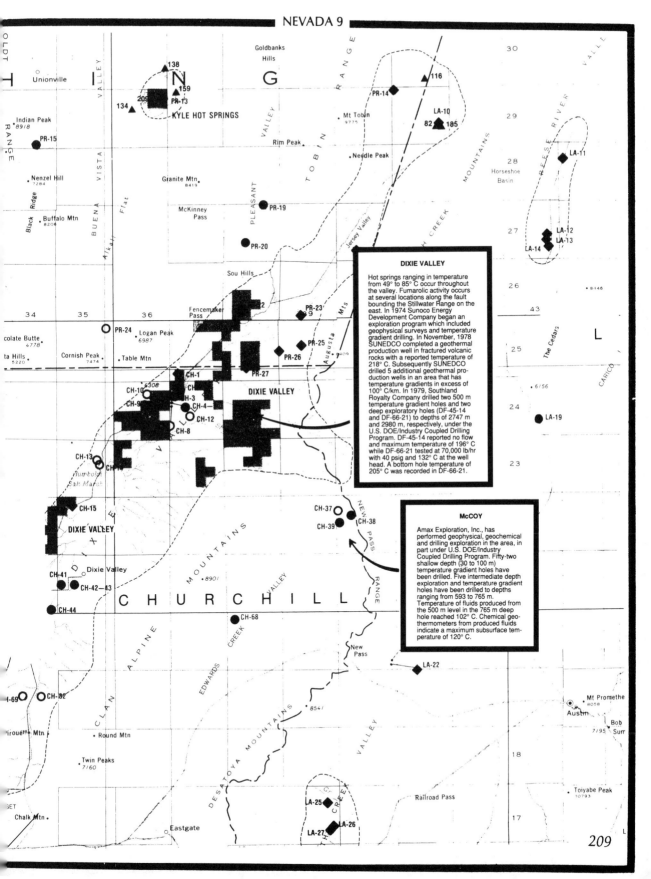

DIXIE VALLEY

Hot springs ranging in temperature from 49° to 85° C occur throughout the valley. Fumarolic activity occurs at several locations along the fault bounding the Stillwater Range on the east. In 1974 Sunoco Energy Development Company began an exploration program which included geophysical surveys and temperature gradient drilling. In November, 1978 SUNEDCO completed a geothermal production well in fractured volcanic rocks with a reported temperature of 218° C. Subsequently SUNEDCO drilled 5 additional geothermal production wells in an area that has temperature gradients in excess of 100° C/km. In 1979, Southland Royalty Company drilled two 500 m temperature gradient holes and two deep exploratory holes (DF-45-14 and DF-66-21) to depths of 2747 m and 2980 m, respectively, under the U.S. DOE/Industry Coupled Drilling Program. DF-45-14 reported no flow and maximum temperature of 196° C while DF-66-21 tested at 70,000 lb/hr with 40 psig and 132° C at the well head. A bottom hole temperature of 205° C was recorded in DF-66-21.

McCOY

Amax Exploration, Inc., has performed geophysical, geochemical and drilling exploration in the area, in part under U.S. DOE/Industry Coupled Drilling Program. Fifty-two shallow depth (30 to 100 m) temperature gradient holes have been drilled. Five intermediate depth exploration and temperature gradient holes have been drilled to depths ranging from 593 to 765 m. Temperature of fluids produced from the 500 m level in the 765 m deep hole reached 102° C. Chemical geothermometers from produced fluids indicate a maximum subsurface temperature of 120° C.

209

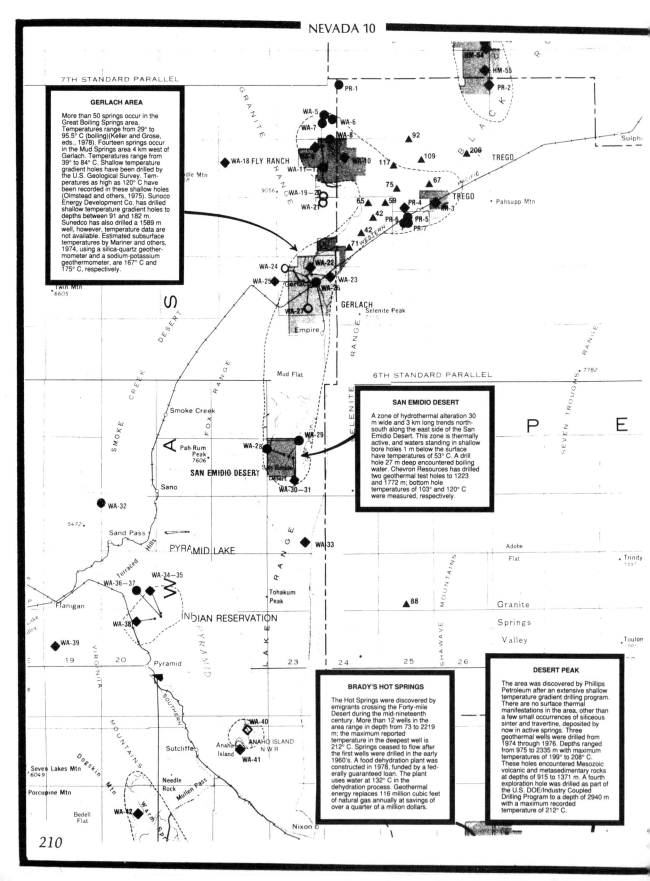

GERLACH AREA

More than 50 springs occur in the Great Boiling Springs area. Temperatures range from 29° to 95.5° C (boiling) (Keller and Grose, eds., 1978). Fourteen springs occur in the Mud Springs area 4 km west of Gerlach. Temperatures range from 39° to 84° C. Shallow temperature gradient holes have been drilled by the U.S. Geological Survey. Temperatures as high as 120° C have been recorded in these shallow holes (Olmstead and others, 1975). Sunoco Energy Development Co. has drilled shallow temperature gradient holes to depths between 91 and 182 m. Sunedco has also drilled a 1589 m well, however, temperature data are not available. Estimated subsurface temperatures by Mariner and others, 1974, using a silica-quartz geothermometer and a sodium-potassium geothermometer, are 167° C and 175° C, respectively.

SAN EMIDIO DESERT

A zone of hydrothermal alteration 30 m wide and 3 km long trends north-south along the east side of the San Emidio Desert. This zone is thermally active, and waters standing in shallow bore holes 1 m below the surface have temperatures of 53° C. A drill hole 27 m deep encountered boiling water. Chevron Resources has drilled two geothermal test holes to 1223 and 1772 m; bottom hole temperatures of 103° and 120° C were measured, respectively.

BRADY'S HOT SPRINGS

The Hot Springs were discovered by emigrants crossing the Forty-mile Desert during the mid-nineteenth century. More than 12 wells in the area range in depth from 73 to 2219 m; the maximum reported temperature in the deepest well is 212° C. Springs ceased to flow after the first wells were drilled in the early 1960's. A food dehydration plant was constructed in 1978, funded by a federally guaranteed loan. The plant uses water at 132° C in the dehydration process. Geothermal energy replaces 116 million cubic feet of natural gas annually at savings of over a quarter of a million dollars.

DESERT PEAK

The area was discovered by Phillips Petroleum after an extensive shallow temperature gradient drilling program. There are no surface thermal manifestations in the area, other than a few small occurrences of siliceous sinter and travertine, deposited by now in active springs. Three geothermal wells were drilled from 1974 through 1976. Depths ranged from 975 to 2335 m with maximum temperatures of 199° to 208° C. These holes encountered Mesozoic volcanic and metasedimentary rocks at depths of 915 to 1371 m. A fourth exploration hole was drilled as part of the U.S. DOE/Industry Coupled Drilling Program to a depth of 2940 m with a maximum recorded temperature of 212° C.

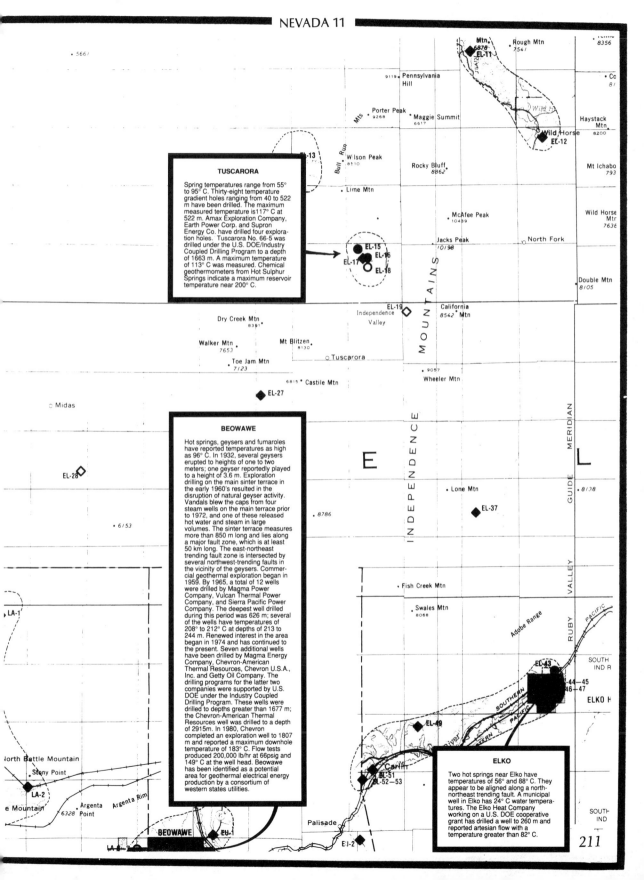

TUSCARORA

Spring temperatures range from 55° to 95° C. Thirty-eight temperature gradient holes ranging from 40 to 522 m have been drilled. The maximum measured temperature is 117° C at 522 m. Amax Exploration Company, Earth Power Corp. and Supron Energy Co. have drilled four exploration holes. Tuscarora No. 66-5 was drilled under the U.S. DOE/Industry Coupled Drilling Program to a depth of 1663 m. A maximum temperature of 113° C was measured. Chemical geothermometers from Hot Sulphur Springs indicate a maximum reservoir temperature near 200° C.

BEOWAWE

Hot springs, geysers and fumaroles have reported temperatures as high as 96° C. In 1932, several geysers erupted to heights of one to two meters; one geyser reportedly played to a height of 3.6 m. Exploration drilling on the main sinter terrace in the early 1960's resulted in the disruption of natural geyser activity. Vandals blew the caps from four steam wells on the main terrace prior to 1972, and one of these released hot water and steam in large volumes. The sinter terrace measures more than 850 m long and lies along a major fault zone, which is at least 50 km long. The east-northeast trending fault zone is intersected by several northwest-trending faults in the vicinity of the geysers. Commercial geothermal exploration began in 1959. By 1965, a total of 12 wells were drilled by Magma Power Company, Vulcan Thermal Power Company, and Sierra Pacific Power Company. The deepest well drilled during this period was 626 m; several of the wells have temperatures of 208° to 212° C at depths of 213 to 244 m. Renewed interest in the area began in 1974 and has continued to the present. Seven additional wells have been drilled by Magma Energy Company, Chevron-American Thermal Resources, Chevron U.S.A., Inc. and Getty Oil Company. The drilling programs for the latter two companies were supported by U.S. DOE under the Industry Coupled Drilling Program. These wells were drilled to depths greater than 1677 m; the Chevron-American Thermal Resources well was drilled to a depth of 2915m. In 1980, Chevron completed an exploration well to 1807 m and reported a maximum downhole temperature of 183° C. Flow tests produced 200,000 lb/hr at 66psig and 149° C at the well head. Beowawe has been identified as a potential area for geothermal electrical energy production by a consortium of western states utilities.

ELKO

Two hot springs near Elko have temperatures of 56° and 88° C. They appear to be aligned along a north-northeast trending fault. A municipal well in Elko has 24° C water temperatures. The Elko Heat Company working on a U.S. DOE cooperative grant has drilled a well to 260 m and reported artesian flow with a temperature greater than 82° C.

211

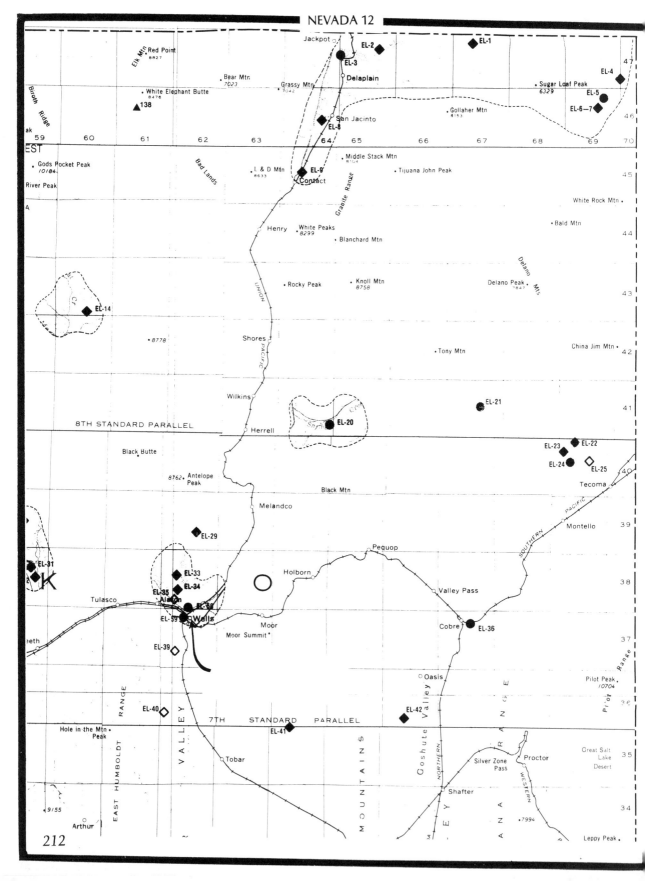

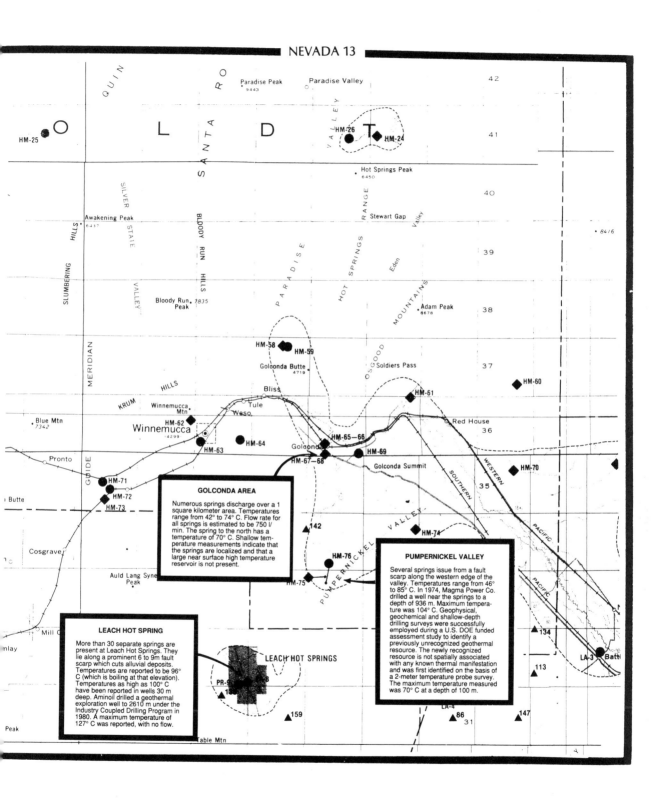

GOLCONDA AREA

Numerous springs discharge over a 1 square kilometer area. Temperatures range from 42° to 74° C. Flow rate for all springs is estimated to be 750 l/min. The spring to the north has a temperature of 70° C. Shallow temperature measurements indicate that the springs are localized and that a large near surface high temperature reservoir is not present.

PUMPERNICKEL VALLEY

Several springs issue from a fault scarp along the western edge of the valley. Temperatures range from 46° to 85° C. In 1974, Magma Power Co. drilled a well near the springs to a depth of 936 m. Maximum temperature was 104° C. Geophysical, geochemical and shallow-depth drilling surveys were successfully employed during a U.S. DOE funded assessment study to identify a previously unrecognized geothermal resource. The newly recognized resource is not spatially associated with any known thermal manifestation and was first identified on the basis of a 2-meter temperature probe survey. The maximum temperature measured was 70° C at a depth of 100 m.

LEACH HOT SPRING

More than 30 separate springs are present at Leach Hot Springs. They lie along a prominent 6 to 9m fault scarp which cuts alluvial deposits. Temperatures are reported to be 96° C (which is boiling at that elevation). Temperatures as high as 100° C have been reported in wells 30 m deep. Aminoil drilled a geothermal exploration well to 2610 m under the Industry Coupled Drilling Program in 1980. A maximum temperature of 127° C was reported, with no flow.

213

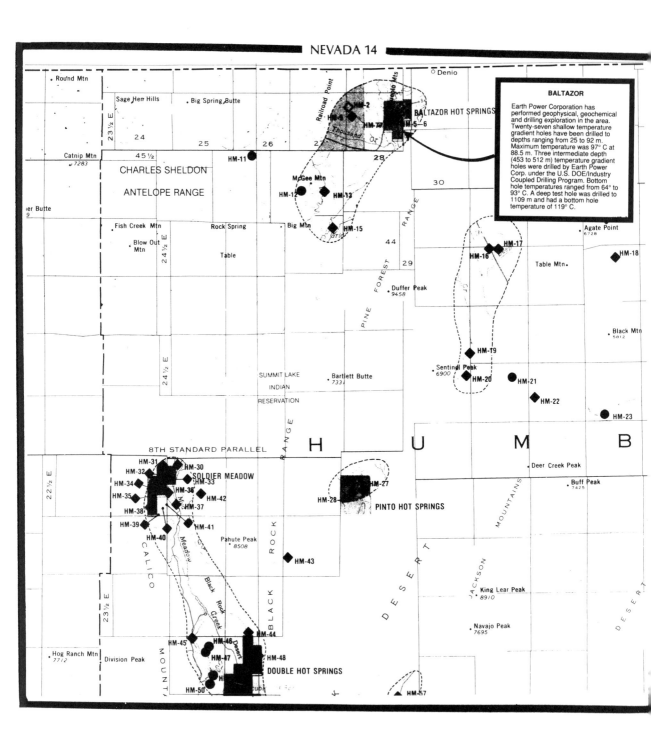

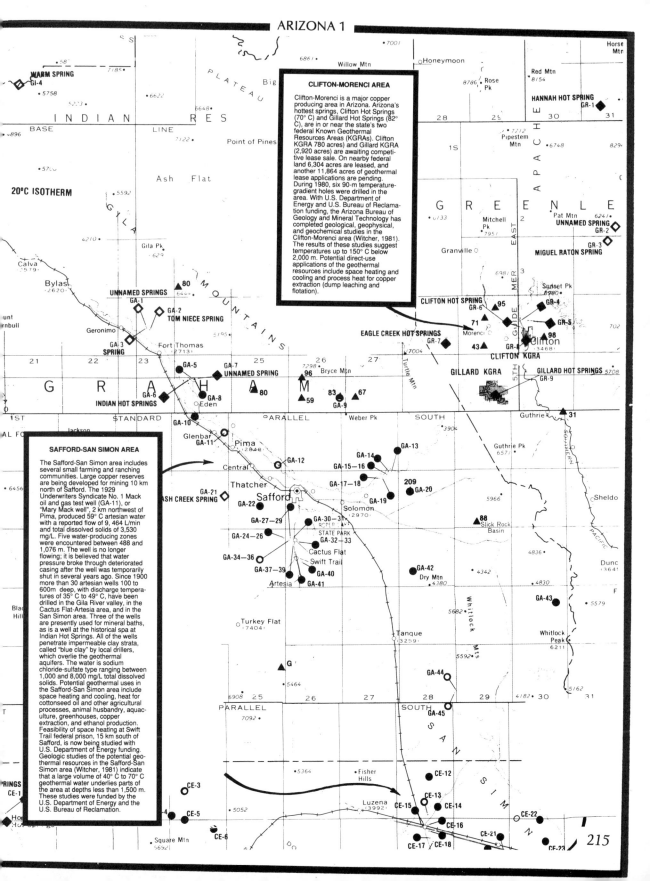

CLIFTON-MORENCI AREA

Clifton-Morenci is a major copper producing area in Arizona. Arizona's hottest springs, Clifton Hot Springs (70° C) and Gillard Hot Springs (82° C), are in or near the state's two federal Known Geothermal Resources Areas (KGRAs). Clifton KGRA 780 acres) and Gillard KGRA (2,920 acres) are awaiting competitive lease sale. On nearby federal land 6,304 acres are leased, and another 11,864 acres of geothermal lease applications are pending. During 1980, six 90-m temperature-gradient holes were drilled in the area. With U.S. Department of Energy and U.S. Bureau of Reclamation funding, the Arizona Bureau of Geology and Mineral Technology has completed geological, geophysical, and geochemical studies in the Clifton-Morenci area (Witcher, 1981). The results of these studies suggest temperatures up to 150° C below 2,000 m. Potential direct-use applications of the geothermal resources include space heating and cooling and process heat for copper extraction (dump leaching and flotation).

SAFFORD-SAN SIMON AREA

The Safford-San Simon area includes several small farming and ranching communities. Large copper reserves are being developed for mining 10 km north of Safford. The 1929 Underwriters Syndicate No. 1 Mack oil and gas test well (GA-11), or "Mary Mack well", 2 km northwest of Pima, produced 59° C artesian water with a reported flow of 9, 464 L/min and total dissolved solids of 3,530 mg/L. Five water-producing zones were encountered between 488 and 1,076 m. The well is no longer flowing; it is believed that water pressure broke through deteriorated casing after the well was temporarily shut in several years ago. Since 1900 more than 30 artesian wells 100 to 600m deep, with discharge temperatures of 35° C to 49° C, have been drilled in the Gila River valley, in the Cactus Flat-Artesia area, and in the San Simon area. Three of the wells are presently used for mineral baths, as is a well at the historical spa at Indian Hot Springs. All of the wells penetrate impermeable clay strata, called "blue clay" by local drillers, which overlie the geothermal aquifers. The water is sodium chloride-sulfate type ranging between 1,000 and 8,000 mg/L total dissolved solids. Potential geothermal uses in the Safford-San Simon area include space heating and cooling, heat for cottonseed oil and other agricultural processes, animal husbandry, aquaculture, greenhouses, copper extraction, and ethanol production. Feasibility of space heating at Swift Trail federal prison, 15 km south of Safford, is now being studied with U.S. Department of Energy funding. Geologic studies of the potential geothermal resources in the Safford-San Simon area (Witcher, 1981) indicate that a large volume of 40° C to 70° C geothermal water underlies parts of the area at depths less than 1,500 m. These studies were funded by the U.S. Department of Energy and the U.S. Bureau of Reclamation.

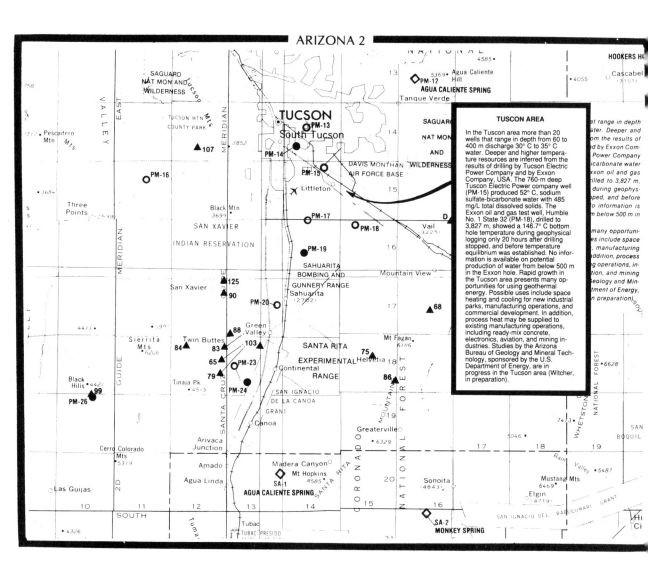

TUSCON AREA

In the Tuscon area more than 20 wells that range in depth from 60 to 400 m discharge 30° C to 35° C water. Deeper and higher temperature resources are inferred from the results of drilling by Tucson Electric Power Company and by Exxon Company, USA. The 760-m deep Tuscon Electric Power company well (PM-15) produced 52° C, sodium sulfate-bicarbonate water with 485 mg/L total dissolved solids. The Exxon oil and gas test well, Humble No. 1 State 32 (PM-18), drilled to 3,827 m, showed a 146.7° C bottom hole temperature during geophysical logging only 20 hours after drilling stopped, and before temperature equilibrium was established. No information is available on potential production of water from below 500 m in the Exxon hole. Rapid growth in the Tucson area presents many opportunities for using geothermal energy. Possible uses include space heating and cooling for new industrial parks, manufacturing operations, and commercial development. In addition, process heat may be supplied to existing manufacturing operations, including ready-mix concrete, electronics, aviation, and mining industries. Studies by the Arizona Bureau of Geology and Mineral Technology, sponsored by the U.S. Department of Energy, are in progress in the Tucson area (Witcher, in preparation).

CASTLE HOT SPRINGS

Geologists at Arizona State University, Tempe, have completed geological and geochemical studies at Castle Hot Springs. These show that the springs are the principal manifestations of a geothermal system contained in a two-km-long segment of a major fault zone. Measured surface temperatures at Castle Hot Springs range from 48° C to 55° C. The springs have an aggregate flow rate of 1,300 L/min. The water is sodium chloride-sulfate type, with 700 to 800 mg/L total dissolved solids. This geothermal resource has potential uses for space heating and cooling of the Arizona State University Foundation conference center at Castle Hot Springs. Geothermal evaluation (Sheridan, Satkin, and Wohletz, 1980) was funded by the U.S. Department of Energy through the Arizona Bureau of Geology and Mineral Technology.

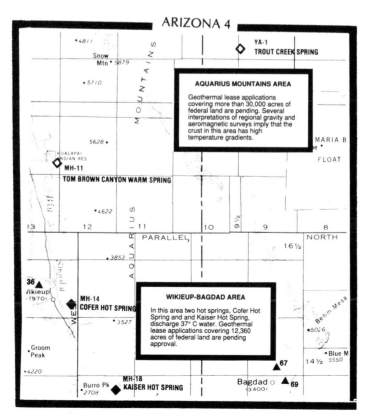

AQUARIUS MOUNTAINS AREA

Geothermal lease applications covering more than 30,000 acres of federal land are pending. Several interpretations of regional gravity and aeromagnetic surveys imply that the crust in this area has high temperature gradients.

WIKIEUP-BAGDAD AREA

In this area two hot springs, Cofer Hot Spring and and Kaiser Hot Spring, discharge 37° C water. Geothermal lease applications covering 12,360 acres of federal land are pending approval.

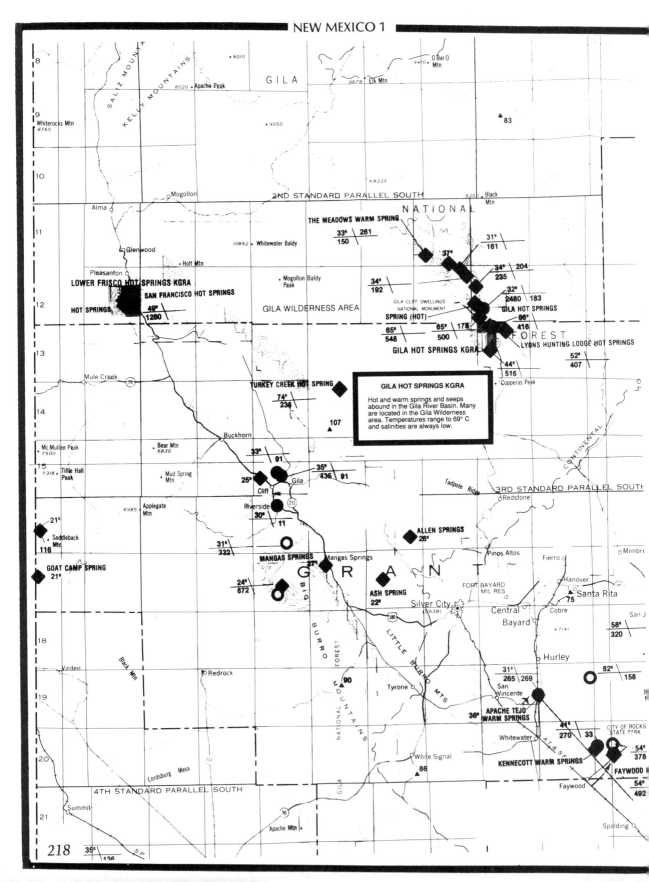

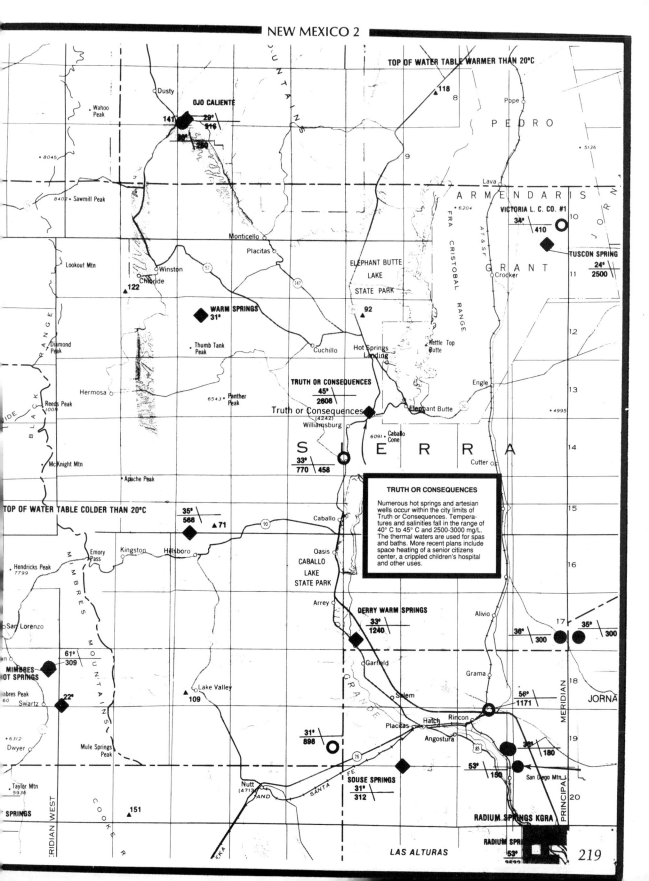

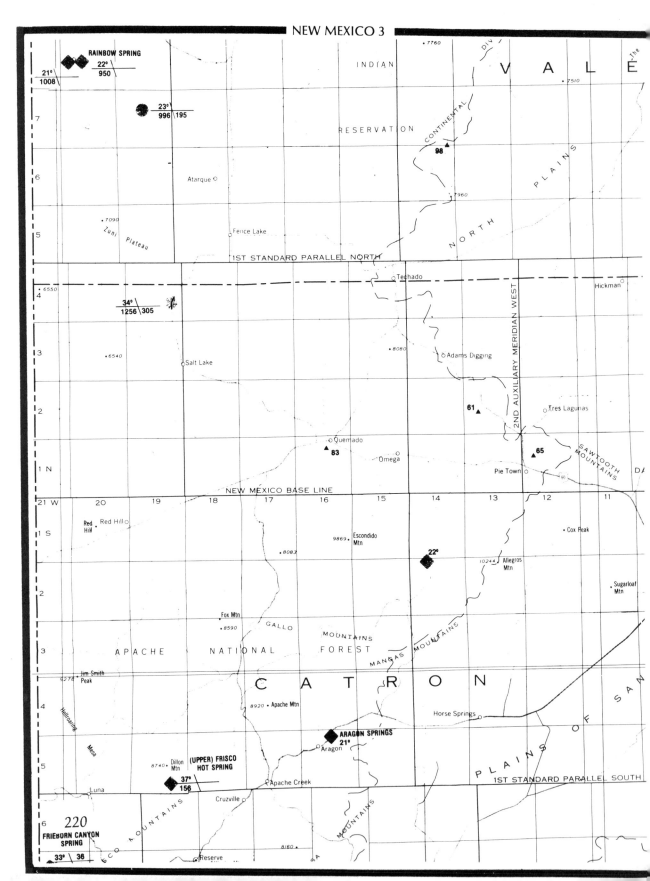

RAINBOW SPRING

21°
1008

22°
950

23°
996 \ 195

INDIAN

VALE

7760

7510

RESERVATION

98

7960

Atarque ○

NORTH

PLAINS

7090

Zuni Plateau

○ Fence Lake

1ST STANDARD PARALLEL NORTH

○ Techado

Hickman ○

6550

34°
1256 \ 305

6540

○ Salt Lake

8080

○ Adams Digging

2ND AUXILIARY MERIDIAN WEST

61 ▲

Tres Lagunas

○ Quemado

83 ▲

65 ▲

SAWTOOTH MOUNTAINS

DA

○ Omega

Pie Town

NEW MEXICO BASE LINE

21 W   20   19   18   17   16   15   14   13   12   11

Red Hill   Red Hill ○

Cox Peak

Escondido
Mtn

9869

8083

22°

10244   Allegros
Mtn

Sugarloaf
Mtn

Fox Mtn

8590

GALLO

MOUNTAINS

MANGAS   MOUNTAINS

APACHE   NATIONAL   FOREST

CATRON

Jim Smith
Peak

8278

8920 • Apache Mtn

Horse Springs ○

PLAINS   OF   SAN

Hellroaring

Mesa

8740 • Dillon
Mtn

(UPPER) FRISCO
HOT SPRING

ARAGON SPRINGS
21°

Aragon

Luna

37°
156

○ Apache Creek

1ST STANDARD PARALLEL SOUTH

Cruzville ○

220

FRIEBORN CANYON
SPRING

33°   36

Reserve

8160

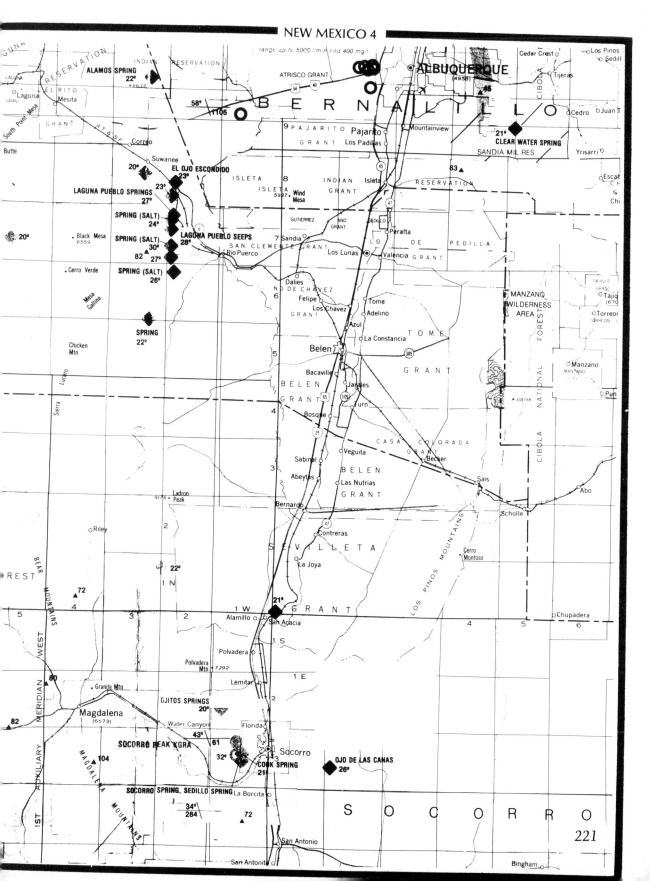

range up to 5000 l/min and 400 mg/l

BERNALILLO

ALAMOS SPRING 22°

Laguna
Mesita
El Rito
Correo
Suwanee
20°
EL OJO ESCONDIDO 23°
LAGUNA PUEBLO SPRINGS 27°
SPRING (SALT) 24°
LAGUNA PUEBLO SEEPS 28°
SPRING (SALT) 30°
82 27°
SPRING (SALT) 26°
SPRING 22°

ATRISCO GRANT

ALBUQUERQUE (4958)

Cedar Crest
Los Pinos
Sedill
Tijeras
Cedro
Juan T
Mountainview
21° CLEAR WATER SPRING
SANDIA MIL RES
Yrisarri
63
Escab
Chi

PAJARITO GRANT Pajarito
Los Padillas

ISLETA
INDIAN GRANT
Isleta
RESERVATION
Wind Mesa
Sandia
GUTIERREZ
SAN CLEMENTE GRANT
Rio Puerco
Los Lunas
Peralta
SEDILLO
LO DE PEDILLA
Dalies
NO DE CHAVEZ GRANT
Felipe
Los Chavez
Tome
Adelino
Azul
La Constancia
TOME GRANT
Belen
Bacaville
Jarales
BELEN GRANT
Turn
Bosque
Veguita
CASA COLORADA GRANT
Becker
Sabinal
Abeytas
BELEN GRANT
Las Nutrias
Bernardo
Sais
Scholle
Abo
Contreras
SEVILLETA GRANT
La Joya
Chupadera

MANZANO WILDERNESS AREA
CIBOLA NATIONAL FOREST
Tajiq
Torreon
Manzano
Pun

Black Mesa 6559
20°
Cerro Verde
Mesa Gallina
Chicken Mtn
SPRING 22°
72
80
Magdalena (6573)
82
Riley
Ladron Peak 9176
Granite Mtn
OJITOS SPRINGS 20°
Water Canyon
43°
SOCORRO PEAK KGRA
104
COOK SPRING 21°
61
32°
Florida
Socorro
OJO DE LAS CANAS 26°
SOCORRO SPRING, SEDILLO SPRING La Borcita
34°/284
72
San Antonio
San Antonit
Bingham

Sierra Lucero
BEAR MOUNTAINS
WEST
MERIDIAN
AUXILIARY
MAGDALENA MOUNTAINS
1ST
Alamillo
San Acacia
Polvadera
Polvadera Mtn 7292
Lemitar
21°
1 W
1 S
1 E

SOCORRO

221

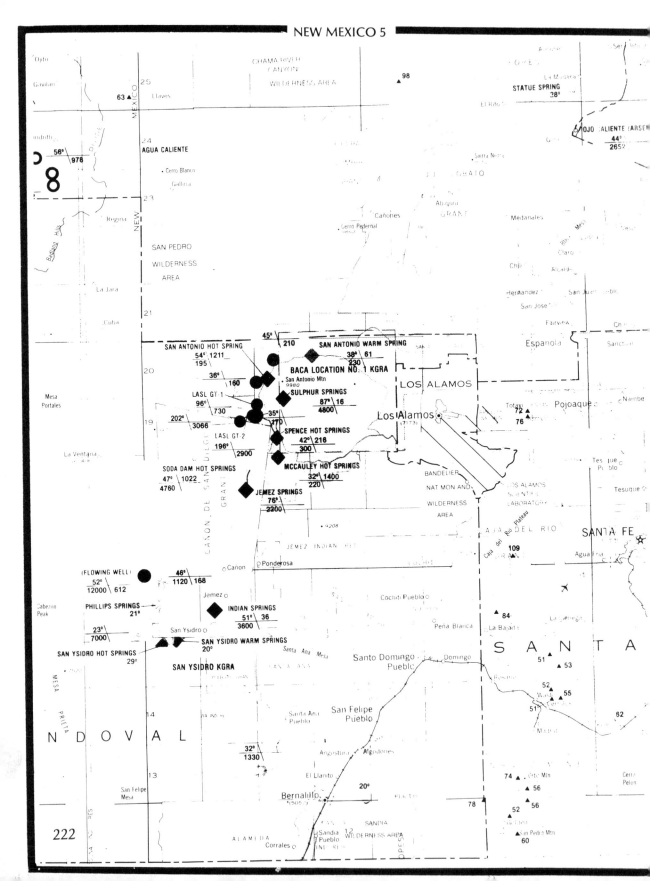

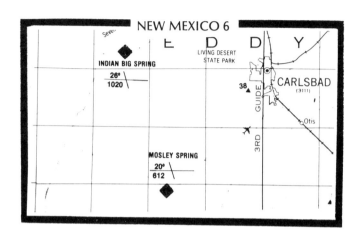